JUNIOR HIGH

MINISTRY

Updated & Expanded

MINISTRY
Updated & Expanded

A guide to early adolescence for youth workers

Wayne Rice

Youth Specialties

≝ ZondervanPublishingHouse
Grand Rapids, Michigan
A Division of HarperCollins*Publishers*

Junior High Ministry, Updated & Expanded: A guide to early adolescence for youth workers

© 1998 by Wayne Rice

Youth Specialties Books, 300 S. Pierce St., El Cajon, CA 92020, are published by Zondervan Publishing House, 5300 Patterson Ave. S.E., Grand Rapids, MI 49530.

Library of Congress Cataloging-in-Publication Data
Rice, Wayne.
    Junior high ministry : a guide to early adolescence for youth workers / Wayne Rice. — Updated and expanded ed.
        p.   cm.
    Includes bibliographical references and index.
    ISBN 0-310-22442-X
    1. Church work with teenagers. 2. Church work with children. 3. Junior high school students—Religious life. I. Title.
BV1475.9.R52
259'.23—dc21

97-32389
CIP

Edited by Sheri Stanley
Cover and interior design by Rogers Design & Associates

Printed in the United States of America

05 06/ /12 11 10 9 8

CONTENTS

PREFACE

I was in college studying to become an architect when I was asked by my local Youth for Christ director to try my hand at working with junior high kids. I was given the assignment primarily because I didn't have enough experience to work with high school students. The idea was for me to learn how to do youth ministry by practicing on junior highers—then I could move up to the big time.

I learned, all right. I learned, first of all, that I was wasting my time studying architecture. I had been smitten by these junior high kids (was *that* the call of God?). The next thing I knew I was trading in my drafting tools for a guitar and a silk screen. (Back in those days, folk music was the rage and those silk-screened psychedelic posters were hot.) I was definitely on my way to a career in youth ministry.

But I also learned a couple of other things. First, I learned that junior highers deserve more than inexperienced, untrained youth workers. Second, I discovered that contrary to popular opinion, junior highers are people, too—special people, in fact—who are going through a very special time of life. Having made this discovery, I decided to become a junior high specialist. I eventually got my promotion to the big time (I did get to work with high schoolers), but over the years, my passion has remained junior high ministry.

I hope that this book will help you to understand where that passion comes from. As you read I hope you'll be able to sense the high regard I have for both junior highers and the adults who work with them. I also hope you notice that I have a little different take on adolescence than many people who write books about today's young people. Because I am not a psychologist who spends a disproportionate amount of time around troubled teenagers, I don't consider troubled teenagers to be the norm. I believe that the vast majority of teenagers are great kids who are basically doing fine—or at least *could* do fine with a little adult support and guidance along the way. Many adults nowadays avoid teenagers because of the bad publicity they have been getting. I believe a major reason teenagers today are involved in more negative behaviors than ever before is because they have been labeled as a uniquely rotten generation. In recent times, they have been called Baby Busters, Generation X-ers, Slackers, and all sorts of derogatory names that only discourage kids. It is my opinion that kids will live up—or down—to whatever expectations we have of them. If we stereotype kids and expect them to be bad, we shouldn't be surprised when they do bad things. But if we treat them with respect and give them the support they deserve, we may be surprised to see how much good they can do. I am bullish on teenagers, and I am convinced that the crucial time for helping teenagers become all that they can be is during early adolescence—the junior high and middle school years.

This book is based largely on my personal experience, but I have attempted to reinforce my experience with the experience of hundreds of other youth workers who have taught me a great deal over the years. I am also a student of adolescence. I am constantly trying to learn more about kids as I watch them, talk with them, and listen to what they are saying. In addition I have benefitted greatly from reading and studying the current research on adolescence and the many good books and other resources that are now available.

It has been said that one of the best ways to learn about something is to teach it, and I have discovered this is true. I have been teaching people how to work with junior highers for almost a quarter of a century. Being a teacher of junior high ministry has forced me to organize my thoughts on this subject and this book is a direct result of that.

This is the third edition of *Junior High Ministry*. The first edition was written in 1978, the second in 1987. The times have changed, and so has junior high ministry. I'm a little older (well, actually, a *lot* older), hopefully a little wiser, and I now have had the additional experience of raising a few junior highers of my own. So because of the changes in junior high ministry, and changes in me, this book bears little resemblance to the original. This edition contains several new chapters, including one on involving parents in junior high ministry, and another on developing a mentoring program. There is new material on programming for junior highers, youth culture trends, faith development, and a new listing of resources. And throughout the book, I have edited, updated, deleted, refined, and clarified. Hopefully you'll agree that the net result is a greatly improved book.

> Twenty years ago junior high ministry was the bad joke of youth work.

I must say that I have been encouraged overall by what has been happening in junior high ministry since the original book was written 20 years ago. At that time, few people took junior high ministry seriously. It was more or less the bad joke of youth work. For those who did take it seriously, there were few resources to use. But that has changed. More people are getting involved in junior high work and more quality resources are being published. Today it is safe to say that a major trend in youth work is an increased awareness of and commitment to junior high ministry.

While I have tried to be thorough in this book, it is not intended to be exhaustive or the final word on junior high ministry. Nor is it intended to replace any of the outstanding books currently available on adolescent psychology and youth ministry. It is a look at junior high ministry in the local church from one veteran's point of view. I only hope that this book will complement the work of others. It covers most of the basics, as I see them, and is designed to stimulate and to challenge both the experienced and the inexperienced junior high worker in the church. Of course, my greatest hope is that a lot of junior high kids will benefit.

For the purpose of this book, I have defined a *junior higher* as any young person between the ages of 10 and 14. Usually I am talking about sixth, seventh, and eighth graders—so in this book you won't see the term *junior higher* refer strictly to students attending a junior high school. In fact, most junior highers now attend middle schools. In general, youth workers tend to speak of *junior highers* even if those students attend middle schools—so I will, too.

Another term that I frequently use to describe this group is *early adolescents*—a more common practice in the academic community. Sometimes I call them *kids*, which some people object to because they think it sounds too young for this age group. But *kids* is the term many junior highers use to refer to themselves, so I have no problem using it here. *Students* is another, more neutral term I sometimes use in this book.

It is interesting, by the way, that there really isn't a name for this group that is exclusively theirs. There is no term that adequately identifies 10-to-14-year-olds except those that imply they are *not* something else. The term *junior higher* actually means that they are not quite high schoolers; *early adolescent* means that they are not quite adolescents. *Middle schooler* means they are not quite either. In the book *The Vanishing Adolescent*, Edgar Friedenberg made the point that if a society has no word for something, it either doesn't matter to them, or it scares them to talk about it. Maybe we need to come up with a better name for our 10-to-14-year-olds. A few authors tried using the term *Quicksilvers* a few years ago, but I don't think anyone could figure out what it meant. A psychologist named Eichhorn coined the term *transcescent*—a cross between the words *transition* and *adolescent*—but it's hard to say and sounds a little like a sexual identity problem. I don't think his word caught on.

A common question I continue to hear from junior high workers has to do with the sixth grade problem. Ever since middle schools came into existence, junior high workers have been faced with a dilemma—whether or not to include sixth-graders in their junior high groups. This problem is especially thorny when you have both junior high schools and middle schools in the same community.

In this book I've assumed that sixth-graders are part of your junior high ministry—even though they may not be officially a part of it. Whether the sixth-graders of your church are in your junior high group, or whether they remain in the children's department, they are still early adolescents who are a lot more like junior highers than children. Regardless of who ministers to them, they need the same attention and thoughtful ministry that junior highers deserve. True, sixth-graders are generally on the less-mature end of the early adolescent spectrum, but in today's accelerated culture, they aren't that different from any other junior high kids. Therefore, I include sixth-graders throughout this book. Only in a few cases will I make special reference to them.

> **Whether or not your church's sixth-graders are in your junior high group, they are still early adolescents.**

By the way, if you aren't sure whether to include sixth-graders in your junior high ministry, it might be a good idea to consult with both the youth and the parents to see how they feel about it. If sixth-graders primarily attend grammar schools in your community, you may want to wait until sixth-grade graduation before allowing them entry into the junior high group. But if the majority attend middle schools, then the reverse would be recommended. Middle schoolers as a general rule don't like being kept back in the children's or juniors' group. Some churches have successfully allowed students to choose either option. They can choose to be a part of whichever group is most comfortable for them. There is no clear-cut best way to do it. We had the same problem with ninth-graders 30 years ago.

I want to express my gratitude to the voices who have inspired me and helped shape my thinking about junior high ministry over the years. Some of my heroes and mentors have been people like David Elkind, Robert Coles, H. Stephen Glenn, Tony Campolo, Rick Little, Marie Wynn, and Joan Lipsitz. Early and very important influences included Laura Baughman, Jerry Riddle, Sam McCreery, Don Goehner, Sonny Salsbury, Jay Kesler, Jim Slevcove, Bill Wennerholm, Tom Goble, and E.G. Von Trutschler. As iron sharpens iron, I have benefitted tremendously from my association over the years with colleagues in youth ministry like Jim Burns, Duffy Robbins, Bill McNabb, Steve Dickey, Ray Johnston, Darrell Pearson, Rich Van Pelt, Dave Curtiss, Bill Rowley, Stan Beard, Dave Veerman, Chuck Workman, Rob Mahan, Miles McPherson, the gang at Youth Specialties, and many others. Thank you all for your friendship. I also want to thank David Jeremiah, Ray Benton, John Ruhlman, and Ken Elben at Shadow Mountain Community Church for your encouragement and for allowing me to serve in such a wonderful church. And thanks also to Ken and Elizabeth Kitson for the use of their Mexican retreat as a sanctuary while working on this revision. To my wife, Marci, God's best gift to me besides himself—my deepest appreciation for your prayers and support over the years. You have been so good to me. And to my grown-up children, Nathan, Amber, and Corey—thank you for bringing me so much joy. Again, I'll take this opportunity to say to my family: I love you.

• O N E •

A CASE FOR JUNIOR HIGH MINISTRY

If children are not reached with the gospel by age 13, the chances of their accepting the gospel after that point are greatly reduced.
—George Barna

Most people still refer to them as *junior highers*—after that uniquely American educational institution called the junior high school—even though middle schools continue to replace and outnumber junior high schools in many areas of the country. In the middle of the 20th century, young adolescents approximately 10 to 14 years old were isolated as a category, and schools were created especially for them because it was recognized that early adolescence is unique. Ten-to-14-year-olds are not the same as elementary school children. But neither are they like the adolescents who attend high school. They are the in-between group, and they belong in a category all their own.

But simply labeling or categorizing them is not enough. Junior highers need special attention and junior high (or middle) schools need to be more than mere holding tanks—scaled-down versions of the high school where kids wait until they are old enough to transfer into the real thing. It is ironic that there are few people who dispute the significance of early adolescence as a stage of life; yet it is safe to say that junior highers remain one of the most neglected (if not despised) groups of people in society.[1] "Grownups don't think you're very important if you are over 10 and under 14," a 12-year-old girl wrote. "But if you're younger than 10 and older than 14, then you're important. When I was 11, I thought I was important, but after the first couple of months I found out that I'm just a plain old boring kid."

My objective in this book is to demonstrate that this age group is indeed important and to suggest some practical ways for the church to reverse the trend of neglect that has characterized the vast majority of youth ministries. In fact, it is my conviction that there is *no higher calling* than to work with junior high students. I don't mean that other ministries are less important, but only that ministry to junior high students is singularly strategic. Researcher George Barna studied thousands of youths and came to the conclusion that unless students

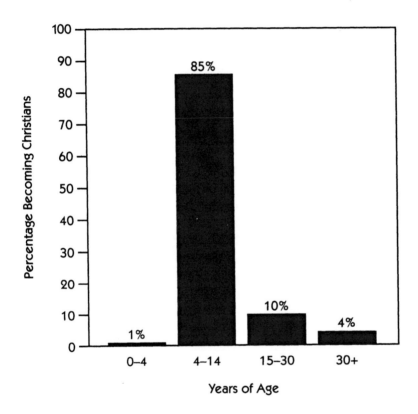

are reached by junior high school, there is little chance of reaching them at all.[2] The International Bulletin of Ministry Research published similar findings that are overwhelming. According to their research, 86 percent of all Christians make their commitments of faith before the age of 15.[3]

More and more educators, parents, policy makers, and researchers are agreeing with each other that early adolescence is the "last best chance" to significantly influence in a positive way the paths that young people will take in their development.[4] Increasingly youth workers across North America have come to realize that high school ministry has essentially become rehabilitation work. Many high school students have already made serious life-changing decisions that are beyond intervention or influence. It is simply too late. But this is generally not the case with junior highers. In this book, I will explain why this it true and I hope that you—the pastor, the youth director, the volunteer—will catch the vision for effective junior high ministry and understand better how to meet the needs of early adolescent youth.

A Time of Neglect

Usually when youth ministry is considered in the church, the primary concern is with high school or college students, even though the number of junior high students may be greater. It is not uncommon for a church to spend a substantial amount of money on programming and professional staff to meet the needs of senior highers without ever considering the same for its junior highers. The children's department of the church naturally concerns itself only with children up through the fifth grade, since the sixth- or seventh-grader is viewed as having outgrown all the old methods and is now ready for something else. The problem is that few people seem to know what that something else is. So the end result is that the junior higher is more often than not put on hold; we wait for him to pass through this stage and to grow up into someone to whom we are better equipped to minister.

There are many reasons why junior highers have been traditionally neglected in the church. Perhaps the most obvious one is that many, if not most, adults dislike junior high kids. They simply don't like being around them. Others suffer from what has been called *ephebiphobia*, a *fear* of adolescents.[5] They are frightened by the unpredictability of junior highers and the negative stereotypes they believe about them. Many parents I know would be delighted if somehow their own kids were able to skip the junior high years altogether. I have written another book for parents entitled *Enjoy Your Middle Schooler.*[6] Some people think the title is an oxymoron. They find it hard to believe that you can actually enjoy your children when they become early adolescents.

People don't feel this way about older teenagers or younger children. Senior highers appear to be, in many ways, a lot like young adults. They are somewhat predictable and are able to communicate on a relatively mature level. They can drive, they have money, and they are often willing to work and to take on many leadership responsibilities—all of which makes the youth worker's job a great deal easier. Junior highers generally offer none of the above, and this unfortunately discourages many people from getting involved in junior high ministry.

Similarly, the prospect of working with or teaching the younger children in the church poses no real threat or problem for the adult who wishes to serve in some way. To the youngster, the adult represents authority, knowledge, power, and deserves respect. Most adults enjoy this kind of recognition. Little kids are, for the most part, manageable, cute, and they believe most everything you tell them. Not so with junior highers. Much to everyone's dismay, they love to challenge authority, and they have a knack for asking disturbing questions that are often difficult, if not impossible, to answer.

According to Don Wells, principal of the Carolina Friends School and member of the Task Force on Middle Schools (National Association of Independent Schools), junior highers are neglected by adults for the following reasons:

1. Early adolescents defy being defined, and that's irritating. We can set some hazy marks about them on a scale relative to any act, value, skill, or any other single thing, but the result is either as useful as a definitive description of all bubbles, or so definitive as to classify all bubbles, save one, the exception. And those things we can't define, can't make sound predictions about, indeed those things that even resist our efforts to classify them by the effrontery of simply being themselves, we tend to avoid. In the case of the early adolescent, we have avoided.

2. Because of our inability to define, the holder of the needed information is a child, and what adult wants to be dependent on a *child* as his resource person? Precious few it seems.

3. The number of persons who had a positive, healthy, happy early adolescence in a supportive, caring environment equals the number of adults presently whole enough to creatively and maturely identify with an early adolescent toward the goal of successful interaction. Such persons were an endangered species long before the blue whale.

4. We all have fragile egos, and we all play to the audience out there. When we have our druthers, we pick good audiences because they tend to make us feel good. Early adolescents are very unpredictable audiences, and many times they hiss and boo. Not because they don't like you, but because they aren't sure they like themselves; not because they want to corporately hurt you, but because they aren't thinking corporately but individually; not because they understand and reject, but because they don't understand that you don't understand.

5. To appreciate the world of the early adolescent, one must "become" in the world of the early adolescent. Such total immersion is not as necessary when working with other age groups, for we readily accept that we can never experience early childhood again and we delight in our ability to enjoy, nurture, and support the childhood experience. We also revel in the fact that we can have adult dialogue with children beyond early adolescence, and although we then have to take full cognizance of their burgeoning physical and mental prowess, they do seem eminently more reasonable than they were just a few years back. Early adolescence cannot be dealt with so neatly, for it has been the stage in our lives replete with terror, anxiety, fear, loneliness, hate, love, joy, desperation, all expressed (or experienced) with the intensity of adulthood yet devoid of adult perspective. It is an age of vulnerability, and vulnerability implies potential pain; adults know that pain hurts, and they don't often willingly enter a domain in which they will be hurt. So we avoid (deny) because we as adults cannot again handle adolescence.

6. Early adolescents are easily identifiable as imperfect specimens of the human condition. They are not the epitome of anything we can define as "good" from our adult perspective. Since they aren't consistent, they can't reach perfection on our terms. We don't use positive superlatives in describing them. All of us, however, generally prefer dealing with those who have "made it" in the superlative sense. Therefore, because early adolescents are moving in such constant flux, they never make it to a desirous end within that stage. Dealing with early adolescents does not afford us the satisfaction of experiencing a finished product, and we lose vision and perspective easily. (And so do they.)[7]

In other words most people avoid junior high ministry because most people avoid things that are unpleasant. People don't usually stand in line to sign up for a bad time. Junior highers are generally stereotyped as being rowdy, restless, silly, impossible to handle, moody, vulgar, disrespectful, and worst of all, unpredictable. Unfortunately all of these characteristics may be true at times, but to be completely fair, the truth is that junior highers offer more than enough to offset whatever hazards may exist in working with them. They are, for example, tremendously enthusiastic, fun, loyal, energetic, open, and, most importantly, ready to learn just as much as the creative youth worker is willing to help them learn. The personal satisfaction and sense of accomplishment that are part of working with junior highers are unequaled anywhere else.

I have served in several churches and parachurch organizations in a variety of roles and have worked with most age groups in just about every context—leading children's church and summer camps to teaching Bible studies and preaching. And I have to say that I enjoy most working with people closer to my own age. I am, after all, an adult and can identify in more ways with adults than with kids.

Yet if I were to select the most challenging and rewarding area of ministry in the church, it would have to be working with junior highers.

Most church staffs are hierarchical in nature. That is, the senior pastor's office is where most of the power and authority resides, and presumably he or she has the most significant ministry in the church. All the other positions in the church are of lesser importance (which is usually reflected by the size of the paycheck). This may or may not be warranted. But consider this: in most cases, senior pastors spend their time meeting the needs of adults—people who are pretty much set in their ways. Adults have generally made all the big decisions about everything important in their lives. They have already decided on their careers, lifestyles, value systems, husbands and wives, and religious beliefs. These will probably not be changed.

Junior high workers, on the other hand, minister to people who still have all those important decisions lying out in front of them.

17

Unlike the pastor who works primarily with adults, the junior high worker gets to *influence* all those decisions—*before* they are made, not after. Maybe we underestimate just how important junior high ministry is in the church.

There are still quite a few people, however, who view junior high ministry as a kind of glorified baby-sitting. They believe that all you can really expect to do is keep an eye on them, give them enough activity to hold their attention, and wait until they grow up. Junior highers, after all, just aren't mature enough for any kind of serious ministry now, they say. To expend a great deal of effort working with junior highers is like throwing pearls before swine. It is better stewardship of both time and money to wait until you can really do some good. Wait until they get older. Wait until they reach high school.

My answer to that is a story: There was a pathway that ended abruptly at the edge of a high cliff, and for some unknown reason, day after day people would walk off the end of the pathway without stopping and fall off the cliff onto the jagged rocks below. After years of losing citizens to this problem, the local authorities finally decided to do something about it. They brought in a team of experts to assess the situation and to make some recommendations. After much study and discussion, the experts decided that the best thing to do would be to *build a hospital at the bottom of the cliff!*

What makes this story so ridiculous, of course, is that the problem is not at the bottom of the cliff, but at the top. Anyone can see that what needs to be done is to find some way to keep people from falling off the cliff. I believe that junior highers stand precisely at the top of the cliff. To wait until they are older is like building hospitals at the bottom of dangerous cliffs. Junior highers need help now, not later. If we wait until they are older, we may not get the opportunity to help them. Most surveys I have seen indicate that the person most likely to drop out of church is a ninth-grader. It is during the junior high years that many young people decide that they are tired of being baby-sat.

A Time of Transition

I read a story in the newspaper a few years ago about a European traveler who wanted to get to Oakland, California. He bought a ticket in Frankfurt, Germany, to Los Angeles International Airport, with a connecting flight to Oakland. When he arrived in Los Angeles, he got lost and told someone at the ticket counter that he wanted to go to Oakland. Because of the traveler's poor English, the person at the counter thought he said "Auckland." Incredibly, the traveler mistakenly bought a ticket and boarded a plane bound for Auckland, New Zealand, instead of Oakland, California. Fifteen hours later he found himself halfway around the world in a country he had no desire to visit at all.

The moral of the story? *Watch your connections.* Changes can be very important, not only in airports, but in life. And of course, some of the biggest changes in life take place during the junior high years. Early adolescence is something like a busy airport terminal. Children arrive looking for the plane to adulthood. Unfortunately, they sometimes end up on the wrong plane.

> Like travelers at a busy airport, children arrive at early adolescence looking for the plane to adulthood.

The years between 10 and 15 are without a doubt the most unsettling in a person's life. This is when puberty occurs—when a person changes physically from a child to an adult. But there are many other changes as well. During this period there is a tremendous amount of upheaval and it takes many different forms. This once-in-a-lifetime metamorphosis and most of the resulting changes will be discussed in greater detail later in this book.

Misconceptions often abound regarding puberty. It is not a disease, so it doesn't need a cure. Everyone experiences it, so it's perfectly normal, even though it results in what appears to be abnormal behavior.

For example, it is not uncommon for a junior higher to catch a sudden case of the giggles or to erupt into tears without warning. Or he might be bursting with energy one moment, yet for no apparent reason become lethargic and lazy the next. He will sometimes act very much like an adult and at other times act like a child. He may become unusually preoccupied with the mirror and worry to the point of depression about every supposed defect in his physical appearance. He may decide to do something one moment and then immediately change his mind and do precisely the opposite—hardly what one would call normal behavior. Actually when working with junior highers, it is a good idea to keep in mind that the abnormal is the normal most of the time.

This once-in-a-lifetime transition called *adolescence* is like living in two different worlds at the same time. It can be both wonderful and terrifying. Frederick Buechner once described it this way:

> The ancient Druids are said to have taken a special interest in in-between things like mistletoe, which is neither quite a plant nor quite a tree, and mist, which is neither quite rain nor quite air, and dreams, which are neither quite waking nor quite sleep. They

believed that in such things as those they were able to glimpse the mystery of two worlds at once.

Adolescents can have the same glimpse by looking in the full length mirror on back of the bathroom door. The opaque glance and the pimples. The fancy new nakedness they're all dressed up in with no place to go. The eyes full of secrets they have a strong hunch everybody is on to. The shadowed brow. Being not quite a child and not quite a grown-up either is hard work, and they look it. Living in two worlds at once is no picnic.[8]

For some junior highers, the new experiences they encounter during early adolescence will be of no consequence and go practically unnoticed by the casual observer. But for others puberty sets off a chain reaction of difficulties and complications. The renowned adolescent psychologist Erik Erikson has written that it is not until adolescence that "the individual begins to see himself as having a past and a future that are exclusively his. Early adolescence is thus a pivotal time of review and anticipation."[9] In other words, kids have their eyes opened. This is when children attempt to put away childish things in their quest to become persons with unique identities, and most of the time these efforts result in struggle, stress, and sometimes—as Erikson points out—crisis. As junior highers begin to break away from parental domination, to seek autonomy and a degree of independence, they find themselves frustrated. Parents are naturally reluctant to let go, and they often don't understand what is going on. Meanwhile, young people are certain that they're not being allowed to grow up and that the only possible solution is to rebel.

And sometimes they do. The juvenile crime rate soars during the early adolescent years. There is much in the news these days about teenage runaways, teenage drug abusers, teenage pregnancy, and teenage suicide, and much of that news is about young people under the age of 15. Without belaboring the point, there is more than enough evidence to prove that the junior high years are uniquely troublesome and require *more*, not less, of the church's concern and attention.

It is both ironic and tragic that the reality of *transition* during early adolescence is also one of the primary reasons why junior highers are so neglected. There are those who would say that since junior highers are in transition—neither one thing nor the other (in-between-agers)—then the best thing we can do is to wait for them to grow out of it. Just wait for them to settle down. Trying to minister effectively to junior highers, they say, is like trying to hit a moving target. They are, after all, in transition.

But they don't simply grow out of it. The changes that take place during early adolescence, and the supervision and guidance (or lack of it) they receive during this time, leave an indelible mark on their lives far into adulthood. The experiences of early adolescence are life shaping and life changing. "The growth events of adolescence," Erikson writes, "are in large measure determined by what has happened before and *they determine much of what follows after* [italics mine]."[10] This is why early adolescence is such a pivotal time in a person's life.

A Time of Questioning

During early adolescence young people learn to think in new ways, causing them to call into question much of what they have been taught. Many childhood myths crumble as they discover new ways of perceiving reality. They no longer consider everything their parents or teachers tell them to be true; they want to understand everything for themselves.

A 14-year-old girl describes the conflict between her old and new perspective: "I had a whole philosophy of how the world worked. I was very religious, and I believed that there was unity and harmony and that everything had its proper place. I used to imagine rocks in the right places on all the right beaches. It was all very neat, and God ordained it all, but now it seems absolutely ridiculous."[11]

It is not at all uncommon for junior highers to suspend temporarily or even to reject entirely the values and beliefs acquired during childhood. This questioning continues until they are able to determine whether these values and beliefs have any validity or relevance to their new young adult lives. Just as Santa Claus and the stork were discarded years earlier, so the God of the Old Testament and the Christ of the New Testament seem not quite as believable as they once were. This is no cause for alarm; in most cases it is normal for youth to discard their childhood assumptions as they seek to arrive at their own conclusions, their own faith and values. (We will discuss this more fully in chapter 8.)

Our point for now is this: it would seem foolish for the church merely to occupy junior highers with activity rather than to offer them thoughtful and honest answers to the questions that flow out of their emerging faith. There is certainly a danger here of losing them entirely with little chance of reclaiming them later.

A Time of Openness

Early adolescence has often been called the Wonder Years, and for a good reason. Junior highers are extremely open to new ideas and experiences. The world of adulthood is coming into focus and their eyes are wide open. They want to try everything, experience everything, and believe every new idea that comes along. They are open to good ideas and bad ideas, positive behaviors and negative ones. They are in the middle of a complicated trial-and-error process of identity formation that will help them determine what kind of person they will eventually be.

I remember Darrin, a 12-year-old who came to youth group one day wearing a T-shirt with the name of his favorite rock band emblazoned across the front. He said he wanted to become a rock star and was saving his money to buy a set of drums. A few days later, Darrin's shop teacher at school told him that the mahogany chessboard he made in class was really outstanding, and suggested that Darrin enter it in the fair. Darrin immediately decided that he would become a carpenter and would now buy himself some carpenter's tools instead of drums. But it wasn't long after that when a speaker came to church and challenged the youth to "do something important with their lives for God," so Darrin went forward to make a decision to become a missionary. He put all his money in the offering plate.

It sounds like Darrin can't make up his mind exactly what he wants to do. If he were 35 years old, we'd call him unreliable or unstable. But at 12 years old, we simply call him normal. Junior highers typically try on personalities, convictions, and behaviors one day and then discard them the next for just the opposite. For many junior highers, a long-term goal often has a life span of about three hours. A life's dream frequently lasts a week. Kids this age will try out all kinds of roles and behaviors to see how they feel and to see what kind of feedback they get from others. They test the waters to determine what they like or don't like and what other people like or don't like. This is why a junior higher's entire demeanor can change from one week to the next. This of course makes junior highers rather unpredictable—but *predictably* unpredictable. It's an important part of the growing-up process. For the junior higher, life is like a big jigsaw puzzle with a lot of the pieces missing. Her job is to find all the pieces and put them into place.

> If he were 35, we'd call him unreliable or unstable. At 12 years old, we call him normal.

Senior high students, by comparison, are nearing the completion of this process and will often be much more predictable and even rather rigid and set in their ways. By the time teenagers graduate from high school, many if not most have already adopted the personality, lifestyle, and values that will be theirs for the rest of their lives. This is why it is so easy to make relatively accurate predictions about high school seniors.

I remember attending my high school reunion, which brought together most of my graduating class. It was good to see my old friends and classmates once again, but it was also kind of eerie. I had the strange feeling all evening that I had been put into a time machine as I renewed old acquaintances and watched the action on the dance floor. It was like being back in high school all over again because everyone was so much *the same.* I discovered that, with few exceptions, I could have made very accurate predictions as to what those high school graduates would be like 10 or 20 years down the road. The introverts were still introverts; the extroverts had become insurance salesmen or politicians; the high achievers had become successful in business or education; the class flakes were still flakes.

This is in stark contrast to the openness, flexibility, and unpredictability of junior highers. Trying to pin them down is like trying to nail Jell-O to a wall. They remain open to all kinds of possibilities for their lives.

One explanation for the openness of junior highers is offered by H. Stephen Glenn, who suggested that children develop their values and beliefs in a cyclical manner. This chart describes the cycle:

Cycle One		Cycle Two	
Age 0–4	Discovery	Age 12–14	Discovery
Age 5–8	Testing Out	Age 15–17	Testing Out
Age 9–12	Concluding	Age 18+	Concluding

According to Glenn, the first stage in cycle one is a time of discovery for the very young child, when the world is being explored for the first time. Newborns to four-year-olds are at great risk because they are constantly sticking things into their mouths, crawling into places they don't belong, and scaring parents out of their wits.

The second stage is a time of testing out (age five to eight), when knowledge is tested on others to determine such things as right from wrong, true from false, and appropriate from inappropriate behavior. A six-year-old will lie or steal just to see if he can get away with it.

The final stage of cycle one is a time of drawing conclusions. Ten-year-olds are quite secure in their perceptions and opinions about everything, having organized their lives in an orderly and systematic way. "They feel certain that they know how life works," Glenn writes. "'We are Presbyterians. They are Catholics. We don't eat pizza. We don't have those kinds of friends. We don't watch those kinds of shows.' There is little equivocation in the mind of a 10-year-old."[12]

Then puberty comes along and wipes out the whole thing. The blackboard is erased, so to speak, and the cycle essentially repeats. As adulthood looms large in front of young adolescents, they once again go through a time of discovery. Junior highers are notorious for exploring and experiencing everything, trying things on for size just like a small child. If you have ever noticed a similarity between junior highers and preschoolers, this may partially explain it. Junior highers, like small children, are undeniably inquisitive and have a need to check out for themselves everything they can.

This time of discovery is followed once again by a time of testing out and a time of concluding. But it is during early adolescence when we find young people most open to new ideas, new experiences, new ways of thinking.

Of course, this openness often takes the form of gullibility or vulnerability. They are not always the most discriminating people in the world and will try almost anything, at least once. This is why so many early adolescents are considered to be at risk. Whatever is going around has to be tried. Fads are big on junior high and middle school campuses. Whatever the new fad, every junior higher has to try it. These kids are easy targets for advertisers, rock-n-roll disc jockeys, drug pushers, and anyone else selling just about anything. This age group is willing to buy things and take risks that older teens and adults would certainly think twice about. As one news magazine reported:

> Too old for Ronald McDonald, too young for the car keys. Yet today's 25 million "tweens" from nine to 15 no longer are viewed by Madison Avenue as the $2 allowance crowd. More marketers are pitching products directly at youngsters. And it is not just cereal. . . . To marketers, these impressionable and seemingly insatiable kids, who buy or influence the purchase of $45 billion worth of goods a year, represent not only a treasure trove but an opportunity to convert an entire generation to brands they might buy for life.[13]

Several years ago, I heard the chairman and CEO of MTV say in an interview, "We own 13-year-olds." These people are very intentional about reaching the early adolescent market with their products and values, because they know that by reaching them now, they are hooking them for life.

I believe that the church has just as much potential as the world to capture the attention of this age group. Junior highers are open not only to fads and bad influences; they are also open to positive guidance and direction for their lives. All they need is for someone to take them seriously and to treat them with a little respect, and they will respond. It is doubtful that there will ever again be a better or more strategic time to reach young people for Jesus Christ.

A Time of Decision

A national survey of more than 8,000 early adolescents revealed that the *value* that increases the most between the fifth and the ninth grades is "to make my own decisions."[14] As junior highers approach adulthood, they covet the one major characteristic of adulthood that has until now eluded them: the ability to make their own decisions.

While they were children, parents, guardians, and other authority figures made all of their important decisions for them. But now they want the right to begin making these decisions for themselves. This does not mean that junior highers want to be *independent*. Actually, what they want is *autonomy*, the right to make decisions about things that are important to them. They want to decide who their friends will be, what clothes they will wear, what music they will listen to, and so on. Likewise they are anxious to make decisions about their values, faith, and other commitments. Their quest for autonomy pushes them to make as many of the decisions that govern their lives as possible.

While it is true that junior highers are making a *lot* of decisions, it is safe to say that not all of them are *lasting* decisions. Erikson maintained that early adolescents between the ages of 11 and 15 are simply not ready to "install lasting idols or ideals as guardians of a final identity."[15] He believed that young adolescents are in a kind of fact-finding period, making the majority of their assumptions, conclusions, and decisions fragile and temporary. You don't have to spend a lot of time around junior highers to know that there is a lot of truth to this. Junior highers are notorious for deciding something now and undeciding it later. They often make decisions without thinking them through or counting the cost. They use the "ready, fire, aim" method of making decisions: decide first and ask questions later.

> Junior highers are notorious for using the "Ready, fire, aim!" method of decision making.

Trial-and-error decision making works fine for choosing whether to take guitar lessons or not, but it's a dangerous way to choose whether to take drugs or not, or whether to have sex or not. Unfortunately, some of the decisions being made by junior highers today are not insignificant. "I am trying to get parents, the community, and educators to recognize one critical fact," said Dr. John Liechty, director of middle schools for the Los Angeles Unified School District. "Every single 10-to-15-year-old is at risk—regardless of the language they speak, their socioeconomical status, their ethnicity, their academic standing—because during that five-year period, they are going to make decisions that will impact the quality of the rest of their lives. The belief system they develop now about themselves and their potential is difficult, if not impossible, to change later."[16]

We must neither overreact or underrespond. Yes, junior highers are making decisions—some of them temporary, some of them life changing, hopefully none of them fatal. Many, in fact, will be positive.

We all know, for instance, of people who decided to follow Christ while they were in junior high. We can't say with any certainty which decisions will be made during early adolescence, but we can be certain that the decision-making process begins (or at least gains impetus) during early adolescence, and that some of the decisions made by early adolescents will receive enough confirmation and support in the years ahead to last.

We need to understand that junior highers have reached a very important crossroad. They are now ready to take some responsibility for their lives. They can begin making good decisions or bad ones. Does this mean that we should push junior highers to make decisions for Christ at this age? Not necessarily. I really don't believe that our job as junior high workers is to try to get junior highers to make final decisions about anything. Priority should be given to teaching junior highers how to think, how to make good decisions, how to exercise good judgment, how to understand the consequences of their decisions. We should allow junior highers the freedom to make decisions on their own without coercion or manipulation on our part. If their decisions are going to have any meaning at all, they must come as a result of their own reasoning, understanding, and process of elimination.

I imagine the role of a junior high worker as being something like a traffic cop at a fork in the road. The road leading out of childhood is straight and sure. Young children journey along that road without

having to make many decisions of their own. Most of their decisions are made by the significant adults in their lives—usually their parents. Then they arrive at that fork in the road called *early adolescence*. Now it's time to make decisions of their own and the first big one is to decide which road to take. One road is the road marked *good decisions* and the other road is the one marked *bad decisions.*

We all know young people who have chosen the road of bad decisions. Some have journeyed far down that road, now almost out of sight. Likewise, we know many young people who have made good decisions. They are following Christ. They are doing their best to live in a God-honoring manner.

As junior high workers, our job is simply to help kids get on the right road. We may never see them arrive at their final destination, but we can point them in the right direction—help them learn to make good decisions. And we can give them *opportunities* to make them as well. I can remember as a junior higher "accepting Jesus Christ as my personal Savior" dozens of times at camps and youth rallies and evangelistic services. Most of those decisions lasted at least . . . until I got home. Which of those decisions was the true decision for Christ? Was it the first one? Or was it the last one? I really don't know, but I have a feeling that somehow, the sum total of all those decisions added up to my becoming a follower of Jesus Christ. That may not be very good theology, but it's very good junior high ministry. Early adolescents should be taught to make decisions for Christ every day.

Again, I want to emphasize that the job of the junior high worker is not to produce large numbers of decisions, but to take seriously the fact that junior highers are capable of making them. We must not fall into the trap of using such decisions as a way to determine success and failure in our ministries. Significant decisions can and will be made by the junior highers in your church, but it is wiser to teach the kids *how* to make them and then allow those decisions to come on their own.

A Time of Exigency

A generation ago, *youth ministry* was virtually synonymous with *high school ministry.* All of the major Christian youth movements, such as Youth for Christ and Young Life, were aimed at high school teenagers, and in many aspects, still are. Junior highers were still considered children—too immature. But times have changed. It was in 1979 that Dr. Urie Bronfenbrenner of Cornell University observed, "The adolescents today are the 12-year-olds, and the 11-year-olds, and the 10-year-olds. That is, they are having the experiences that five years earlier, adolescents didn't have until they were 13, 14, and 15; and they, in turn, are having the experiences that adolescents used to have when they were 16, 17, and 18."[17]

A few years later Dr. Victor Stursburger of the American Academy of Pediatrics wrote: "Short of being in a war, these are the most dangerous times adolescents have ever had to face. There are more choices teens have to make at younger ages and less guidance to make those choices. Now, 14-year-olds are having to decide 'Am I going to have sex or not? Am I going to use drugs or not? Am I going to drink alcohol or not?' Two generations ago those decisions were made in college. A generation ago they were made in high school. Now they're being made in junior high school."[18]

And the trend has continued. All of us know of eight-, nine-, and 10-year-olds who are struggling with issues that in previous generations were reserved for the teen years and beyond.

The cutting edge of youth ministry in today's church is at the junior high and middle school level. This is not to say that high school ministry is any less important now than it ever has been—but more and more youth workers are recognizing that if youth ministry is to be taken seriously at all, then junior high ministry has to be given a higher priority.

On the Niagara River, there is a place called Redemption Point. It is this spot that is considered to be the last reasonable rescue opportunity for people who have been caught adrift in the river. If people are swept into the river and drift beyond Redemption Point, attempts to fish them out will be fruitless; they will plunge over the raging waterfall and most surely die. All resources, therefore, are implemented to snatch people from the river before Redemption Point.

I believe that junior highers have reached Redemption Point. It is here that their developmental course will largely be set for life. Too many young people at this age are in danger of "going over the falls" with little chance of rescue. Now is the time for the church to implement every available resource to reach out to these kids before we lose them.

Adolescent psychologist Gary Downing, who has also served as a church youth minister, expresses it well:

> Because early adolescent growth has accelerated so much over the last 20 years . . . we must rethink our assumptions, our strategies, and our programs in order to respond to the changing needs of kids. We must overcome our ignorance, apathy, and our stereotypes so that we do not lose a whole generation of people so desperately in need of our love and concern. We cannot afford to dismiss this young subculture as "too squirrelly, too energetic, too disrespectful, or too shallow" to be worthy of our time and resources. We cannot expect to "warehouse" this group for several years and expect that they will be waiting for us when we decide we are ready for them. They won't be there tomorrow because we aren't here today when they need us the most.[19]

The junior high years offer us a unique opportunity for ministry in the local church. At no other time in a person's life are so many options considered, changes made, and lives shaped. It is not a time for baby-sitting but for loving attention. We need to surround our junior highers with caring adults who are interested in them and willing to mentor them in the Christian faith. "The most cost-effective program in any church is a strong junior high department," says Doug Murren, a pastor and leader in the modern church-growth movement. "Junior high school is the make-it-or-break-it time for children, in my opinion. . . . Our best efforts and budgeting need to be aimed at doing a good job with kids in this age bracket."[20]

I have always loved the picture that Scripture provides of the boy Jesus, coming of age as a young adolescent. Luke tells the story—perhaps with a smile on his face as he writes—of a 12-year-old boy separating from his parents (literally) and beginning his preparation for life as an adult.

When Mary and Joseph finally catch up with him, they find him in the temple courts sitting with the teachers, "listening to them and asking them questions." He wasn't shown to the playground or led off to the youth group for fun and games. Instead he was treated with dignity and respect and given the attention that he deserved. And remember that these teachers didn't realize who he was. They didn't know they were talking to the Son of God. That's why Luke comments that "they were amazed at his understanding." I am impressed with these teachers who were willing to take time to listen to a 12-year-old boy.

> Every year his parents went to Jerusalem for the Feast of the Passover. When he was 12 years old, they went up to the Feast, according to the custom. After the Feast was over, while his parents were returning home, the boy Jesus stayed behind in Jerusalem, but they were unaware of it. Thinking he was in their company, they traveled on for a day. Then they began looking for him among their relatives and friends. When they did not find him, they went back to Jerusalem to look for him. After three days they found him in the temple courts, sitting among the teachers, listening to them and asking them questions. Everyone who heard him was amazed at his understanding and his answers.
>
> —Luke 2:41-47

What do you expect from junior highers? Too many people in the church answer, "Not much." But the time has come for a new way of thinking about this age group. I believe that if we start taking junior highers seriously, and begin to give them the kind of attention they deserve, even skeptics will be amazed.

Notes

1. From a study conducted by the Family Resource Coalition and Search Institute. Of 659 family-serving organizations, only half have a mission statement that includes the period of early adolescence. See Search Institute, "Source" newsletter, Vol. XIII, Number 1, February 1997, p. 3.

2. George Barna, *Generation Next* (Gospel Light, 1995), p. 30.

3. From the International Bulletin of Ministry Research, quoted in *CE National News and Notes*, Volume 10, No. 4, Winter 1996-97, p. 3.

4. Carnegie Council on Adolescent Development, *Turning Points: Preparing American Youth for the 21st Century* (Carnegie Council, 1989), p. 8.

5. From the Greek (*ephebe* or "young man"). See Mike Males, *The Scapegoat Generation* (Common Courage Press, 1996), p. 16.

6. Wayne Rice, *Enjoy Your Middle Schooler* (Zondervan, 1994).

7. Donald A. Wells, "The Educational Plight of the Early Adolescent," unpublished manuscript, 1976. Used by permission.

8. Frederick Buechner, *Whistling in the Dark* (Harper & Row, 1988), p. 1.

9. Eric Erikson, *Identity, Youth and Crisis* (W. W. Norton, 1968), p. 91.

10. Erikson, p. 23.

11. Jerome Kagan, "A Conception of Early Adolescence," *Twelve to Sixteen: Early Adolescence*, Robert Coles and others (eds.) (W.W. Norton, 1972), p. 94.

12. H. Stephen Glenn and Jane Nelson, *Raising Self-Reliant Children in a Self- Indulgent World* (Prima, 1989), p. 161.

13. *U.S. News and World Report*, March 20, 1989.

14. Search Institute, "Young Adolescents and their Parents," *Project Report* (Search Institute, 1984), p. 12.

15. Erikson, p. 54.

16. "Middle School Solution to Turbulent Age Group," in *The Los Angeles Times*, October 13, 1992, p. C2.

17. Urie Bronfenbrenner, cited in "Options in Education," program #95: *Portrait of American Adolescence* (National Public Radio, 1979).

18. Victor Stursburger, quoted in *Youthworker Update*, Volume 1, No. 6, February 1987, p. 1.

19. Gary Downing, "Is There Life after Confirmation?" Unpublished manuscript, 1985.

20. Doug Murren, *The Baby Boomerang* (Regal Books, 1990), p. 23.

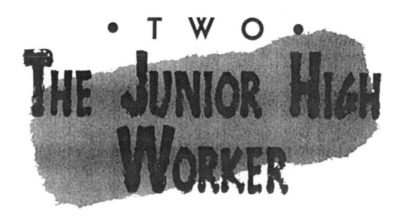

• T W O •
The Junior High Worker

Learn to run a junior high group and you can rule the world.

—Bill Wennerholm

Junior high ministry is about people, not programs. The junior high worker is absolutely central to the success or failure of programs and methodologies. Junior high ministry is essentially relational, making the people involved in it the main ingredient.

Today there are all kinds of resources, ideas, curricula, and books available for junior high programming (believe it or not). A lot of it is very good. But the truth is—none of it will work without good people to make it work. If the kids don't like or can't relate to the people involved in the programs and activities, the ministry will fail.

But there is good news. The reverse is also true. That is, if you are the kind of person who relates well to junior highers and if you are able to communicate with them reasonably well, then it is likely that you could use almost any resource or new idea successfully. This, of course, doesn't mean that the junior high workers who relate well to junior highers don't have to be selective about resources, but they do have a distinct advantage.

Junior high students nearly always describe their youth programs or classes in terms of who leads them. The leader is the one who makes the class great or terrible. It is interesting that high school and college students almost always select their classes by *subject*—after they have looked over the course offerings. But with junior highers, there is little concern about content. The important question for junior highers is not *"What* did you get?" but *"Who* did you get?" The goal is to get the good teachers and avoid the bad ones.

Educator Edward Martin comments about attempts to separate the teaching from the teacher:

> Curriculum reform projects of the past 10 years in the academic disciplines have tried to improve junior high schools by producing better materials, some of which could be taught by any teacher. Most of them now realize that with a bad teacher, students will feel the new course is just as bad as the old.[1]

If we want good junior high ministry, then we need good junior high workers. This is not optional. Junior high ministry simply can't be done by anyone. It would be convenient if everyone who was willing or available could do the job, but unfortunately there are some people who just can't work with junior high kids. They don't have the right stuff.

Before you get too discouraged and assume that I must be referring to you, let me urge you to read on. Don't close the book yet. The right stuff is probably not what you think it is. The qualifications required for junior high ministry are not outside the grasp of ordinary people like you and me.

What are those qualifications?

First, a word about some unqualifications. Take, for example, the stereotype of the typical junior high worker—a handsome, young, entertaining, athletic, single college student who dresses very hip, owns a custom-built van with surround sound, and has an apartment at the beach. Even with all these "assets," this guy could be hopelessly unqualified to work with junior highers. It is possible, of course, to win the affection and admiration of junior highers for a while by being cool or by having a great personality, good looks, and the latest clothing styles, but most good junior high workers that I know possess few of these. That doesn't mean you cannot be young, beautiful, and talented—but you certainly don't have to be in order to relate well and minister effectively to junior highers. Sometimes those positive assets can actually work against you if kids perceive that you have it all together and they don't. They may feel threatened by you unless you let them know that you have faults and imperfections just like they do. Kids will like you and listen to you not because you happen to be hip or glamorous, but because you like them and listen to them.

Now on to the qualifications.

Certainly we have to begin with a basic prerequisite for ministry to junior highers (or anyone else for that matter)—spiritual maturity. I assume that anyone who takes on a position of leadership in the church has a meaningful relationship with Christ that can be communicated to others. This does not mean, of course, that a junior high worker has to be a spiritual giant. It means instead that he or she has a faith that is alive and growing. It is inappropriate for someone who does not have this basic foundation to teach or otherwise minister to others in the church.

At a workshop on junior high ministry a few years ago, a group of overzealous youth workers brainstormed a list of characteristics of an effective junior high worker and came up with 27 different items. Just looking at that list made me feel discouraged. Since the perfect junior high worker doesn't exist, I'll spare you those 27 characteristics, and narrow it down to the six I consider the most important. You must—

- Understand junior high kids
- Like junior high kids
- Be patient
- Be a good listener
- Be a positive person
- Have time to do it

Chances are good that you fit this description. If you don't, keep in mind that all of these qualifications can be learned. People do not naturally possess a liking for junior highers or good listening skills, but they can be acquired. Few junior high workers will score high on all six of the above characteristics. It's okay to be a positive person who needs to improve on listening skills. On the other hand, it would be safe to say that a person who flunks out on any one of these six qualifications is going to encounter some real difficulty relating and ministering to junior highers. Let's look at them one by one.

Learning to Understand Them

Good junior high workers understand junior high students. They are able to identify with early adolescents; they can empathize. Most adults can't. To most adults junior highers are beyond their understanding. They can't understand why junior highers are so moody, noisy, angry, disrespectful, irreverent, smart-mouthed, and lazy. All of these behaviors may be true about particular junior highers, but usually there are good reasons for them. What junior highers want from adults is someone who looks beyond their behavior and tries to understand. Without this understanding communication becomes almost impossible.

Every adult has one very good point of identification with junior highers: we were all, once upon a time, junior high kids, too. Even though the world that today's junior highers are growing up in has changed, most of the problems they face today are not that different from the problems we faced when we were their age. All of us, regardless of race, creed, color, or economic class, know what it's like to be a young adolescent. We've all been there; adolescence is a universal, shared experience.

But psychologists tell us that there is a problem for normal adults when it comes to remembering that adolescent experience. They call it *repression*: "rejection from consciousness of painful or disagreeable ideas, memories, and feelings"—a kind of adult amnesia. To make life more endurable, the brain automatically tries to forget—or at least blocks from memory—painful experiences from the past. Those painful experiences are never lost completely from consciousness, however; they are just pushed back into the recesses of the mind and rarely, if ever, recalled. It is common for therapists to use hypnosis or some other method to help people remember and deal with repressed events.

What does repression have to do with junior high ministry? Simply this: psychologists tell us that some of life's most painful experiences occur during early adolescence—while we are junior highers. So we repress our early adolescence. We block it from memory. Once we leave those adolescent years behind, we forget them.

Some have compared the adolescent experience with childbirth. Most women endure quite a bit of pain when they give birth to a child. But it usually doesn't take long for them to forget (or repress) it. Jesus described this kind of forgetfulness when he remarked that "a woman giving birth to a child has pain because her time has come; but when her baby is born, she forgets the anguish because of her joy that a child is born into the world" (John 16:21). In the same way, most people go through the pain of early adolescence and then block it from their memory when adulthood comes. Educator John A. Rice wrote this:

> . . . but where is one who does not wince at the memory of his adolescence? Women say they cannot remember the pangs of childbirth. Crafty nature blots them, lest there be no more children. So also one does not remember one's second birth . . . from childhood into youth. This second birth becomes in memory a dull pain.[2]

So what's so painful about early adolescence, you ask? (Have you forgotten?) Consider the embarrassment and humiliation of having to dress for that first P.E. class, the struggle with parents for independence, the times when you were not accepted into the right group of kids, the rejection you felt, the guilt feelings brought on by new awareness of your sexuality, puzzling questions from a developing mind, love triangles and broken hearts, and the list could go on and on. No one wants to go through life with all *that* on his mind, so it is repressed. The average adult's inability to understand and empathize with junior highers can be attributed simply to the fact that he just doesn't remember.

The best way for you to understand junior highers is to get in touch with your own early adolescent years. Sure it's hard to reach back and relive events and recall feelings from a long time ago, but it isn't impossible and it does wonders to help you empathize with kids.

Understanding junior highers does not mean that you need to be an expert on youth or youth culture; it just means that you need to develop a good memory. Your memory can be one of your greatest resources as a junior high worker. There have been many occasions when I have looked into the face of a 12- or 13-year-old who was having a problem of one kind or another and felt for a moment like I was looking into a mirror. I recognized myself as a boy around that age. That realization helped me tremendously as I listened and attempted to relate to him and offer guidance.

If your memory and you cannot cooperate, it's not likely that you will need to go to a psychiatrist or a hypnotist for therapy. Sometimes just being around junior highers will do the trick. You might talk to people who knew you well when you were a junior higher (like your parents, if possible). Sometimes it's helpful to try and write down as much as you can remember about those years. In my office I have a picture of myself when I was in the eighth grade. It's a constant reminder that I was once a junior high kid.

Regardless of your ability to instantly recall your youth, it is wise to read as many books and articles on adolescence as you can. Check your public library. The chapters in this book dealing with the characteristics of junior highers will hopefully be helpful to you as well, and I have listed other resources for further reading in the back of this book. Doing some homework is an excellent way not only to stay informed, but also to jolt the memory when remembering does not come easily.

Keep in mind that the reason for all this remembering and reading is to bring about a better understanding of junior highers and an identification with their problems and feelings. Without this it becomes very difficult to relate to junior highers. Young adolescents will often exaggerate their miseries and overdramatize their suffering, and it's hard to be supportive when deep down we just don't believe things are as bad as they let on. And, of course, it's entirely possible that they may not be. But to junior highers, their suffering is very real, and adult advice, criticism, and analysis is the last thing they need in a moment of crisis. When a person is hurting, he needs a soothing balm, some encouragement, a shoulder to cry on, someone who will listen and understand. When a junior higher tells

> When a junior higher tells you that she is the ugliest person in her peer group, believe it. Your acceptance must come first; advice, reason, and perspective can come later.

you that she is the ugliest person in her peer group, believe it. You have been given an important piece of information. Your acceptance must come first; advice, reason, and perspective can come later.

I can especially identify with the crises of junior highers when I reflect on my own romantic experiences at that age. Whenever I would fall in love with the girl who sat on the other side of the classroom, or with the pastor's daughter, or whoever the lucky girl happened to be at the time, I was certain that it was the real thing. Someday we would be married, have children, and live happily ever after. But the adults in my life, parents especially, would only smile and to my great dismay classify it as puppy love. I can't describe how much that hurt. In retrospect, they were right. It *was* puppy love. But puppy love is very real to puppies.

Learning to Like Them

A few years ago I conducted a survey of approximately 700 junior high kids from all over the United States, and I asked each young person to answer a number of questions. One of the questions was this: *If you could ask any question and get a straight answer, what would it be?*

Naturally, I received many different responses, but there was one that appeared more than all the others. The big question on the minds of many, if not most, junior highers is simply "Do you like me?"

They want to know if they are liked and accepted. They aren't concerned about the theological issues of the day, or about how they can be better Christians at school, or about what the future holds. The real issue that gets top priority with so many junior highers today is "What do you think about me? Am I okay?"

More recent studies conducted by Search Institute have shown that not being liked is ranked among the top three worries of early adolescents, even ahead of dying.[3] Being accepted by others is very important to junior highers, and more often than not they will pledge absolute loyalty to whoever gives that acceptance to them. Like nearly everyone else, they like to be liked, but their insecurities give this need a greater significance. Their need to be liked is linked closely with their emerging adulthood and their quest for independence. They are not certain whether they are likable, which they perceive to be an important prerequisite for success in the adult world.

The implications for junior high ministry should be obvious. A good junior high worker is one who genuinely likes junior high kids—a necessity for anyone hoping for a meaningful and productive ministry with junior highers. Understanding is important, but unless you like to be around them, understanding becomes merely an academic exercise. There are many experts in the field of early adolescence who have never developed a liking for the young people they know so much about. I have asked many junior high principals to name the most important characteristic of good junior high teachers. The typical reply? "They've got to like junior high kids."

There are degrees of liking, of course. You may be one who likes junior highers a great deal or only mildly (that's okay), but the important thing is that what you have comes through for the kids to see. It's not enough to simply announce "I like you" now and then and leave it at that. Words rarely make a good substitute for actions. Junior highers need to see words translated into actions. *Show* them that you really like them whenever you can.

Practically speaking this means that you should try to develop friendships with kids individually. Learn their names. I have discovered the hard way that forgetting a junior higher's name can be extremely detrimental to a developing relationship. Find out each one's likes and dislikes, interests, and concerns. Visit their homes, meet their parents, and learn their family situations. Sometimes the best way to get to know a junior higher is to get a guided tour of his bedroom. You can learn a lot by looking at all the posters and other paraphernalia on the walls and shelves.

> I can't recall much of those Sunday night youth meetings 40 years ago, but I'll never forget Jerry picking us up to shoot baskets or go bowling.

I have found that one of the best ways to show junior highers that you really like them is to do things with them that are not required of you. After all, they know that you are going to be involved with them in programs and meetings, teaching classes, and even visiting them on occasion—because it's your job. That's what you are expected to do as a youth leader. But when you are willing to give up some of your own free time to be with them, that's different. Only a friend would do that.

Perhaps you could take a junior higher or two on a fishing, camping, or backpacking trip, or invite some of them (even on short notice) to a ball game or movie some evening. Try taking kids shopping with you on a Saturday afternoon, or inviting them to your home during the week, or hosting a slumber party. These are all good ways to let kids know that you enjoy their company.

When I was in junior high school, my family went to a small church that didn't have much of a youth program except for a Sunday night youth meeting just before the evening service. Our pastor's younger brother, Jerry, was given the responsibility of leading those youth group meetings for several years. Today I can't recall much of what happened at any of those Sunday night meetings of almost 40 years ago, but I'll never forget Jerry. I remember well that every Saturday Jerry would come around in his car and pick up several of us boys and we would shoot baskets, or go bowling, or head for the beach, or just mess around. As a junior higher, I considered him one of my best friends, even though he was a lot older than me, and I know I would have done almost anything for Jerry. During those years when I was having a great deal of trouble finding acceptance from adults and being treated like a real person, Jerry liked me and was my friend. That was more important than great youth meetings. I realize now that Jerry played a big role in my development both as a person and as a Christian.

Left to their own devices, young adolescents will gravitate toward the oldest person who will take them seriously.

Anytime you can give personal attention to your junior highers, you are letting them know that you are serious when you say that you care about them. Sometimes all it takes is a phone call during the week thanking them for something, asking a favor of them, or just checking up on how they are doing. Calling someone for no particular reason is something that a friend would do. I have used the mail in much the same way. Junior highers love to get mail, and a personal, affirming note now and then helps tremendously to show kids that you think of them more than on Sundays only.

You can be a friend to a junior higher without acting like a junior high kid. It is important to retain your identity as an adult. You are not an overgrown kid. Likewise, junior highers need encouragement just to be themselves and not try to be little adults. Your role should be that of an adult friend who sincerely likes them, cares about them, listens to them, and tries to help whenever possible. H. Stephen Glenn, coauthor of *Raising Self-Reliant Children in a Self-Indulgent World* once remarked that young adolescents—left to their own devices—will always gravitate toward the oldest person they can find who will take them seriously and treat them with dignity and respect. This of course flies in the face of the common belief that adolescents hate adults and want nothing to do with them. Granted many youth *are* turned off by adults who they perceive as being hostile toward them—a sizable group. But they are very responsive to older adults who show a genuine interest in them and will look to those people for guidance and support.

Liking junior highers is not always something that comes naturally, especially as you grow older. Still, most of the time, building a relationship with them is easier than you might think. It does require a commitment—as most relationships do—and it also requires cultivation and care to help it along. In other words, it's no different from any other kind of relationship. You have to work at it.

Learning Patience

Junior high workers need patience—lots of it. I have known many people who went into junior high ministry with plenty of enthusiasm and zeal, only to quit a few months later because they lacked patience. Junior highers will test your patience. They are famous for it.

"They're testing everybody," explained a middle school principal." If, for example, I said that for a week we're going to have a new tardy policy that calls for a machine gun on the top of the building and when the tardy bell rings we're going to strafe, I guarantee you that even if I gave six months advance notice I would lose three or four hundred kids on the first day of tardy. Because every junior high school age youngster needs to test whether you really mean what you say."[4]

Not only will they test your patience, but junior highers rarely provide you with the kinds of results you need to feel successful. If there was ever a ministry of sowing, this is it. Somebody else usually does the reaping. In many ways the patience you need to do junior high ministry is a lot like faith. It is "being sure of what we hope for and certain of what we do not see" (Hebrews 11:1). The dictionary says *patience* is "endurance, fortitude, or persistent courage in trying circumstances." No question that junior high workers need *that* kind of patience. Why? Because in junior high ministry, *success* and *results* are almost nonexistent—at least in the ways most people understand those two words.

Ralph Waldo Emerson said this about success: "I look on that man as happy who, when there is a question of success, looks into his work for a reply." People are happy when they stand back from their work and find they have accomplished something significant and worthwhile. It's a good feeling.

But if your work is junior high ministry, you may look into it and not find anything at all that looks or feels like success. In some ways, it more closely resembles failure. It's hard to find results in

> **Junior high ministry is like growing and tending sequoias—you won't be around when the trees mature.**

junior high ministry.

I'm not saying that junior high ministry is not fruitful. Results will come, but they won't be *short-term* results. Junior high ministry is like growing and tending sequoias—those giant redwoods in California that take thousands of years to grow. There is little chance that the person who plants sequoia seedlings will be around when the trees mature.

Similarly junior high workers rarely see the results or the end product—what I call the *visible impact*—of their work. Most people in the ministry want to think that their efforts actually make a difference in other people's lives. They would like for their ministry to bear fruit and produce tangible, visible results. It is encouraging for pastors and teachers to know that their words are being taken to heart and put into practice. It is gratifying for counselors to know that an individual took their words of advice seriously and is now benefiting from them. Without a certain amount of visible impact, it would be difficult to continue.

But visible impact such as this is rarely found in junior high ministry. You can get kids to repeat all the right words, to make all kinds of decisions, and to behave themselves for varying periods of time. But real, lasting results will rarely be evident while the kids are still in your junior high group.

A friend of mine recently took his junior high group on a mission trip to Mexico. The trip was one part of a six-week discipleship course on Christian values. By allowing the kids to see for themselves the poverty and the suffering of the poor people of Mexico, he hoped that his junior highers would be able to make better decisions about their values and priorities. And it seemed to work. When they debriefed their Mexico experience, they were unanimous in their commitment to become more concerned about the plight of the poor and the oppressed.

Two weeks later, the same junior highers conducted a fundraising activity, after which my friend asked them to make a choice. They could use the money they had raised to help feed and clothe the poor people they had visited in Mexico—or they could use it for a fun trip to an amusement park. The decision was theirs.

The group voted unanimously to go to the amusement park.

When something like this happens, it makes you wonder whether your work is making any difference at all. Normally, you

> **Knock yourself out for junior highers, and instead of strokes you'll get sneers and snores.**

hope that you see results reflected in some kind of positive behavior; but with junior highers, you just can't count on it. And it rarely has anything to do with how well or how poorly you are doing your job. Learning and growth in junior highers will be taking place even when their behavior seems to indicate otherwise.

I like to tell junior high workers that their ministry is a lot like the ministry that Jesus had while he was on earth. Jesus spent three years with his disciples, yet he saw little in the way of results while he was with them. You can imagine the frustration Jesus must have felt when his disciples bickered among themselves, fell asleep on the job, or failed to remember what he taught them. Most of the disciples deserted Jesus when he needed them the most. He went to the cross without seeing his ministry come to fruition. It was not until many years later that the *visible impact* of Christ's earthly ministry was realized. So it is with junior high ministry. That's why patience is so important.

Patience is also required because junior high workers receive little in the way of affirmation and praise for what they do. Everyone—especially those who volunteer—needs to be stroked a little bit. But in junior high ministry, strokes are most often in short supply.

I love working with little children once in a while. It's great for the ego. Little children are so easy to please. They listen attentively and respond with enthusiasm. Do something nice for them and they'll make you feel like a hero. They hug your leg and write you love letters. Little children are wonderful.

Likewise I enjoy the opportunities when I get to work with adults. Adults are generally gracious and polite. Even when I do poorly, at least a few will go out of their way to show their appreciation, shake my hand, and offer some words of encouragement.

But with junior highers, it's a different story. It's not uncommon to knock yourself out for them and instead of getting strokes, you get

> ### A Retelling of Matthew 5
>
> Then Jesus took his disciples up the mountain and gathering them around him, he taught them saying:
>
> "Blessed are the meek, for theirs is the Kingdom of God; blessed are they who mourn; blessed are the merciful; blessed are they who thirst for justice; blessed are you when persecuted; blessed are you when you suffer; be glad and rejoice, for great will your reward be in heaven."
>
> Then Simon Peter said, "Are we supposed to remember this?"
>
> And Andrew said, "Do we need to write this down?"
>
> And James said, "I don't have any paper."
>
> And Phillip said, "Are we going to have a test on this?"
>
> And Bartholomew said, "Will you make Thomas stop hitting me?"
>
> And John said, "The other disciples didn't have to learn this."
>
> And Matthew said, "Can I go to the bathroom?"
>
> And Judas said, "Boooooring!"
>
> And Jesus wept.

discipline problems. Instead of applause, you get sneers, snores, insults, and outright rejection. Nobody calls to tell you what a great job you did. Instead, you get calls from parents who make unreasonable demands on you. Unless you are thick-skinned, this kind of affirmation can be very frustrating.

Patience is needed, but resilience may be needed even more." Keep giving young adolescents the chance to reject you," Peter Scales advises.[5] Hang in there. It's helpful to remember that junior highers actually have a higher regard for the adults who work with them than any other age group—even though they have funny ways of expressing it. It usually takes a few years, however, before they fully realize just how significant those adults are (or were).

Learning to Listen

Junior highers are at a point in their lives when they need someone who will listen to them. The maxim that children should be seen and not heard doesn't go over very well with early adolescents. They want to be heard. They want to be taken seriously, and of course, the best way to take them seriously is to listen to what they have to say.

Listening has rightly been called the language of love, and in junior high ministry, it is also the key to a young person's heart. H. Stephen Glenn put it this way: "Take a young adolescent seriously—by listening to him or to her—and that young adolescent will give you a great deal of power and authority over him or her."[6] Be careful here—don't interpret that to mean that the purpose of listening is to control or dominate junior highers. What it means is that when a junior higher is taken seriously by an adult, then that young person is likely to give back to the adult *the right* to exercise power and authority over him. Put another way—if you will listen to junior highers, they will listen to you.

An old bit of wisdom says that there are two ways to open an egg. The first is to break it. The second is to warm it. The first is preferred if you want to eat the egg. The second is preferred if you want it to live. If we want our junior highers to live and to grow, then we must warm them with our ears—by being good listeners. If we will listen to them, they will open themselves up to what we have to say. They will respect us and look to us for leadership and guidance. Junior high workers who want to have a significant impact on the lives of young people would be well advised to develop their listening skills.

A Positive Attitude and a Sense of Humor

When junior highers describe school teachers they don't like, they often say, "He's such a grouch." Junior highers interpret grouchiness in adults as a personal dislike for them. But they are attracted to those adults who greet them with a smile and who seem to possess a positive attitude and a warm sense of humor.

This doesn't mean that you have to be a comedian to be an effective junior high worker. You don't have to be like the stereotypical youth worker whose biggest asset is the ability to tell jokes and take a pie in the face. Junior high ministry is a lot more than fun and games. But it does mean that you are mature enough not to take yourself or your ministry too seriously. You just need to be able to loosen up a bit.

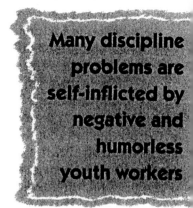

Many discipline problems are self-inflicted by negative and humorless youth workers

I have met many junior high workers who see themselves primarily as disciplinarians. Their job is to maintain law and order. The problem with that attitude is that many (if not most) discipline problems in junior high ministry are self-inflicted by junior high workers who are essentially negative and humorless. Those who approach junior high ministry with a drill sergeant mentality won't last very long. There are times when it is much better to try to see the humor in some of the outlandish or disruptive things that junior highers do than to try to stop them with reprimands and threats of punishment.

When I first began running junior high camps and retreats, I learned very quickly that the campers enjoyed most those activities that were clearly against the rules, such as conducting midnight raids on each others' cabins, having water balloon wars, and setting booby traps around their cabins. Rather than cracking down and punishing those who participated in such activities, we legalized virtually all of it. We had giant water balloon fights, we allowed secret raids each evening on unsuspecting cabins, and we even gave an award each day for the most inventive booby trap set by a cabin group. The results were quite positive, and the kids had a great camping experience.

There are some people who by nature have a tendency to always see the proverbial sugar bowl as being half empty rather than half full. Effective junior high workers usually come from the second group. They are able to look beyond the faults and inconsistencies of early adolescents to see the big picture. Junior highers need people who will laugh with them at their mistakes and who will let them know they are loved (and enjoyed) even when they mess up.

It Takes Time—*Your* Time

You may have sensed by now that good junior high ministry could require a sizable portion of your time. It takes time, after all, to build relationships with individual students while organizing all the meetings, classes, outings, and so on. Time is a very important factor in the potential effectiveness of a junior high worker in the church, and the time demands can be discouraging. Rarely does anyone have more than enough time. With today's busy schedules, the problem is usually finding any time at all.

Speaking from personal experience, this shortage of time can be the downfall of any well-intentioned junior high worker. You may like junior highers and have a strong desire to minister to them, but just be too busy to put that desire into practice. For this reason, I always list as a prerequisite for the junior high worker a willingness to allocate enough time to do an adequate job. The actual amount of time will vary a great deal from person to person, but it is certain that it will take more than an hour or two on Sunday.

Time plays such an important role because it is tied up with the fact that junior highers view things pretty much in black and white categories. That is, you are either a friend to them or you are not. When you say one thing and fail (or are unable) to back it up with your actions, you run the risk of being categorized as a hypocrite. That, of course, is not always accurate, but proving otherwise can sometimes be difficult. Junior highers characteristically fail to understand adult obligations, and they often take this to mean that some other task is more important than they are.

The bottom line here is that junior high ministry must be more than good intentions. It does require time. When I look for someone to help with a junior high group, I try to find someone who is not already committed to dozens of other jobs in the church, since I don't want these other jobs to rob them of the time they are going to need to be with junior high kids.

On the other hand, I have learned that a little bit of time is always better than no time at all. If you are a volunteer, as most junior high workers are, you may have only one or two hours a week to do junior high ministry. You may have time to call or visit only two kids all month. But that's great! Chances are that's more time than anyone else was able to give to those two kids all month, and God will bless that. Jesus fed a multitude with two fish; he can also work wonders with two hours.

Get Help When You Need It

You may be the kind of person who can do everything yourself, but it is more likely that if you are single-handedly ministering to the junior highers in your church, regardless of the size of the group, you could benefit from some help. Junior high ministry is always best when it is a team ministry. If you are a youth director or Christian education director responsible for a number of age groups, no doubt you are also in need of other adults who can serve as junior high sponsors or leaders.

How many? Usually the size of the group will dictate the exact number that is required. A good ratio is approximately one adult for every eight junior highers, although every group should have at least two adult leaders—one male and one female. The 1:8 ratio, although arbitrary, is based on the idea that it is difficult to establish relationships with many more than eight. It can be done, of course, but it's much more difficult, especially with the many other responsibilities of adult life. If you hope to be able to give some quality time to each person, it is wise not to bite off more than you can chew.

Another important consideration is the male-female balance of the group. If you are a male but your group is made up of quite a few girls, you should have a female coworker who can relate to those girls as only another female can. Junior high girls are just beginning to deal with their emerging womanhood, and they need adult women whom they can trust and confide in. The same is true for boys. It's not being sexist to recognize that boys should have men they can relate to and look up to and girls should have women. Early adolescence is an important time of gender identification, and it helps to have good adult role models available.

A related problem for many young male junior high workers is how to handle junior high girls who become infatuated with them, who "have a crush" on them. This is not uncommon, and it also happens, although less frequently, with female junior high workers and junior high boys. I don't have an easy solution for this, but I have found that it is very helpful (if you are male) to have a woman coworker who can minister to the girls in the group, and vice versa.

The problem, of course, is not usually the failure to know when more help is needed. The problem is knowing whom to enlist. For reasons already stated, there is rarely a waiting list of people who want to work with junior high kids. Usually those who do emerge are the chronic volunteers—people who volunteer for everything. They're usually fine folks, but they are more than likely volunteering for the wrong reasons. To wait around for volunteers is usually not the best way to get the best people. The best way is to take the initiative yourself and seek out people who you have reason to believe would make outstanding junior high workers. You have to recruit them.

Again, keep in mind that we're not talking about people who have lots of youth ministry experience, or who are young and talented. We are looking for people who possess to some degree the qualifications previously described in this chapter. Again, no one has to be perfect. As a rule of thumb, I usually seek people who have the time and the willingness to give junior high ministry a try and who seem like the kind of people who haven't repressed their own adolescence so much that they find it impossible to relate to junior highers. From that point, other necessary or helpful skills may be developed.

When looking for junior high workers, I have found that it is generally best to rule out high school students. They usually lack the maturity to take on the responsibility for junior high ministry. That doesn't mean that high school students can't be involved in the junior high ministry in some very effective ways. I have used high school students for leading music, doing dramas, helping out with games and skits, even teaching. It's good for junior highers to see older teenagers serving Christ, using their gifts and talents in ministry, and being leaders and role models for them. But high school students are simply too close in age to the junior high students to be reliable junior high workers.

When I worked as a junior high camp director, I always had the most difficulty with church groups that used high school-aged cabin counselors. We frequently had to discipline male counselors who had become overzealous about "counseling" some of the female campers long after the evening meetings were over. High school students may be fully capable of assisting in many areas of the junior high program, but in most cases it is better to seek more mature leadership.

College students often make very good junior high workers, but there are problems common to this age group as well. One is that they are rather transient—here this semester, gone the next, or away for the summer. It is best to find people who can give the junior high group a degree of stability over two or three years if possible.

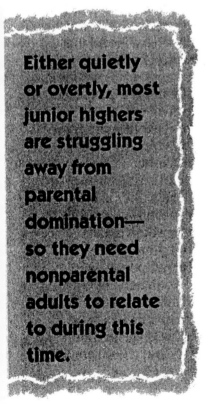

Either quietly or overtly, most junior highers are struggling away from parental domination—so they need nonparental adults to relate to during this time.

One middle school ministry that I am familiar with requires a three-year commitment from its adult leaders. A male leader, for example, at the beginning of this term is given a group of six to eight sixth-grade boys, and he works with those boys for three full years (through sixth, seventh, and eighth grade) until they move on to the high school department of the church. Of course, in practice, this model is no more free from breakdown than any other, but the reasoning is sound. For three years, each kid in the group has someone who knows him well and notices whenever he is having difficulty or is making progress. The end result of such a plan should be a lower dropout rate as well as a more effective ministry.

Parents often are willing to work with the junior high group and, depending on who the parents are, that can be either good or bad. Some parents volunteer to work with the junior high group simply because they have a vested interest in what's going on. They may want to keep an eye on their kids, or they may want to keep an eye on you. Needless to say, this is not the best motivation for doing junior high ministry.

Parents can and should be involved in the junior high program in some way, but there are potential problems with parents doubling as junior high workers. They may be overly protective of their own children or perhaps too close to them to deal with them in an objective manner. It's difficult to be neutral with your own kids. You can give objective, empathetic advice to other people's kids, but it's difficult to do that with your own.

A bigger problem is that kids are often intimidated by the presence of their parents in the youth group, which prevents them from opening up as they might under normal conditions. Most junior highers are involved, either quietly or overtly, in a struggle to free themselves from parental domination, and they usually need adults other than their parents to relate to during this time. For this reason, it's a good idea to ask students how they feel about having their parents involved in the youth group. You may be surprised to find that some of your junior highers have no problem with it at all. In fact, some students actually *want* their parents to be involved.

Despite the potential problems, I would not rule out parents of junior highers as leaders for the junior high group, especially if they sincerely want to be involved and appear to be qualified to do a good job. It's strictly a judgment call. I'll have more to say about the role of parents later in this book.

When I am looking for junior high workers, I generally like to recruit young adults, either single or married, in their 20s and 30s. Young couples with no children or with young children often make wonderful husband/wife teams. I also like to go after older adults—whose children have grown, or those of retirement age. So long as they enjoy the kids and are able to understand and communicate with them, they have all that it takes. Many times kids will love and respect older folks more than those closer to their own age.

One of the most creative junior high workers I have ever met is in his 60s. He teaches a Sunday school class of seventh-grade boys in a small town in Oregon. Once a month he has his class wear old clothes to church and instead of attending services that week, they all climb into the back of his camper and go fishing. He provides the boys with bait, tackle, and even shows them how to tie flies. And according to this junior high worker, he gets more teaching done along the banks of a stream once a month than he is able to accomplish during the remaining three weeks of the month spent in the classroom. I wouldn't doubt it at all.

Mentors for Junior Highers

So far in this chapter, we have primarily concerned ourselves with adults as junior high workers—people who take responsibility for leading, teaching, or otherwise participating in the overall junior high ministry of the church. But there is another very important role that adults in the church can play in the junior high ministry, and that is to simply become a *mentor* to one or more junior high students. Mentors don't have to be involved in the programs and weekly activities that typically make up a junior high ministry. Instead, they are adults in the church who get to know individual junior highers on a one-to-one basis. They are, for your junior highers, adult *friends*.

I will discuss mentoring in more detail in chapter 11, but for now it is important to note that a primary goal of effective junior high ministry in today's church is to connect kids with caring Christian adults who will take them seriously and treat them with dignity and respect. When that happens, young people not only come to know Christ, but they come to know someone older and wiser who will help them to grow strong and mature in the Christian faith.

In the past it was not uncommon for a church to hire one youth minister who was expected to do it all. I remember well my first job as a youth pastor. I was regarded by most people in the church as a hired gun who was expected to attract, entertain, and teach the kids what they needed to know about the Christian faith. My job was to give the youth a program of their own—to get the kids out of everyone else's hair. But thankfully, most of us who have worked with kids for more than just a few years have discovered how counterproductive such an approach to youth ministry really is.

Today the emphasis is on the professional youth worker as an equipper of the church, one who helps the entire church to love and care for its young people. The role of the youth worker is to find ways to bring adults and youth together again, rather than separate them with programs of their own. While programs and activities designed exclusively for junior highers are still important and serve many useful purposes, they are not the central focus of an effective junior high ministry. The purpose of programming is to provide opportunities for youth and adults to be together in positive ways so that relationships may develop and mentoring can take place.

Any adult in the church can be a mentor to a junior higher. All that is required is a willingness to get to know one kid and to find ways to nurture that relationship over a period of time. As I said before, mentors don't have to attend meetings, teach classes or lead games—unless they want to, of course. They simply assume the role of an adult friend who encourages, offers guidance and support, and prays.

All the qualifications of a junior high worker that we have discussed in this chapter apply to mentors. They should be people who are understanding, likable, patient, good listeners, positive, and willing to give of their time. Again, no one is perfect, but with a little encouragement, everyone can develop these assets. For this reason, when recruiting mentors, it's important to provide training to help these adults understand their role and to develop their mentoring skills.

Every junior high worker is a mentor, of course, but not all mentors are junior high workers. Some are ordinary adults who do nothing more than care about one kid. Those kind of people are very special and they will make your job a whole lot easier.

Other Places to Go for Help

The important thing to remember is that you don't have to rely on your own effort to do effective junior high ministry. You need to take advantage of the many people who can help you and the many resources that are available these days. You will, of course, have to go after them. Help rarely comes calling on its own.

There is now an abundance of printed resources that are loaded with ideas to make the programming end of junior high ministry a lot less time-consuming. You don't have to be original with everything you do. I have always maintained that the essence of creativity is the ability to copy well what has already been done, and this holds true with youth work as well. Why reinvent the wheel? Many hundreds of hours have gone into developing the resources that are at your disposal, and the more you use other people's good ideas, the easier it becomes to create ideas of your own.

There are numerous seminars, workshops, and training events held at various times of the year all over the country, sponsored by many different denominations and by independent youth ministry organizations like Youth Specialties. It's not always convenient to attend events that require a great deal of travel, time, or expense, but these conferences are excellent ways to get a shot in the arm when you may be needing it most.

In addition there are undoubtedly junior high workers from other churches in your area who would probably appreciate getting together with you periodically for sharing ideas and support. At times you will find that you are able to pool resources with other churches and possibly schedule some activities together. This is especially beneficial for smaller youth groups.

You may also find it helpful to form a support group of parents and other interested persons in the church who are able to meet with you whenever necessary to discuss some of your concerns, to help with planning, and to pray for the junior high ministry of the church. There are probably a number of people in your congregation who are unable to work with the junior highers week after week but who have much to offer in an advisory or supporting role.

The kids themselves can be a big help to you as well. You don't have to do everything for them. Junior highers are capable of taking on some responsibility, and they usually enjoy it. It's a good rule of thumb, however, not to give them more than they can handle or complete within a reasonable length of time. They can become easily frustrated or bored with the whole thing if it seems too big. Junior highers are great starters and lousy finishers. But be on the lookout for ways they can be involved. Not only will the kids benefit, they will also save you a lot of work in the process.

A final note on this subject: Remember that your greatest resource is God. Junior high ministry is a calling from God, and he will provide you with the strength and the resources to pull it off. If you feel inadequate, great! God will be able to use you much more than the person who thinks he needs nothing more than all of his incredible talents, abilities, and resources. Be yourself and let God do the rest.

Bathe your junior high ministry in prayer. Pray for each of your young people by name and seek God's direction for your programming decisions. Depend upon God to take whatever you are able to do, and then bless and multiply it.

Notes

1. Edward Martin, "The Early Adolescent in School," *Twelve to Sixteen: Early Adolescence*, Robert Coles and others (eds.) (W. W. Norton, 1972), p.180.

2. John A. Rice, *I Came out of the Eighteenth Century* (Harper & Bros., 1942), p. 121.

3. Search Institute, "Young Adolescents and Their Parents," *Project Report* (Search Institute, 1984), p. 97.

4. John Liechty, interviewed in "Middle School Solution to Turbulent Age Group," *The Los Angeles Times*, October 13, 1992.

5. Peter Scales, *Boxed In and Bored* (Search Institute, 1996), p. 20.

6. H. Stephen Glenn, *Developing Capable Young People* (Humansphere, Inc., 1983). Audio recording.

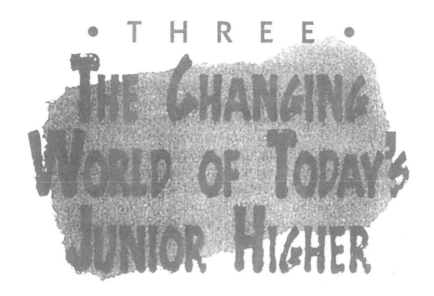

• T H R E E •

The Changing World of Today's Junior Higher

Young adolescents are experiencing a period of change more rapid than at any time other than infancy.

—Peter Scales

Who are junior highers? What exactly does a junior higher look like? Why do junior highers act the way they do? How are junior highers unique from other age groups? And how are today's junior highers different from junior highers of a generation ago? These are questions we'll try to answer in the next few chapters as we look at the specific characteristics and developmental needs of junior highers.

We'll examine how junior highers develop physically, socially, intellectually, emotionally, spiritually, and so on. While it is convenient to discuss each of these areas individually, it is important to keep in mind that these categories are quite artificial. Life can't be neatly divided up that way. But in the interest of clarity, it helps to take each of these areas one by one.

As we look at these areas and discuss the characteristics of junior highers, we will also deal with their implications. Our goal will be to connect what we know about junior highers with applications for junior high ministry in the church. It is not enough to merely describe junior high kids. Most of us know what one looks and acts like. Only Yogi Berra would put it this way: "You can observe a lot just by watching." But having information about junior highers is one thing; applying it is another. We want to learn about junior highers so that we will be able to use our knowledge in a positive and powerful way to minister to kids.

Need-Based Ministry

When you are trying to decide on a ministry strategy it always makes good sense to start with needs. Need-based ministry is simply taking time to discover or define a person's specific needs, and then trying, if possible, to find effective ways to meet those needs. To use a comparison, a doctor will diagnose a patient carefully before treating that person or before prescribing a cure. Obviously not every patient requires the same kind of treatment. What is good for one may be disastrous for another. Just because something worked for one patient doesn't mean it will be helpful for all. The doctor must begin with each patient's specific needs.

I heard a story once about a young boy who got an archery set for his birthday. A few days later, the boy ran into the house and excitedly asked his father to come look where he had been shooting arrows into the side of an old barn. His father went outside and was amazed by what he saw. There on the side of the barn were several targets, and dead center in the bull's-eye of each target was one of the boy's arrows. The father was naturally impressed and very proud of his young Robin Hood. He asked the boy how he had learned so fast to shoot so straight.

"It was easy," the boy replied. "I just shot the arrows first, and then drew the targets around each one."

Some people take that approach when it comes to youth work. Programs are a lot like arrows; people are like targets. The tendency is often to draw people around programs, rather than to create programs that are truly on target, meeting needs. This is no doubt encouraged by all the "It worked for me and it will work for you" books and seminars that offer the very latest in techniques, ideas, strategies, and the like. Program ideas are very important and helpful, of course (some of my favorites are included in this book), but that's not the place to start. Every idea or method should be carefully chosen on the basis of whether or not it meets the particular needs of the individuals in the group. There are many ideas that work, but not all of them meet needs.

This brings us back to the characteristics of junior high kids—our target group. Early adolescents offer us a variety of needs that have to be dealt with if effective ministry is to take place. Junior highers differ significantly from other age groups. A good junior high worker should know what those differences are and then act or program accordingly, in the best interests of the kids.

Unfortunately there remains a considerable gap between what we know about junior highers and how we treat them. This is true not only in our churches but in the public schools as well. According to Don Wells, principal of the Carolina Friends School:

> When attempting to construct a program for early adolescents, one is immediately struck by the disparity between the data we have on the early adolescent and the programmatic responses we devise.
>
> • Fact: Early adolescents need to try on a variety of roles. Response: We class them in few roles to make them a manageable lot.
>
> • Fact: Early adolescents vary enormously in physical, mental, and emotional maturity and capability. Response: In schools, chronological age is still the overwhelming factor used in grouping students.
>
> • Fact: During early adolescence the development of control over one's life through conscious decision making is crucial. Response: Adults make all meaningful decisions for almost all early adolescents almost all of the time, but do give the early adolescent the freedom to make safe decisions.
>
> • Fact: Early adolescence is an age where all natural forces (muscular, intellectual, glandular, emotional) are causing precipitous peaks and troughs in their entire being. Response: We demand internal consistency of the early adolescent, and in schools even punish some for not achieving this consistent state despite the fact that it is totally impossible for many to achieve at this point in development.
>
> • Fact: Early adolescents need space and experience to "be" different persons at different times. Response: We expect them to "be" what they said they were last week because otherwise we cannot use forethought in dealing with them.
>
> • Fact: Early adolescents are preoccupied by physical and sexual concerns, frightened by their perceived inadequacy. Response: We operate with them each day not as though this were a minor matter in their lives, but as though such concerns did not exist at all.
>
> • Fact: Early adolescents need a distinct feeling of present importance, a present relevancy of their own lives now. Response: We place them in institutions called junior high schools, which out of hand stress their subordinate status to their next maturational stage, and then feed them a diet of watered down "real stuff."[1]

In this book we will examine many of the characteristics of early adolescents that have relevance for junior high workers in the church and that demand our attention. Keep in mind that I do not intend to duplicate or replace any of the outstanding material on early adolescence by leading doctors, psychologists, educators, and researchers. All of these people are more qualified than I to give the subject a more scholarly and thorough treatment. In fact I cannot overemphasize to you the importance of reading as much as you can about this age group from other sources. Although we will only be scratching the surface, we will try to cover, in as much depth as necessary, those areas of special significance to the junior high worker in the church.

The Changing Early Adolescent

Perhaps no other word better describes early adolescence than the word *change*. As we discussed in chapter one, early adolescence is a time of transition—a time of enormous change. Everything is changing for junior highers—their bodies, their brains, their friends, their relationship with their parents, their demands, their feelings, their expectations. These changes reflect the metamorphosis that is taking place in their lives as they leave childhood behind and become adults. Most of these changes are internal—that is, they take place inside the life of the early adolescent. These are not changes imposed on them by others. These changes are simply part of the process of growing up. At no other time in a person's life does more change take place.

This is why it is important for parents and other adults to do whatever they can to reduce the number of *external* changes going on in the life of the early adolescent. By external change, I am talking about such things as a divorce or other family crisis, a move to another city, or a change in schools. These are changes that are imposed on the youngster from the outside, usually by other people. When external changes occur simultaneously with internal changes, a great deal more stress is put upon the young person, and they are at a significantly greater risk of suffering emotional distress or other problems. "The period of early adolescence is one of continual change and transition," wrote researcher Richard Lerner. "However, when these multiple changes occur simultaneously (e.g., when menarche occurs at the same time as a school transition), there is a greater risk of problems occurring in the youth's development."[2]

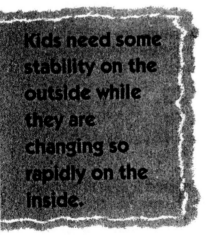

Kids need some stability on the outside while they are changing so rapidly on the inside.

One of the original reasons for the creation of the middle school (grades six through eight) had to do with this issue. Middle schools were created to help reduce the stress placed on students who were making the transition from elementary school to the junior high. Many seventh-graders were having difficulty with their adjustment to a new school environment. Since, on average, there are more *internal* changes going on in the life of a seventh-grader than a sixth-grader, the transition was lowered, from the seventh grade to the sixth.[3] Whether in fact sixth-graders in middle schools actually experience less difficulty adjusting to their new school than seventh-graders in a junior high school is not certain. But conceptually it makes a lot of sense. I often advise parents to wait—if they possibly can—until their sons and daughters are out of junior high school before they make any huge changes in their family life. Kids need some stability on the outside while they are changing so rapidly on the inside.

The Variability of Early Adolescence

Throughout this book I make quite a few generalizations about junior highers, which is a very dangerous thing to do whenever you are talking about people. It's especially hazardous when talking about junior highers, since no two junior highers are alike. In fact, the preceding sentence is about the only generalization that can be made about junior highers with any real accuracy.

A key word to remember when dealing with this age group is *variability.* Junior highers vary tremendously from one person to the next. To know that a young person is 13 is to know virtually nothing important about that person, except perhaps his grade in school.[4] Most 13-year-olds are in the eighth grade. Other than that, there isn't much you can say about that young person with any accuracy. She could be a fast developer, a slow developer, or somewhere in between.

Joan Lipsitz has noted that it is not unusual to find a six-year difference in biological age between slowly developing boys and rapidly developing girls in the same classroom.[5] This observation is based on the fact that it is normal for there to be a four-year spread in the average age of the onset of puberty. Add to that the fact that it is normal for girls to be about two years ahead of boys. This means that there could be a six-year developmental difference between a late-blooming 13-year-old boy and an early-developing 13-year-old girl.

Most of us who have worked with junior highers for any length of time have seen this phenomenon firsthand. There in your eighth grade Sunday school class is a girl who looks old enough to be dating college guys (and she could be). And sitting right behind her is a freckle-faced boy with a high-pitched voice who looks about nine years old. Which one is the real eighth-grader? Which of these young people do you choose your eighth-grade Sunday school curriculum for? These are questions that will continue to plague those who work with this age group and unfortunately there are no simple answers. "And here we are considering only biological age," adds Lipsitz. "There is such extreme variability among individuals who are changing not only physically, but also socially, emotionally, and intellectually, that the label of chronological age . . . may be the most misleading social organizer that we have adopted."[6]

This is one of the reasons it is important that you do not look at your junior high group as a "group." Instead, you must see them as Jason, Michelle, Christen, Geoffrey, Jennifer, and Nick. Your group is a collection of persons who are all at different places in their development and who have different needs at different times. We will be saying a lot more in this book about the importance of relationships, but as you can see, the need for a personal, one-on-one kind of ministry becomes obvious when you consider the variability of this age group.

Additionally we may need to find better ways to group junior highers than by age or grade in school. There is much debate over the appropriateness of grouping sixth-graders with seventh- and eighth-graders in middle school programs. Do sixth-graders belong with older kids or with younger? What about ninth-graders? Where do they belong?

Some junior high ministries have experimented with grouping kids according to maturity level. Others have tried grouping kids according to interest, using a variety of electives and other activities from which kids could choose. Some churches allow kids to simply choose the group they feel most comfortable in. It is doubtful that there exists a simple, clear-cut method that takes the variability of this age group into consideration and works for everyone. One thing is clear: The junior high worker who is concerned about individual kids will do a better job meeting their needs than the one who is more concerned about groups.

Nevertheless there are some things that can be said about junior high kids in general, and in this book I won't hesitate to say them. While we cannot say that all kids are the same, we can say that the majority of young people between the ages of 11 and 14 do have many developmental characteristics and needs in common. But don't try to put the kids you work with in a box. Some kids will be way ahead of schedule, others far behind, and some kids will skip certain stages altogether.

Are Today's Junior Highers Different?

Having worked with junior highers for several decades now, I've often reflected on how today's early adolescents are different from the ones I worked with back in the 1960s. There *are* differences, of course, but most of them have little to do with the developmental characteristics of junior highers that we will be discussing in the next few chapters. If you were to read the original version of this book, which I wrote over 20 years ago, you would find that most of what I have to say about junior highers hasn't changed much.

We need to remember that despite how much the world has changed in recent decades, junior highers today are really not that much different from junior highers of the past. They still are young emerging adults, going through the biggest transition of their lives—from childhood into adulthood—and they are asking the same fundamental questions that you and I asked when we were their age: "Who am I? What am I going to become? Does anybody like me? Am I okay?" Just as early adolescents of every generation have had to come to terms with their identity, purpose, and meaning in life, so are the kids who inhabit our youth groups today. They may look different, use a different language, and they may be experiencing a different world around them, but in the most important ways, they are the same. That's why it is possible for adults to relate to junior highers simply by *remembering* their own junior high years, as we discussed in chapter two. If we can stay in touch with our own early adolescence, we can understand much of what our kids are feeling.

But while it is true that junior highers today are a lot like junior highers of the past, the same cannot be said for the world in which they live.

A Changing World

To deal with all the changes that have taken place in society and culture during the last 20 or 30 years would require writing another book. However, in order to provide a background for discussing today's junior highers, I want to highlight just a few trends that I believe have had a significant impact on the youth and families who attend our churches and live in our neighborhoods today.

> ### The Good Old Days
>
> I see no hope for the future of our people if they are dependent upon the frivolous youth of today, for certainly all youth are reckless beyond words. When I was a boy, we were taught to be discreet and respectful of elders, but the present youth are exceedingly wild and impatient of restraint.
> —the Greek poet Hestes, eighth century B.C.
>
> Youth today loves luxury. They have bad manners, contempt for authority, no respect for older people, and talk nonsense when they should work. Young people do not stand up any longer when adults enter the room. They contradict their parents, talk too much in company, guzzle their food, lay their legs on the table and tyrannize their elders.
> —Socrates, fifth century B.C.

Abandonment

Today's youth have been abandoned by the adult world. They grow up without the kinds of natural built-in support systems that generations of the past enjoyed. The extended family has virtually disappeared. Rites of passage that once permitted entry for youth into the adult world have vanished. Our cities and towns can no longer literally be called *communities*. Even the nuclear family has been replaced by what David Elkind calls the "Postmodern Permeable Family"—one that no longer assumes traditional parent-child bonds.[7] It is estimated that 50 percent of all American children and youth will have spent some time in a single-parent home.[8] As one young writer put it, "Friends have become the family we never had."[9]

A recent nine-year study by the Carnegie Council on Adolescent Development found that America's 19 million young adolescents are being neglected to such an extent that "half of them may be irrevocably damaging their chances for healthy and productive futures." According to the study,

> Ten-to-14-year-olds are being abandoned by their governments, communities, schools, and parents just when they most need guidance and support. They are in danger of becoming "lifelong casualties" of drug and alcohol abuse, violence, suicide, AIDS, teen pregnancy, and failed educations. . . . The report's statistics are alarming. The rate of suicide among young adolescents increased 120 percent from 1980 to 1992; the firearm-homicide rate for 10-to-14-year-olds more than doubled between 1985 and 1992; the smoking rate for 10-to-14-year-olds rose 30 percent from 1991 to 1994; two-thirds of eighth-graders report that they have tried alcohol, and 28 percent say they have been drunk at least once; pregnancy rates for girls younger than 15 rose 4.1 percent between 1980 and 1988.[10]

There may be no better way to describe youth in today's world than to say that they are growing up virtually alone—what some have called *relational deprivation*. Since birth, many of them have been left alone to care for themselves and to find their own way to adulthood. As William Mahedy and Janet Bernardi have noted in their book *A Generation Alone*, today's youth have been abandoned by their parents, their families, their culture, and their world—and it is this abandonment that has become the root cause for practically every disorder that we see in today's kids.[11]

Marginalization

Today's youth have for the most part been relegated to the margins of society. In the past, adolescents had an important role to play. They were needed; they were viewed as *assets*. In the past, when children became adolescents, they took their place alongside adults and made a contribution to society. They had jobs to do on the family farm or the family business. But today, there is no place for them. Youth are viewed more as liabilities than assets. Edward A. Wynne and Thomas Einstein of the University of Chicago wrote this about today's kids:

> The most typical characteristic of adolescents today is that no one really needs them. And they know it . . . This does not mean that most adolescents are not loved or enjoyed. But their roles are largely ornamental. If most of them died, the immediate day-to-day work of the world would continue.[12]

Indeed the only disruption to the day-to-day work of the world would be in those areas where youth are needed as consumers. The entertainment industry, the fast-food industry, the clothing and sneaker industry would likely be disrupted by the disappearance of adolescents, but little else. "Today's generation of young people are the first in history to be totally unnecessary," says Tony Campolo.[13]

We see additional evidence of the marginalization of youth in the loss of physical space allotted to them in which to grow up. In rural cultures, children had acres of land to use as a playground or a place to explore. Even in the city, neighborhoods and parks were safe havens for youth in need of space to run and play. But the land is no longer available and the safety of the neighborhood is gone.

"Fifty years ago it was possible to tell children to go out and play, even in urban areas," David Elkind remembers. "But today, many urban and suburban communities are no longer safe for children."[14] In recent years youth have turned to the shopping malls of America for a place to hang out, but even those are now becoming off-limits for kids. Many of the largest shopping malls have already pulled up the welcome mat for teenagers and now require them to be accompanied by an adult.[15]

Enmity

I spoke recently with a junior high boy who had sadly come to the conclusion that adults simply hated them. In some ways he is not far from the truth. Today more than ever before, there is enmity (hostility) between the generations. A generation ago youth loathed the adult world (the Establishment) and declared a universal distrust of anyone over 30. But those same youth—who are all now over 30—have turned the tables on today's kids and won't have anything to do with them. Adults loathe teenagers and teenagers know it. According to Mike Males, writing in his book *The Scapegoat Generation*:

> American adults have regarded adolescents with hope and foreboding throughout this century. What is transpiring today is new and ominous. . . . The message Nineties American adults have spent two decades sending to youths is: You are not our kids. We don't care about you.[16]

And the feeling is mutual, of course. As adults have disconnected from youth, youth have disconnected from adults. The rise of youth gangs, runaway culture, and the like are a testimony to this unfortunate reality. More and more the media portrays youth in a negative light, resulting in unfair stereotyping of youth and an abiding fear of them. And this only causes the vicious cycle of abandonment and marginalization to continue.

Exploitation

In his book *The Disappearance of Childhood,* Neil Postman argues that childhood and adolescence is—or at least was—a time when kids were protected and shielded from certain kinds of information.[17] There was a time when young people were given a safe and stress-free environment in which to grow and develop, without having to deal with the kinds of pressure that adults face. But today even very young children are exposed to every sort of human depravity and vice under the mistaken assumption that having a bad experience will somehow prepare them better for adulthood. But in reality, the reverse is true. As Elkind has written, *a good experience is the best preparation for a bad experience.*[18] Regular exposure to disturbing information only traumatizes children and creates stress that interferes with their progress. William Mahedy, a college chaplain who also served in the Vietnam War, has noticed in many of today's kids the same type of post-traumatic stress disorder that is common among war veterans.[19] Today's kids have simply seen too much, experienced too much, and done too much. That's why they have been called the Been There, Done That generation. They've lost their innocence.

Ambiguity

Kids who grow up in today's world no longer automatically learn the difference between right and wrong, good and bad, true and false. A generation or two ago, there was something of a national consensus regarding values, but today, the only value that is held in high regard is the value of *tolerance.* There is no longer agreement on what is black or white; everything is a shade of gray, and it's up to the individual to decide. This, of course, creates added stress on children who need the security of boundaries and limits. They need to know that certain behaviors are right and that others are wrong. They need to know that certain things are good for them and that other things are harmful. It is increasingly difficult in today's world to teach kids right from wrong in a society whose television networks advertise their programming with slogans like "Guaranteed to break at least 20 percent more commandments than any other lineup!"[20]

Disillusionment

Stemming perhaps from the trends we've already discussed, youth today have grown more and more disillusioned about the future. "I'm destined to end up in jail or a bum," one youth says. "Sometimes the future seems okay, but most of the time, I can't see any future at all."[21] Not all young people feel this way, of course, but too many of them today have become extremely cynical about what life holds for them in the future, and they are much less hopeful about their chances for success.

Kids today are less trusting of other people and they are especially less trusting of institutions—creating an even greater challenge for the church. Depression among children and youth is a growing problem in this country, and rather than providing hope for our kids, we are medicating them. *The Wall Street Journal* reported that "the makers of Prozac, Zoloft, Paxil and other antidepressants are taking aim at a controversial new market: children." According to the *WSJ*, an estimated three million to four million kids in the U.S. suffer from depression and the drug makers are simply "responding to an urgent need."[22]

Keep in mind that all of the trends we have described here are sweeping generalizations that are neither absolute nor exhaustive. They are broad brush strokes describing a few changes in our culture that have impacted many youth and families—but not all of them, all the time, or in the same way. And remember that the purpose of such an analysis is not to provoke outrage or a wringing of the hands over everything that is wrong with the world. On the contrary our purpose is to encourage responsive junior high ministry. We can, for example, provide care and support for kids who feel abandoned. We can provide a place of significance for youth who have been marginalized. We can give friendship, respect, and a loving relationship with God to kids who have felt the sting of rejection. We can speak the truth in love to kids who have been exploited and left tossing in a sea of ambiguity. And for kids who have lost hope, we can share with them the good news of the resurrected Christ—who forgives, heals, empowers, and provides life everlasting. In reality, the worse the world looks, the better the gospel looks. Light always shines brightest in the darkness. Whenever we take a close look at the damage that has been done to young people because of an increasingly hostile world, we should be encouraged and highly motivated to respond positively as ambassadors of Christ. Today is a great day for doing junior high ministry. We can't help but make a difference in the lives of kids.

Notes

1. Donald A. Wells, "The Educational Plight of the Early Adolescent," unpublished manuscript, 1976. Used by permission.

2. Richard M. Lerner, *Early Adolescence: Perspectives on Research, Policy and Intervention,* (Lawrence Earlbaum, 1993), p. 4.

3. Joan Lipsitz, *Growing Up Forgotten* (Lexington Books, 1977), p. 96. See also Donald Eichhorn, "The School" in *Toward Adolescence: The Middle School Years* (University of Chicago Press, 1980), p. 60.

4. James M. Tanner, "Sequence and Tempo in the Somatic Changes in Puberty," *The Control of the Onset of Puberty,* Melvin M. Grumback, Gilman D. Grave, and Florence S. Mayer (eds.) (John Wiley and Sons, 1974), p. 455.

5. Joan Lipsitz, "The Age Group," *Toward Adolescence: The Middle School Years,* Mauritz Johnson (ed.) (University of Chicago Press, 1980), p. 21.

6. Lipsitz, "The Age Group," p. 21.

7. David Elkind, *Ties That Stress: The New Family Imbalance* (Harvard University Press, 1994), pp. 1-14.

8. *The American Family under Siege* (American Research Council, 1989).

9. Kevin Graham Ford, *Jesus for a New Generation* (InterVarsity Press, 1995), p. 79.

10. Steve Wulf reporting in *Time,* October 23, 1995, "A Generation Excluded," p. 86, on the release of "Great Transitions," a report by the Carnegie Council on Adolescent Development's 27-member panel of scholars, scientists, members of Congress, and former Cabinet officers.

11. William Mahedy and Janet Bernardi, *A Generation Alone* (InterVarsity Press, 1995), p. 14.

12. Edward A. Wynne and Thomas Weinstein in *The Chicago Tribune* (March 28, 1995). Quoted in *Youthworker Update,* June, 1995, p. 8.

13. From an address presented at the Youth Specialties National Youth Workers Convention, about 1985.

14. Elkind, *Ties That Stress,* p. 133.

15. "To Keep Them Away, Malls Turn Snooty," *The Wall Street Journal,* October 17, 1996, p. B1.

16. Mike Males, *The Scapegoat Generation* (Common Courage Press, 1996), p. 43.

17. Neil Postman, *The Disappearance of Childhood* (Delacorte, 1982).

18. David Elkind, *All Grown Up and No Place to Go,* (Addison Wesley Longman, 1984), p. 100.

19. Mahedy and Bernardi, *A Generation Alone,* p. 34.

20. From an ad for the USA Network in *TV Guide,* quoted in *Media Update,* Volume 16, No. 3, p. 1.

21. Adrienne Salinger, *In My Room: Teenagers in Their Bedrooms* (Chronicle Books, 1996), p. 90.

22. "Antidepressant Makers Study Kids' Market," *The Wall Street Journal,* April 4, 1997, p. B1.

• F O U R •

PHYSICAL DEVELOPMENT IN JUNIOR HIGHERS

Puberty is when massive doses of progesterone and testosterone come roaring into the body, setting off a biophysical disaster of unprecedented proportions.

—H. Stephen Glenn

Young adolescents are going through some enormous physical changes. They are in the process of being transformed—literally—from children into adults. It can be compared to a butterfly coming out of a cocoon. It only happens once in a person's life, and it usually happens during the junior high years. In this chapter, we will take a close look at what happens to a typical junior higher's body.

This transformation is brought about, of course, by puberty—which, "next to birth itself, is the most drastic change we experience in life," writes Donald Wells, "but unlike birth, we are acutely aware of the exciting transitions through which we pass."[1] The changes brought about by puberty are most definitely enormous—which, of course, is all by design. God created us to be first, children; and then at puberty to be transformed into adults. Puberty is quite normal and, for most young people, a positive experience as they grow into the new bodies they will inhabit for the rest of their lives. Not everyone is completely satisfied with the final result, but most get through puberty with few difficulties.

In the United States, the average age for menarche—when a girl has her first menstrual period—is anywhere from 12.1 to 12.9 years. The female adolescent growth spurt actually begins much earlier—

around 9.6 years, although recent research has found that many girls (almost 50 percent of black girls and 15 percent of white girls) begin the onset of puberty by the age of eight.[2] Its peak velocity is around age 11. Comparable milestones occur almost two years later for boys.[3] This is why girls are usually bigger and more fully developed than boys during early adolescence. The boys don't catch up with the girls physically until around age 15. (See the chart on page 67.) This, of course, creates some awkward moments in communication and relationships between the boys and the girls. The boys are starting to take an interest in the girls (finally), but to their chagrin, most of the girls are more interested in older boys.

While the above figures are fairly accurate, they are not absolute. As I noted earlier, it is not unusual for two boys who are the same age to be as much as four years apart in physical development during early adolescence.

Most people are aware that the average age for the onset of puberty is lower today than it was, say, a hundred years ago. Studies in the United States have shown that in the year 1900, the average age of menarche was 14.2 years, compared with today's 12.9.[4] In other countries, the downward trend has been even more severe as they have become more industrialized or more modernized. Coinciding with this earlier maturation has been an increase in height and weight. This has led many experts to think that modern society's eating habits—better nutrition, more protein and calories—have been a major contributor to earlier puberty. Bigger people seem to experience puberty earlier. But no one seems to know the exact reason for earlier maturation. Likewise, no one seems to know whether this trend will continue, although recent evidence suggests that things have stabilized considerably over the last 25 years and that there has been no significant change.[5] Let's hope so. Otherwise, we may see the day when kids go through puberty before they enter kindergarten.

Regardless of when it happens, the bottom line is that children are in the process of becoming adults physically. It is unfortunate that in our culture this very important and significant event in the life of a young person is hardly noticed at all. Or if it is acknowledged, it is only in a negative context. A friend of mine whose daughter turned 12 told me a humorous incident that occurred not long ago in his home. Both he and his wife noticed a foul smell in the room. The discerning mother took her daughter aside and explained to her that it was time for her to start using a deodorant because of her body odor. When she heard this, the 12-year-old girl grinned broadly and yelled "Hooray!" For this girl, being allowed to use a deodorant was a welcome symbolic rite of passage that signaled her entry into womanhood.

In many ancient cultures (and in some cultures today), there

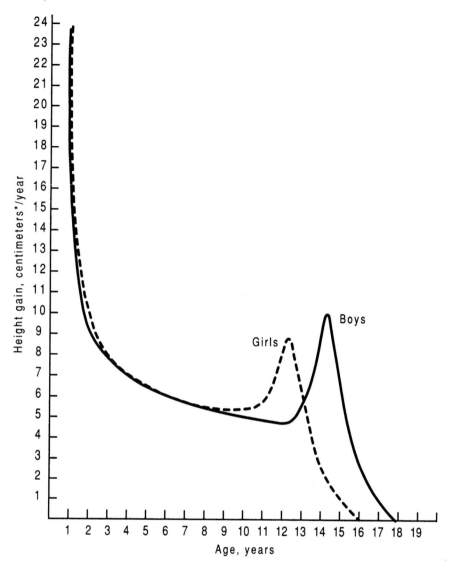

Typical velocity curves for length or height in boys and girls. These curves represent the velocity of the typical boy or girl at a given instant. From J. M. Tanner, R. H. Whitehouse, and M. Takaishi, "Standards from Birth to Maturity for Height, Weight Height Velocity and Weight Velocity; British Children, 1965," *Archives of Disease in Childhood* 41 (1966); 455-71.
*A centimeter equals .39 inch.

were somewhat more noble rites of passage than receiving a stick of deodorant. For example, as soon as a boy or girl manifested the physical signs of adulthood (menarche, pubic hair, and so on), there would be ceremonial rites of passage to make one's transition from childhood into adulthood a matter of public record. For girls these rites often included such events as the celebration of the arrival of the first menstruation, formal training in sexual matters, and instruction in cooking, clothes making, and the like.

Boys, who do not experience such a well-defined and observable event as menarche, would sometimes be taken off in the company of the men, perhaps circumcised, tutored in the duties and privileges of manhood, and allowed to emerge officially as a man. Among some American Indian tribes, a boy would be sent out alone on a *vision quest*. He would then return, reborn, with a new name, his name as a man.[6]

Michael Ventura, writing in *Crossroads: The Quest for Contemporary Rites of Passage,* sheds some light on the meaning of ancient rites of passage:

> Unlike us, tribal people met the extremism of their young (and I'm using "extremism" as a catchall word for the intense psychic cacophony of adolescence) with an equal and focused extremism from adults. Tribal adults didn't run from this moment in [the lives of] their children as we do; they celebrated it. They would assault their adolescents with, quite literally, holy terror: rituals that had been kept secret from the young till that moment—rituals that focused upon the young all the light and darkness of their tribe's collective psyche, all its sense of mystery, all its questions, and all the stories told both to contain and answer those questions.[7]

Ancient rites of passage were major events in the lives of children and families and they were always infused with a sense of mystery and spirituality. When the rites were complete, the young initiates took their places alongside others in the adult world. The boys had become men and the girls had become women, and they were recognized as such by their families, their peers, and their society. In addition, they were given a new set of rights and responsibilities. They had achieved a new status that was both affirming and terrifying. But they knew exactly where they stood.

Our modern culture is one of the few in history without rites of passage for its young, and most researchers and scholars agree that this has had severe consequences.[8] Today's passage from childhood to adulthood is not nearly so clear-cut or brief. Junior highers, who are emerging adults, are simply put on hold and required to wait another eight to 10 years before claiming their adulthood. Even then they aren't sure when they have arrived. This is certainly one reason for many of the problems and frustrations faced by modern teenagers, particularly in the sexual arena. They have adult bodies, but they must put them on ice. They are required to muzzle their natural urges, which for some is a very difficult thing to do.

It is interesting to note that the trend toward an earlier onset of puberty in recent times, combined with modern culture's trend toward later marriages, more education, and the like, has created a special group of people that many cultures never had to deal with before— teenagers. In fact, the term *teenager* was not really a part of the English language until the 1940s, and it was not until then (or later) that youth work began to be perceived as necessary.[9] Until recently there were few books, resources, or organizations concerning themselves with youth ministry because youth ministry was virtually nonexistent. It was created to meet the needs of a whole new category of people who, because of changes in society and changes in physical development, were neither children nor adults.

What's Happening?

The junior higher's body changes in many ways during puberty, and these changes are accompanied by an equal number of puzzling new experiences—some exciting, some embarrassing, and others just plain awful. When these perils of puberty occur, it's hard for many early adolescents to understand them or adjust to them. What makes it even worse is that no one talks much about them either, and those who do are often misinformed.

For girls, the most noticeable of these changes is a general acceleration in both height and weight, a widening of the hips, and the appearance of breasts. At this age, girls become softer, rounder, and grow very concerned about their figures. They want to look good in a bathing suit, and they want boys to notice them.

This can be a very frustrating time for girls who are concerned that they are growing too much or too little in the wrong places and who insist upon comparing themselves with others or the girls they see in the fashion magazines. Breasts in particular have become such a preoccupation in our society that it's not surprising that girls with small breasts often fear that boys will never like them. Girls worry, too, if one breast grows faster than the other, which is not unusual. "When a young girl starts to develop breasts," writes Dr. Maryanne Collins, pediatrician and specialist in adolescent medicine, "one side always enlarges first. Invariably mothers and daughters get concerned because they do not realize that this is normal."[10] Girls also worry if their breasts enlarge too quickly. A girl with "too much" is often the object of considerable ridicule from other girls and some rather unpleasant joking from boys. Most girls could benefit from some assurance at this point that beauty and sex appeal is rarely dependent on the breasts or any other part of the anatomy for that matter. They need to hear that breasts come in all shapes and sizes.

Junior high girls also usually experience their first period, which can be a real shock if they aren't prepared for it. Accidents occur at the worst times and are very embarrassing. Menstruation for junior high girls is just like it is for older women, so it is frequently accompanied by abdominal pains, lack of energy, and occasional irritability. It also takes a while before most girls have their period on a regular 28-day cycle. They might go three months without having a period and then have two very close together. This can cause a lot of worry as well. Hopefully, someone is able to assure them that all this is normal.

For boys, their first frustration with puberty is that they don't develop as early as the girls do. But when they do experience the onset of puberty, they grow rapidly and unevenly. It is not uncommon for boys to grow as much as six inches in height in one year, yet the arms, legs, and trunk may grow disproportionately resulting in awkwardness and clumsiness. Just when a boy is becoming more coordinated, puberty strikes and his forward progress may be set back. Some boys worry because they aren't growing very rapidly and think they are too short. Appetites increase dramatically at this age as well. Most junior high boys can easily outeat adults. Another noticeable change is the deepening of the voice, which creates embarrassing moments when it decides to change right in the middle of a sentence. Acne (pimples on the face) is another peril of puberty that is common to both boys and girls.

Perhaps the most telltale sign of approaching manhood is the emergence of pubic hair. For boys, pubic hair is similar in significance to breasts for girls. Until you grow a crop of pubic hair around the genitals, your manhood remains in doubt. Taking a shower after a P.E. class can be a traumatic experience for a slow developer. I have visited boys' locker rooms at junior high schools where no one took showers at all. When I was running junior high camps, it was not uncommon for boys hoping to avoid embarrassment to go all week without changing their underwear. It was almost comical to watch those who *did* change their clothes do it *inside their sleeping bags* so that no one would see them.

The event for boys that parallels

Physical Changes during Adolescence

MALES

- Development of penis and testicles
- Pubic hair growth
- Involuntary ejaculation
- Enlargement of neck
- Broadening of shoulders
- Growth of armpit hair
- Marked growth of hair on face and body
- Deepening of voice
- Increase in activity of sweat glands
- Growth spurt in height and weight
- Growth of muscle tissue

FEMALES

- Development of ovaries and uterus
- Pubic hair growth
- Onset of menstruation (menarche)
- Breast development
- Widening of hips
- Growth of armpit hair
- Slight growth of hair on face and body
- Slight deepening of voice
- Increase in activity of sweat glands
- Growth spurt in height and weight
- Growth of fat-bearing cells

menarche for girls is the first ejaculation. Usually this occurs while the boy is asleep, hence the term *wet dream.* Unprepared for this, some boys think they just wet the bed—more worry and guilt. Other worries include the size of one's penis (in comparison with others that they have seen or heard about) and spontaneous erections (occurring at the most inappropriate times). Masturbation is also common with this age group.

A friend of mine related to me an incident that illustrates the fence-walking that young adolescents sometimes do between childhood and adulthood during puberty. My friend took a group of junior highers to summer camp, and after arrival, he noticed that one of the kids had left his suitcase on the bus. Unable to find the camper to whom it belonged, he opened up the suitcase to see if there might be a name or some other clue to the camper's identity. Inside the suitcase, among the clothing and other personal articles, he found two very interesting items: a can of Play-Doh and a copy of *Penthouse* magazine. The suitcase belonged to a 12-year-old boy.

> **Inside the 12-year-old's suitcase, the counselor found a *Penthouse*— and a can of Play-Doh**

Early adolescents are experiencing some extraordinary physical changes during the junior high years, and while they are aware of them, they often do not anticipate or understand them. If we really believe in need-centered ministry, then it would seem only natural to consider a junior higher's need to know about the changes taking place in his or her body and the need to be assured that what is happening is good, not bad. God is not trying to make life miserable for them. They need to know that these changes are normal, not something to be ashamed of nor afraid of. Puberty happened to all of us, and we came though it pretty well. So will they.

A New Awareness of Their Bodies

With the onset of puberty comes a newly acquired awareness of the body. Junior highers become very concerned with their appearance—whether or not they are good looking or attractive and whether or not they measure up to others their own age. Peter Scales has noted that "if infancy has its Terrible Twos, then early adolescence has its Terrible Too's: too much, too little, too slow, too fast."[11] They are, in their own secret fears, growing too rapidly, too slowly, too unevenly, or developing too much in all the wrong places. And for many these fears are justified. Physical growth can be very uneven and unpredictable during early adolescence, the source of much anxiety and grief. Recent studies have shown that "worrying about my looks" peaks at the eighth grade: 69 percent of girls and 49 percent of boys in that grade list this as their main worry.[12] Here is how one teenager described what was happening to her:

> Every day, just about, something new seems to be happening to this body of mine and I get scared sometimes. I'll wake up in the middle of the night and I can't go back to sleep, and I toss and I turn and I can't stop my mind; it's racing fast, and everything is coming into it, and I think of my two best friends, and how their faces are all broken out, and I worry mine will break out, too, but so far it hasn't, and I think of my sizes, and I can't get it out of my head—the chest size and the stomach size and what I'll be wearing and whether I'll be able to fit into this kind of dress or the latest swimsuit. Well, it goes on and on, and I'm dizzy, even though it's maybe one o'clock in the morning, and there I am, in bed, so how can you be dizzy?
>
> Everything is growing and changing. I can see my mother watching me. I can see everyone watching me. There are times I think I see people watching me when they really couldn't care less! My dad makes a point of not staring, but he catches his look, I guess. I'm going to be "big-chested"; that's how my mother describes herself. I have to figure out how to dress so I feel better—I mean, so I don't feel strange, with my bosom just sticking out at everyone! I have to decide if I should shave my legs! I will! Damn! I wish a lot of the time I could just go back to being a little girl, without all these problems and these decisions![13]

She describes quite vividly in those two paragraphs how many junior highers feel. They worry tremendously about their appearance, and about how their bodies will turn out when they stop growing. Ordinarily it's not a neurotic kind of worrying. Most kids don't lose sleep over their pimples, but some do. Although there are actual cases on record of young people who have committed suicide (or attempted it) because they perceived themselves as being ugly, such cases are extreme. Usually this worry is a hidden fear that affects the lives of young people in ways they are not even aware of at the time. For example, the slow developer who feels inadequate or out of place may try to compensate by becoming withdrawn or boisterous. Most junior highers require much more privacy than ever before. They will lock themselves in the bathroom for long periods of time while they examine themselves or try to improve their appearance.

Privacy is very important for early adolescents. At junior high camps, it is not uncommon for kids to hang towels and blankets all around the bunk beds in their cabins to have private places to change clothes during the week. This is normal and to be expected because they don't want people to see them with their clothes off. I toured a junior high school a few years ago and noticed that in the bathrooms the doors were missing from all the toilet stalls. I found out later that the school authorities had removed the doors because kids were smoking cigarettes inside the stalls. They believed that removing the doors would prevent such behavior. Unfortunately, what it prevented was not smoking, but using the toilet. They wound up with an entire school full of constipated kids.

Undoubtedly the biggest reason that junior highers are obsessed with their appearance and their physical development is that it dramatically affects their social lives. When my children were younger, they could make instant friends with anyone their own age. At the park, for instance, they would play with any other children who were there, regardless of race, creed, color, looks, or sex. But as children grow older and get closer to the onset of puberty, this innocence fades. Kids become much more selective in their associations. Suddenly there emerges a popular group and an unpopular group. Popular kids don't have much to do with unpopular kids, and vice versa. It's an extremely rigid caste system that lasts for years, and it is particularly noticeable during the junior high years. To be unpopular is terrible in the eyes of most kids, and of course, it's everyone's dream to be counted among the elite. When we are in this select group, acceptance by others, positions of leadership, and life happily ever after are virtually assured.

What is it that makes a person popular or unpopular? Most of the time it will have something to do with physical characteristics, such as how you look or how well developed you are. Early developing boys who are athletic, tall, and good looking tend to be the most popular. Girls who are pretty, have attractive figures, nice hair, and so on are likely to be popular. If you are ugly (or just plain), short, fat, or flat, you are doomed. Unfortunately this is made even worse by modern culture's overemphasis on being beautiful and sexy (as seen on TV and in magazines). For this reason junior highers place a great deal of emphasis on physical characteristics. For them, it's a matter of social survival.

> **For junior highers, physical characteristics are a matter of social survival.**

In Judy Blume's book *Letters to Judy,* there are a number of revealing letters that the author has received from young people who are very unhappy with their bodies. This letter is typical:

> Dear Judy,
> Hi, my name is Emily. I am 12 years old and live in Kansas. In fifth grade I had a lot of boyfriends, but now I am in seventh grade and I have none. It is because I am flat. All the boys tease me and call me Board. Sometimes I feel like crying. All my friends talk about their periods and about shaving. I am afraid to ask my mother for a razor

or a bra or a deodorant. One day I took my brother's deodorant so I would have some for gym.[14]

A junior high girl may become preoccupied with her appearance because she may have the idea that her entire future is dependent on it. She may think that if she isn't attractive, she may face not only being unpopular, but also she won't have dates, she won't get married, she won't be able to get a job or have children. Her life is over! This view of the future, distorted as it may be, leaves some girls in a state of depression and despair. Others will embark on a strenuous program to repair whatever supposed defects they may have with cosmetics, exercises, diets, and an endless quest for that miracle product that will make them look like a supermodel. In recent years, many young adolescent girls have developed serious eating disorders (anorexia and bulimia) because they are afraid of gaining weight. And some trendy parents are giving their daughters gifts of cosmetic surgery for graduation from junior high school.

In the surveys I have taken with junior highers, nearly all list as their heroes the most glamorous people in show business or sports. Their favorite television programs are those featuring heroic, beautiful, sexy, almost superhuman characters who are always successful and, more importantly, admired by everyone. Every junior higher fantasizes about being such a person. In response to the question, "If you could change anything about yourself, what would it be?" young people invariably list physical improvements—a new nose, new hair, new face, new breasts, or a whole new body.

This dissatisfaction with themselves unfortunately causes some young people to have a deep resentment toward God who gets blamed for their lack of physical perfection. I heard one junior higher tell another, "When God was passing out noses, you thought he said roses and asked for a big red one!"

On the other hand, the message of the gospel can be very helpful to junior highers at this very point. They may feel inadequate or inferior because of their failure to measure up to the world's criteria for beauty or success, but Christ offers hope in the midst of all that. No one is plain or ordinary in the sight of God. We are all created in his image, which makes each of us a reflection of the beauty of God. We are special, despite the world's standards, because God loves us.

One youth worker used a very creative object lesson to illustrate to his junior highers that beauty is only skin deep. He wrapped up some garbage in gift-wrapping paper and tied a nice ribbon around it. He also put a very nice gift in a plain paper sack. Then he played a game with his junior highers and told the winner of the game to choose either package as a prize—the gift wrapped in beautiful paper or the paper sack. Naturally the beautifully wrapped package containing the garbage was chosen. The point was not missed by the kids: What is on the outside doesn't always reveal what is on the inside. We sometimes look only at the outward appearances, but God looks into the heart (1 Samuel 16:7). As Christians we need to see things God's way and look for the inner beauty in each other. (By the way, the disappointed young person who chose the garbage was also awarded the paper sack containing the nice prize after the lesson was learned.)

We need to help kids understand the message of the gospel concerning human worth, but we also need to take their feelings seriously. Even though they may be confident that God looks into their hearts, they are also confident that their friends look at their outward appearances, and that carries more weight at this particular time in their lives. Still we need to model for them a different standard of behavior. We cannot let our actions contradict the very gospel that we teach. For example, we need to love the least attractive kids in our youth groups just as much as the most attractive ones. We must avoid using put-downs (slams, chops, dissing) aimed at them or making fun of their physical shortcomings. Put-downs really hurt at this age. We need to treat each person with respect.

We should also be careful about parading in front of them glamorous Christian celebrities—former beauty queens, football heroes, and so on. While there is value in letting kids know that it is possible to be a Christian and be beautiful, famous, or successful, there is even more value in letting kids know that God can use them in significant ways even when they are not.

Avoid Embarrassing an Early Adolescent

Junior highers can be very cruel at times and take every opportunity to point out deficiencies in each other whenever it is to their advantage. They think that by making fun of someone else they can make themselves look superior. Usually junior highers are able to bounce back without any problem after some good-natured ribbing, but put-downs, ridicule, and the accompanying embarrassment can be very damaging to relationships and to self esteem. A few years ago, a tragic story in a small town in Missouri made national headlines when a 12-year-old boy brought his father's gun to school and killed a classmate who had repeatedly called him "Chubby." Then he turned the gun on himself and committed suicide. "He was relentlessly teased about being fat," said his teacher. "But neither of these boys were problem students."[15] While such extreme behavior is rare, it illustrates the magnitude of feelings that young adolescents carry with them when they are struggling with issues regarding their physical appearance. This is why it is so important for us to avoid situations in which kids might be looked down on because of ability, handicap, appearance, or physical development in general.

As a junior higher, I was a slow developer and not as athletic as other boys my age. Because of that I did not enjoy my P.E. classes at school. I enjoyed playing games and good competition as much as the other kids, but I hated when they would choose up teams. I was inevitably chosen last, simply because I wasn't very good at sports, and it was humiliating every time it happened (even though I didn't blame anyone for not choosing me first.) My label as a klutz was difficult to overcome, even though I caught up with most of my classmates in high school and did fairly well in sports later on.

This is why chapter 12 includes some games that are great for junior highers. Almost anyone can play them because they require little in the way of skill or ability. Why make junior highers suffer through games like football, basketball, and volleyball when only a few people can excel at them? There are plenty of other games available that are fun, physical, and very competitive (which junior highers love) but downplay athletic ability. These are the kind of games we should play with junior highers. I visited a junior high gym class recently and watched a seventh-grade coed volleyball game. What a disaster! The kids hated it and couldn't wait for it to be over. Most of them were unable to return the ball successfully over the net. It was humiliating, especially for the boys. I was tempted to step in and show them a few games that were both fun and easy to play.

Despite all that you or anyone else can do, there is no good way to prevent junior highers from experiencing some embarrassment as long as they are around other people. It's normal and inevitable. But a good junior high worker will at least be sensitive in this area, avoid put-downs and ridicule, and try to find ways to help each person feel accepted, liked, and important.

Help Them Find Affirmation in Areas beyond Sports and Looks

When I was in the ninth grade, I was arrested for shoplifting. My best friend and I were caught trying to walk out of a store with our coats lined with merchandise. That ended my brief career as a big-time criminal. Like most adolescent shoplifters, my friend and I never needed anything we took. In fact we usually gave most of it to our friends at school. It was just an exciting game, a challenge, and in retrospect, it was mostly a way for us to prove our manhood—both to ourselves and to others. We hadn't been able to prove it any other way. We had tried out for the freshman football and baseball teams and were unsuccessful. We weren't very popular. So we needed some way to show that we were courageous, adventurous tough guys, and for a while, shoplifting was how we did it. It made us look big in the eyes of our peers.

This kind of thinking is not uncommon with early adolescents who are slow developers or who have deep feelings of inferiority. The drive to be accepted by one's peers is strong and may cause junior highers to try to compensate for their lack of physical prowess in undesirable or self-destructive ways. Smoking, drinking, drug abuse, sexual promiscuity, rowdy behavior, vandalism, foul language, fighting, joining gangs, running away from home, and breaking the law are only some possible manifestations of this.

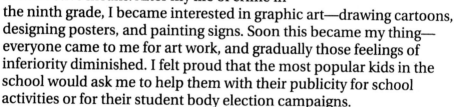

We weren't athletic, we weren't popular. So to prove we were tough, we shoplifted.

On the other hand, it is possible for kids to achieve the peer acceptance and ego satisfaction through positive and constructive means. After my life of crime in the ninth grade, I became interested in graphic art—drawing cartoons, designing posters, and painting signs. Soon this became my thing—everyone came to me for art work, and gradually those feelings of inferiority diminished. I felt proud that the most popular kids in the school would ask me to help them with their publicity for school activities or for their student body election campaigns.

Early adolescents need ways to gain a positive identity and a feeling of self-worth, and an important part of a junior high worker's ministry can be to help kids find ways to accomplish this. Art, music, writing, program planning, public speaking, service, dramatics, leadership, teaching, sports, humor, or just helping out are all possibilities. Slow developers should especially be given opportunities whenever possible to affirm themselves in areas in which they can excel. Build on their assets and help them feel good about themselves even though they may not be winning the battle on the physical front.

Sex and the Single Junior Higher

With the onset of puberty comes the advent of sexual activity. By sexual activity, I mean everything from fantasizing about sex and watching pornographic movies to sexual intercourse. We hear a lot these days about the increasing number of junior highers who are becoming sexually active. One recent study reported that 46 percent of *fifth graders* have had sexual intercourse.[16] Can statistics like these be believed? We need to remember that most of the surveys conducted on sexual behavior rely on the truthfulness of the subjects being surveyed. Author Mike Males in his book *The Scapegoat Generation* has observed that while many studies report high percentages of junior highers having sexual intercourse, only 2 percent of girls under 15 actually get pregnant. That means 98 percent of girls reach age 15 *without* getting pregnant. "Junior highers must be American's most skilled condom deployers," writes Males. "Seventh graders should be enlisted to hold seminars for U.S. grownups, who sport the industrial world's highest rates of unplanned pregnancies."[17] His conclusion: the so-called "junior high sexual revolution" in reality probably consists of junior high kids engaging in wild exaggeration of their sexual behavior.

While there is ample evidence that many young adolescents are in fact becoming sexually active at younger ages these days, it is important to remember that today's young adolescents are not *that* different from adolescents of the past. In 1954, William Carlos Williams wrote, "These kids get to be 12 or 13 and they explode. They'll tell you that—energy is pushing through them, and some say they're going to ride with it, enjoy it, and not worry!"[18] Sexual feelings and desires during early adolescence are not new. They are a normal part of growing up. What is new is that today's young people are living in a very different world. No longer does society feel an obligation to protect children and youth from sexual information they may not be ready to handle. Today's kids are exposed to hundreds of explicit sexual messages every single day—on television and in movies, popular music, advertising, and just about everywhere else. And the messages they get are conflicting. Parents and church leaders tell them that sex is wrong. Health and school officials tell them that sex without protection is wrong. The entertainment media tells them that there's nothing wrong with sex at all. No wonder kids are confused.

"It creates a lot of pressure for me," said a 12-year-old boy. "I need to know what I'm doing, or else there's going to be the really embarrassing situation of it not working and neither of us knowing what to do, even though we want to do it . . . I just don't know what to do."[19]

Teaching Junior Highers about Sex

When I was in junior high school, I was confused about sex, too, but in a different way. I automatically assumed that my sexual feelings were sinful and should be repressed, simply because no one talked about the subject. Sex was a taboo subject at church, and I for one was afraid to ask. Since my parents were Christians, I figured they probably wouldn't want to talk about it either. I was certain there must be a Bible verse somewhere that said, "Verily I say unto you: Sex is dirty, filthy, and nasty; save it for the one you're going to marry."

While a lot has changed over the past 40 years, there is still a reluctance on the part of parents and church leaders to talk about sex in other than condemning tones. To their credit, many schools, both public and private, have attempted to pick up the slack in sex education. But because these "health classes" often approach sex education as an academic subject, they not only fail to answer the most important questions kids have about sex, but they actually make the subject boring. One 14-year-old boy described his sex education class at school as "all these dumb little books . . . I don't think they could teach me anything. Maybe how many sperm are in a drop of semen, but I don't even want to know that. It's not going to help me any."[20]

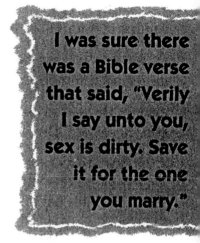

I was sure there was a Bible verse that said, "Verily I say unto you, sex is dirty. Save it for the one you marry."

We cannot assume that parents are accepting the responsibility for teaching their children about sex. Most parents avoid talking to their kids about sex, even though they wish they could. One study found that although most parents believe that sex education belongs in the home, only about one-third of them actually talk with their children about sex.[21] Another study found that 45 percent of America's teenagers say they learn "nothing" from their parents about sex. "Three out of four say it's hard to talk to their fathers, and 57 percent find their mothers tough going. Only about a third (36 percent) say they would ask their parents for any desired sexual information, while almost half (47 percent) would turn to friends, sex partners, or siblings."[22] The following paragraph, written by a 12-year-old girl, is typical:

> My mother decided to finally have the talk with me. But I knew about that subject long before my mother told me about it. When she was telling me, she kept asking me if I had ever heard anything about that. I kept saying no, as if I had never heard a word. But you know how it is, everyone picks everything up on the streets. My mother wasn't the first one to tell me. Actually, she was the last.[23]

Nor can we assume that kids are learning all they need to know from other sources. Even in our present age of enlightenment, there are many early adolescents who remain essentially uninformed and disturbingly ignorant concerning their sexuality and how their bodies are changing. A few years ago while I was speaking at a large junior high conference in the midwest, a 13-year-old girl was rushed to the hospital one night with severe abdominal pain. Everyone thought she was having an attack of appendicitis or something similar. But when she got to the hospital, she had a baby. This surprised everyone, of course, but it surprised the girl even more. She didn't know she was pregnant.

Several years ago I asked over 700 junior highers from church youth groups this question: "Where do you get your information about sex?" Most said school, but it is hard to know whether they meant health education classes at school or friends at school. The second and third most common answers were friends and parents. Other typical answers: "TV. . . .myself, by doing it. . . .the streets. . . .I keep my ears open. . . .wherever I can get it. . . .nowhere. . . .nobody gives me a straight answer." One girl replied, "I refuse to answer that question because it doesn't belong in the church."

Of course, the truth is that questions about sex *do* belong in the church, and kids should be able to get honest and helpful answers to them. The Bible has much to say about sexuality and contrary to popular opinion, it is not all negative. God created our bodies and our sexuality, and he wants us to enjoy it. Like everything God made, sex has its proper place and purpose, but we certainly don't have to be ashamed or embarrassed to talk about it openly within the four walls of the church.

To the church's credit, many denominations and Christian publishing houses have recently developed a number of excellent Christian sex education programs.[24] Despite these new resources, it is safe to say that most church leaders, perhaps because they are afraid of controversy, are still reluctant to discuss the subject of sex with their young people except from a negative, moralistic, or judgmental perspective.

I am not suggesting that every church needs to conduct sex education classes during the Sunday school hour (although it just might increase your Sunday school attendance), but it would certainly seem appropriate and reasonable for church leaders, particularly junior high workers, to let kids know that they can talk openly about sex in the church. They watch people on television talking openly about sex every night of the week. They know that sex exists. The cat is out of the bag. Now they just have questions. Junior highers should be able to get straight answers to their questions from a Christian point of view. They are already getting answers from every other point of view.

Some people, especially parents, think that if they don't bring up the subject, then kids won't be concerned about it. They argue that talking about sex will only make kids more curious or overstimulate them

> Junior highers need straight answers about sex from a Christian point of view. They're already getting every other point of view.

and encourage experimentation. Fortunately it just doesn't work that way. Experimentation is caused by a lack of information, not an abundance of it. Ignoring the subject doesn't make it go away. Sooner or later (usually sooner) there comes a time when kids must have the information they need concerning their bodies, and if they don't get it at home or at church or at school, they'll get it somewhere else.

Yes, You Can Tell Junior Highers the Truth about Sex

As I mentioned earlier, sex-education curriculum written from a Christian perspective is now available. It is not the purpose of this book to offer a detailed junior high sex-education program. I believe, however, that any attempt to deal with the subject in a junior high group should be characterized by openness and honesty. Openness will allow all of the issues to be dealt with in a secure and nonthreatening environment. Honesty will insure that the kids get the straight scoop about sex in a helpful and assuring way, rather than getting half-truths, misinformation, and myths.

Besides dealing with the basic issues of puberty, one of the first steps in teaching sex to junior highers is to help them unlearn some of the myths they have picked up about sex from the media and from other sources. It is truly amazing how much bad information kids have already learned by the time they are 10 or 11 years old.

Here are just a few of those myths.

Myth: Sex is a big problem.
Many kids believe this is true because they hear so much about all the problems that sex brings. Watch daytime television for about five minutes and you'll hear every kind of sex problem imaginable. Listen to radio talk shows and you get the impression that everybody in the world is having problems with sex. Keep listening and you'll hear ads for penile implants and cures for impotence. Bookstores and magazine racks are loaded with stories and advice columns on how to overcome sexual dysfunction. Dr. Ruth and other sex therapists discuss sex problems no matter how bizarre they might be. In light of all this, junior highers need to know that sex is not a horrible problem or a source of stress and anxiety for everyone. They need to know that there are in fact many people who have well-adjusted, enduring, satisfying, (and yes, exciting) sexual relationships within the bonds of marriage.

Myth: Sex is dangerous.
This is a popular message nowadays, and there are definitely elements of truth to it—but it may be sending the wrong message to kids. Adolescents naturally gravitate to risky behaviors, and sex is portrayed today as one of the most risky of all. "Sex can kill you," say some of the

warnings about sexually transmitted diseases. While it is true that certain sexually transmitted diseases, like AIDS, can cause death, sex itself cannot. Kids need to know the difference. As I write this, scientists are getting closer each day to finding cures for many of these diseases, and we can thank God for that. If we rely on the sex-is-dangerous myth to motivate kids to responsible sexual behavior, we may find ourselves looking a little foolish when those cures *are* found.

Myth: Sex is a performance.

Or sex is technique. We hear all the time that you are either "good" or "bad" in bed. What makes a person good in bed? What do they need to know before they have sex? How does one get experience? Truth is, lovemaking involves much more than learning the mechanics of sex. Once sex becomes a performance, it becomes one-dimensional and empty. Sex involves the whole person—mind, body, and soul. It is one part of a relationship that requires time and commitment along with a lot of mutual love and respect. The sex-is-performance myth assumes that the best sex partner is one who has had the most experience. In reality, he or she is the worst. The best way to learn about sex is to learn together with the person you are going to spend the rest of your life with.

Myth: Only people with perfect bodies are good at sex.

Or—unless you have sex with someone who has a perfect body, it won't be very good. Variations of this myth are widespread and extremely harmful. Girls fear that their breasts are too small or that they are a few pounds overweight. Boys are led to believe that their ability to be "good in bed" depends entirely on the length of their penises. Junior highers are not too young to be told the truth—that sex has little to do with body parts and everything to do with love and commitment to another person.

Myth: Everyone is doing it.

This is a very common myth among young people that kids themselves like to perpetuate. This myth puts a tremendous amount of pressure on young people who have not become sexually active because they feel left out. But the truth is—everyone is not doing it. There are many people, teenagers included, who live happy and fulfilling lives without having sex. Some studies indicate that the vast majority of teenagers are having sex, but I'm among those who are suspicious of studies that ask kids to answer questions like, "Are you

> I'm suspicious of studies that ask kids, "Are you sexually active?"

sexually active?" or "Have you had sexual intercourse?" I have known kids who answered yes when they really weren't sure what the question meant. Others, believing the myth, just don't want to admit that they are virgins. It's not cool to admit to that. I'm not saying that all surveys on sexuality are bogus, but I am saying that kids need to hear that it's okay to say "No way." Many people do and they are the smart ones.

Myth: Sex is the most important thing there is.
Due largely to overexposure (literally) in the entertainment media, young people not only believe that sex must be the most important thing there is, but the *only* thing there is. The primary reason there is so much sex in the media is because it gets ratings. The most important things in life rarely do. We need to help kids understand sex in its proper perspective.

Myth: You prove your manhood or womanhood by having sex a lot.
Many young adolescents, especially boys, believe that sexual prowess determines manhood. They see people in movies having sex over and over again, with lots of different people. It might be a good idea to remind them that the world-champion copulators are not people, but rabbits and hamsters. I read one article which pointed out that the most sexual creature on earth is the oyster. It has sex hundreds of times every day. Real men prove their manhood by taking responsibility for their actions and demonstrating good judgment and self-control.

There are other myths as well—for example, the one that *sex is bad* (sinful) or that *sex has no consequences*. These and many other issues need to be challenged and discussed honestly and openly with junior highers.

Before beginning any kind of sex-education program in your church, be sure to plan ahead, decide what you are going to cover in advance, and discuss it with the church leadership and with the parents of the kids. It might be a good idea to actually go through the material that you propose to use with the parents so they will know what you are going to do and give you the support you need. You might want to think of other ways to involve parents in your sex-education program as well.

Regardless of what you do, be honest, open, and biblical when discussing sexuality with your junior highers. Young adolescents are maturing sexually, and they have a natural curiosity about the subject. Let's not allow the media and the world to do our sex education for us by default.

Teaching Junior Highers to Care for Their Bodies

Here's a joke that is often told whenever youth pastors get together. What's the difference between boogers and broccoli? Answer: Junior

Time-honored joke among youth workers: What's the difference between broccoli and boogers? Junior highers don't eat broccoli.

high kids don't eat broccoli.

There's some truth to that. Junior highers don't eat too many green things or anything else that they think is good for them. It's ironic that at the time adolescents are becoming more aware of their bodies and concerned about their appearance and their physical development, they actually do very little to take care of their bodies. Good health seems to be a nonissue for them, perhaps because they believe they are invulnerable—that they will live forever. It's sometimes quite difficult to help kids understand the importance of good nutrition and exercise.

Most churches don't spend much time dealing with health issues, except to condemn such things as smoking, drinking, and drug abuse. Traditionally the church has limited itself to the care of the soul rather than the care of the body. But God gave us our bodies, creating each one in his own image. Since our bodies are in fact a "temple of the Holy Spirit" (1 Corinthians 6:19) and since we are asked to "present our bodies" back to him (Romans 12:1), it would seem consistent with Scripture to help young people stay physically fit.

The Maternal and Child Health Service reports that the three groups most vulnerable to poor nutrition are infants and young children, adolescents, and expectant mothers. Another nutrition survey indicated that young people between the ages of 10 and 16 had the highest rates of unsatisfactory nutritional status, boys more than girls.[25]

It is generally agreed that nutrition hits one of its low points during adolescence. This is especially disturbing when you consider that the adolescent growth spurt is second only to infant growth. The body is developing rapidly, including the brain, which is perhaps the most vulnerable to abuse. There is strong evidence that early malnutrition (in infants) directly affects intellectual competence, but little is known about how nutritional deficiencies affect the brain during later childhood and adolescence.

I'm not suggesting that you substitute a salad bar for your next pizza bash, but I am suggesting that you regularly encourage kids to recognize that their bodies are a gift from God and need to be taken care of. This means that we not only talk about traditional health-related problems such as cigarette smoking, drugs and alcohol, but also proper nutrition, personal hygiene and exercise. You could be doing junior highers in your group a great service by raising their consciousness about these and other important health issues.

Notes

1. Donald A. Wells, "The Educational Plight of the Early Adolescent," unpublished manuscript, 1976. Used by permission.

2. "Girls can start sexual development as early as age 8, study finds" in *The San Diego Union-Tribune,* April 8, 1997, p. A3. This article reported on a study conducted by Marcia Herman-Giddens of the University of North Carolina at Chapel Hill and published in *Pediatrics* (American Academy of Pediatrics) April, 1997.

3. Marcia Herman-Giddens, Eric Slora, and others, "Secondary Sexual Characteristics and Menses in Young Girls Seen in Office Practice: A Study from the Pediatric Research in Office Settings Network," *Pediatrics* (American Academy of Pediatrics) April, 1997, pp. 505-512.

4. J. M. Tanner, "Sequence, Tempo, and Individual Variation," in *Twelve to Sixteen, Early Adolescence,* Robert Coles, et al. (eds.) (W. W. Norton, 1972), p. 22.

5. David Bromberg, Stephen Commins, and Stanford B. Friedman, "Protecting Physical and Mental Health," *Toward Adolescence: The Middle School Years,* Mauritz Johnson (ed.) (University of Chicago Press, 1980), p. 40. Recent research has found evidence that the average age of menarche may be getting slightly lower (Herman-Giddens, 1997; see note 2 above). By studying girls who visited their doctors in 65 pediatric practices across the nation, Herman-Giddens found that the average age of menarche for white girls was 12.88; for black girls, 12.16. She acknowledged, however, that her findings may have been skewed if a significant number of girls were brought to their doctors because of concerns that they were developing sexually too early.

6. Eric W. Johnson, *How to Live through Junior High School* (J. B. Lippincott, 1975), p. 39.

7. Michael Ventura, "The Age of Endarkenment" in *Crossroads: The Quest for Contemporary Rites of Passage,* Louise Caru Mahdi, Nancy Geyer Christopher, and Michael Meade (eds.) (Open Court, 1996), p. 53.

8. Christina Goff, "Rites of Passage: A Necessary Step toward Wholeness," in *Crossroads: The Quest for Contemporary Rites of Passage,* Louise Caru Mahdi, Nancy Geyer Christopher, and Michael Meade (eds.) (Open Court, 1996), p. 6.

9. "Growing Up Goes On and On and On," *The Wall Street Journal,* March 24, 1997, p. B1.

10. Peter Scales, *A Portrait of Young Adolescents in the 1990s* (Search Institute, 1991), p. 9.

11. Scales, p. 9.

12. Search Institute, "Young Adolescents and Their Parents," *Project Report* (Search Institute, 1984), p. 101.

13. Robert Coles and Geoffrey Stokes, *Sex and the American Teenager* (Harper & Row, 1985), p. 2.

14. Judy Blume, *Letters to Judy* (G. P. Putnam's Sons, 1986), p. 166.

15. "Boy, 12, teased for being overweight, kills student, self in classroom" in *The San Diego Union-Tribune*, March 2, 1987, p. A6.

16. From research conducted by the University of Michigan School of Nursing, cited in *Harper's*, January 1997, p. 13.

17. Mike Males, *The Scapegoat Generation* (Common Courage Press, 1996), p. 46.

18. Quoted in Coles and Stokes, *Sex and the American Teenager*, p. 2.

19. From an interview with Amos Hartigan, a 12-year-old boy, in "My Sex Life, Chapter One," *Harper's*, January 1994, p.34.

20. Coles and Stokes, *Sex and the American Teenager*, p. 38.

21. Search Institute, "Young Adolescents and Their Parents," p. 14.

22. Coles and Stokes, *Sex and the American Teenager*, p. 36.

23. Blume, *Letters to Judy*, p. 155.

24. One example is the curriculum "There Is a Season: Studies in Human Sexuality for Youth of Christian Churches and Their Parents," written by Dorothy Williams and published by C. Brown Co. Youth Specialties has also published several resources for teaching youth about sexuality and sexual values.

25. Joan Lipsitz, *Growing Up Forgotten* (Lexington Books, 1977), p. 17.

• F I V E •

SOCIAL DEVELOPMENT IN JUNIOR HIGHERS

The three most important things to a junior higher are (1) their friends, (2) their friends, and (3) their friends.

Just as junior highers are changing from children to adults physically, so they are also becoming much more socially aware and socially mature. They want adultlike relationships. They want friends. When they were younger, they only needed playmates, but now they need and seek out meaningful friendships. Friends are very different from playmates. They are people who can be trusted, who listen to you, and who understand feelings. They are people you can share your life with and learn from. Friends become a necessity of life, and the lack or loss of them becomes a crisis. Loneliness becomes a new experience for junior highers, and the fear of rejection becomes a source of anxiety and often dictates behavior and value choices. Junior highers will usually do whatever is most conducive to making friends and keeping them. It is safe to say that friends are the lifeblood of adolescence.

A few years ago I conducted a survey and asked junior highers this question: "Do you like school?" The vast majority surprisingly responded with a yes. When I asked them to explain, they indicated that they liked school for one reason: School is first and foremost a place to be with friends. Similarly many students who expressed a strong dislike for school cited the absence of friends or the presence of enemies. The quality of the teaching, curricula, facilities, and programs had little to do with their feelings toward school. Friends were, and are, primary. The implications for junior high workers in the church should be obvious. Youth groups need to have a good amount of "redeeming social value" in order for junior highers to enjoy being a part of them. The youth group should be a place where good friends are found.

The Quest for Autonomy

To understand what is actually happening with junior highers in the social dimension of life, we must begin with a stock theme of adolescent psychology. Simply stated, it is a primary task of early adolescence to break ties with the family and to establish an identity that is separate from parents or other authority figures. This is the adolescent quest for autonomy or independence.

Little children tend to be carbon copies of Mom and Dad. They follow their parents around, do what their parents tell them to do, believe what their parents believe. But when children reach adolescence, they want to be their own person, separate from their parents. They want to make their own choices and commitments, to be set free. They want to be treated like adults, or at least to *not* be treated like children. This is when kids become highly critical of their parents and consider them and everything they do and think to be hopelessly old-fashioned. They may be embarrassed by their parents and prefer not to be seen with them in the shopping mall or sit with them in church because they don't want anyone to mistake them for children. While there are certainly exceptions, this behavior is normal and to be expected with early adolescents.

Obviously this accounts for many of the problems between parents and their early adolescent children. Many parents are caught completely off guard by this disturbing development. Some parents take it personally and feel terribly discouraged. They find it hard to understand why they are suddenly "losing control." They never had such problems before. Just when their children are finally learning to be good, obedient boys and girls, they become young adolescents and appear to take a giant step backward. I usually counsel parents that it is helpful to remember that adolescent development progresses via the detour of regression. Sometimes things have to get worse before they get better.

Many parents may understand this but are reluctant to allow it to happen. As their children move toward independence, they become more rigid and refuse to let out any rope. This results in clashes and strained parent-child relationships. Parents often need extra help understanding that their young adolescent child is not viciously turning against them. They need to know that the child is simply seeking autonomy—trying to discover and establish her own identity as an individual, and needs to be given opportunities to do so. This does not mean, on the other hand, that parents should take a *laissez-faire* or hands-off approach; this would be even more disastrous. Parents remain the most important influence on children throughout their adolescent years. They are wise to work with their children, nurturing them by giving them a little more freedom, responsibility, and trust, rather than "provoking them to wrath" while they are trying to grow up.

The Role of Friends

Along with this quest for autonomy comes a change in the nature of the relationships the young adolescent needs and seeks out. A child's primary relationship is with his or her parents. Little children who grow up in healthy homes are generally showered with love, praise, and support from parents, which meets the relational needs of the child. Every child should feel that he is special, that he is the most important person in the world. They believe this because their parents tell them so. There is nothing wrong with this kind of egocentrism. This gives the child security and confidence.

But when children grow into adolescence and begin their quest for autonomy and independence, they realize that the affirmation and support they get from parents is not enough. They need affirmation and support from "out there in the real world." As children are beginning the process of leaving the nest, they want to know if they will feel as secure out of the nest as they did in it. They still need their parents' love, but they also need to find others who will validate their self-image in the world.

That's why, as I wrote earlier in this book, the most important question for a junior higher is "Do you like me?" or "Am I okay?" Junior highers want to know what others think of them. Here, of course, is where friends come in. Friends are the people who say, "Yes I like you; you *are* okay. I want to be with you. You are my friend." For young adolescents, friends are mirrors, reflecting back a glimpse of who they are, and what their self-image looks like. If they can find friends, they feel good about themselves. If they cannot, they feel deep feelings of rejection and inferiority.

> To young adolescents friends are mirrors, reflecting back to them who they are.

The junior higher's passion for friends explains some of the behaviors that we commonly associate with this age group, such as their penchant for self-absorption. They can spend hours in the morning getting ready for school, trying to decide what to wear or coiffing their hair. Psychologist David Elkind believes that every early adolescent plays to an imaginary audience—all those people who are watching him, thinking about him, making judgments about him—and of course, that is everyone in the whole world.[1] So it matters greatly how they look, what they say, who they're with, where they go. The most interesting subject to junior highers is themselves. If you want your junior highers to listen to you, talk about them. Make them the topic. You can be sure that they want to know what you think about them.

The Bridge to Adulthood

Friends are an important part of growing up. They not only provide young people with a sense of who they are, but they also provide them with the confidence and security that they need to eventually become independent, self-reliant adults. The junior higher's cluster of friends, often referred to as the peer group, is something of a bridge to adulthood. It is the place where young adolescents develop their identity as an individual. It is rather ironic, actually, that in order for a young person to come up with his identity as an individual, he must lose his identity by becoming part of a larger group of friends. As Joan Lipsitz has written, "It is one paradox of adolescence that it is possible to achieve this inner, apparently singular, sense of individuality only when one sees oneself in terms of a larger social context."[2] That larger social context is the peer group. Junior highers don't like to stand out from the crowd. They want to blend in. This is why a junior higher will conform to the peer group. What the crowd does, she does. What the crowd likes, she likes. It seems just the opposite of what she wants—to be independent. But it's all part of the process.

This has been described by authors Alvin Howard and George Stoumbis:

> In his desire for independence, the early adolescent appears to become a rigid conformist to the mores, dress, speech, and attitudes of his fellows. Security is found in identifying with the group insofar as is at all possible. If group standards denigrate strong academic performance, the high grades are for "squares" and "goody-goodies." The seventh-grade pupil who was a strong student becomes only an average ninth-grade student, which confuses and shocks his parents and teachers. The early adolescent is almost certain to develop an air, a manner of sophistication or pseudo-sophistication, which he hopes will cover up the worries, doubts, and feelings of uncertainty that are usually with him. During this time the early adolescent is highly susceptible to undesirable influences and individuals—if they are admired by his peer group. To gain status and recognition he must conform to these new standards. The role of the school should be obvious in developing desirable values, attitudes, and standards, and in providing socially approved experiences and situations.[3]

We need to remember that when a junior higher conforms to her peer group, she is subconsciously trying to find out whether or not she is liked and accepted as a unique individual separate from her

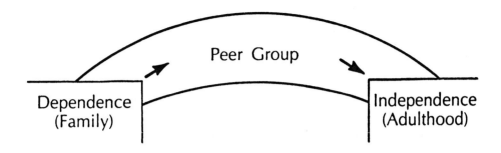

parents. Once she is accepted and feels secure as part of the group, then she is likely to have enough confidence in herself to step out and to experiment with being different—to affirm her identity apart from the group. The peer group becomes in fact the bridge to independence.

Drawing from personal experience once again, I was very much like my parents, as most youngsters are, during my preteen years. My values, beliefs, and tastes were almost identical to those of my parents. I remember as a child listening to country-and-western music (and liking it!) because my mother and father did. I knew all the words to the latest Hank Williams song, and I never missed a broadcast of the "Grand Ole Opry."

But along about the fifth or sixth grade, I noticed that other kids my age did not listen to country music, and for the first time, that had an impact on me. And so, much to my parents' chagrin, through junior high and high school, I listened to the rock music of my era (remember the Coasters and the Shirelles?). Having become so enlightened, I decided that country music was for ignorant hillbillies (parents included), and there was no way I was going to be caught dead listening to it again. My father and I would fight for control of the radio whenever we got into the car. All the other kids liked rock and roll, and so did I. I had a great need to be like my friends and to be accepted by them. To have been different would have been extremely foolish.

Looking back I recall that it was as a senior in high school and during college that I finally dared to be different. By that time I had courage enough to strike out on my own and decide what I liked rather than what the crowd liked. I became a great fan of folk music, then bluegrass and country music. I came full circle, and for my parents it was like the return of the Prodigal Son.

That's the way it usually goes with early adolescence. The pattern is predictable enough to say that it is normal and necessary for junior highers to lose their identities to find them. Failure to conform (even when the group is doing something wrong) can produce feelings of guilt and inadequacy as severe as the feelings involved in going against one's conscience. Caught between a rock and a hard place, so to speak, the result is often a difficult struggle for the junior higher. This is what we usually mean by *peer pressure:* "Should I do what my friends want me to do, or should I do what I know is right?" He or she knows that either of the choices will lead to painful consequences.

It is important for adults, particularly parents, to understand that conformity to one's peer group—or friends—is not *all* bad. It serves a useful purpose. True, junior highers are extremely vulnerable to dangerous influences and they sometimes choose the wrong kind of friends and get involved in behaviors that are unacceptable. But the alternatives are often worse. Better a little bad influence than no friends at all. There are a great many adults who haven't yet "grown up" or who are seriously maladjusted emotionally or psychologically simply because they were never able to find friends as adolescents. It is not uncommon to find adults still conforming to every whim of the crowd, hoping to find the acceptance they never got during their youth.

> **Some adults still conform to every whim of the crowd, hoping for the acceptance they never got during their youth.**

But isn't conformity wrong? Aren't we to encourage kids to be different, to stand apart from the crowd? Yes, there are times when conformity is wrong (if the group is doing something wrong) and there are times when it is necessary to take a stand. But that doesn't mean that the group is always wrong, or that one must always be different. It is counterproductive to overreact to what has to be considered an important part of adolescent development. It doesn't help junior highers to insist that conformity to the peer group is necessarily sinful. That's not the point of Romans 12:2 ("Do not conform . . . ") Paul wasn't writing to teach youth to shun their friends or to be oddballs. Good or bad, having friends and being part of a group is a primary method kids use to socialize themselves into adulthood. In the words of educator Jerome Kagan, "Every young adolescent . . . needs peers to help him sculpt his beliefs, verify his new conclusions, test his new attitudes."[4]

Earlier Forms of the Child-to-Adult Bridge

In recent times the peer group has provided early adolescents with their most important relationships outside the home. This was not always the case. In societies of the past, the peer group rarely served as the primary bridge to adulthood. Adults assumed that role. As I wrote in chapter four, it was common for there to be rites of passage in which children at puberty were initiated or welcomed into the adult community. From then on, adults no longer regarded that young person as a child, strictly under the care of their parents, but as a young adult, ready to become integrated into the world of adults. Adults gave young people a place in society where they could learn the responsibilities of adulthood and receive a controlled introduction to adult life. In colonial America, for example, adolescents were given entry-level jobs in the community. Boys were given apprenticeships from age 14 to 21, girls from 12 to 18. Working alongside adults, they could learn a variety of trades, such as farmer, shipbuilder, barber, hatter, baker, and even candlestick maker.[5]

I don't want to romanticize or glamorize the past too much. There's no denying that adolescents were often badly mistreated in colonial America and throughout history. Still it is clear that historically adults played a much larger role in the lives of adolescents than they do today. Certainly down through history, there have always been peers, peer groups, and peer friendships. But they were never as predominant in the development of adolescent culture as they are today. Generally speaking, peers have completely replaced adults as the primary socializer of children into adulthood. Although adolescents once learned how to become adults from other adults, they now learn about adulthood primarily from each other. This is essentially why "youth culture" exists (a relatively recent phenomenon, as most of us know). Youth culture provides the environment where kids can practice being adults. They practice on each other. It's something of a miniworld, with its own customs, styles, music, dress, and language. It is a middle ground between childhood and adulthood where kids can figure out who they are and what they want to become.

Why has this change taken place? Why is it that adults no longer involve themselves in the lives of youth as they once did? As we discussed in chapter three, one reason is that the world has changed. We no longer live in a rural, agrarian society like the one our ancestors knew. Instead we live in an industrialized, technological society, that puts many new demands and a great deal of pressure on adults as well as

> Although adolescents once learned how to become adults from other adults, they now learn it primarily from each other.

children. As a result today's adults have little time or energy to devote to other people's kids. The sad truth, in fact, is that in today's world many parents hardly have time to devote to their *own* kids.

Psychologist David Elkind, among others, has researched the impact of these changes in society on today's young people. In his book *All Grown Up and No Place to Go,* he writes:

> In today's society we seem unable to accept the fact of adolescence, that there are young people in transition from childhood to adulthood who need adult guidance and direction. . . . In a rapidly changing society, when adults are struggling to adapt to a new social order, few adults are genuinely committed to helping teenagers attain a healthy adulthood. Young people are thus denied the special recognition and protection that society previously accorded their age group. . . . Young people today are quite literally all grown up with no place to go.[6]

Following the San Francisco Bay-area earthquake of 1989, California began the arduous process of retrofitting its thousands of highway overpasses with additional support to prevent damage from future quakes. There is a good analogy here. As we consider the bridge to adulthood that young adolescents need to cross, perhaps the time has come for us to retrofit it with the kind of support that can only be provided by caring adults.

The Myth of Peer Influence

Who or what exerts the greatest influence on today's youth? The popular consensus on this question is pretty much unanimous: the greatest influence on today's kids is the peer group. This conclusion has shaped much of our youth ministry today. We continue to separate kids from adults in an attempt to take advantage of the influence teenagers have on each other. While this strategy works to a certain extent, I believe that there is a better, more effective way to provide guidance for today's youth. But first we have to debunk the myth of peer influence.

Researchers have found that throughout early adolescence, young people continue to look first to their parents for advice and guidance on important issues. Not only that, but parents also remain the primary models for their adolescent children. While the influence of peers most definitely increases dramatically during early adolescence and the influence of parents decreases, the influence of peers never completely outweighs the influence of parents.[7] This should be good news for parents who might be led to think that they no longer have any significant influence on their adolescent children.

After parents, the award for second greatest influence in a person's life goes to other members of the family, especially grandparents. Most people, when asked who influenced them the most (other than their parents) cite grandparents, older brothers and sisters, uncles and aunts, cousins, and others who are part of their extended family. They have influence simply because they are related. They care. When I reflect on my own adolescence, I know that one reason I stayed out of serious trouble was because I simply had too many people to disappoint. There were relatives all around me with a vested interest in how I turned out. The same is true for young people today, when those family members are present.

Next in line—after parents and the extended family—comes *significant adults outside the home*. This includes teachers, coaches, youth workers, neighbors, bosses, parents of friends, and so on. I have asked hundreds of adults to reflect on their adolescence this way: "When you were a teenager, who—besides your parents or other family members—had the greatest influence on you?" Rarely do I hear the name of a member of their peer group—another teenager. Instead, people invariably cite the names of adults—people who were mentors and counselors and friends. Unfortunately many kids today have few such adult relationships. Perhaps that's one reason teenagers today are such celebrity worshipers. In the absence of real adult models, they turn to rock stars, movie stars, and other popular personalities who seem heroic, successful, and admirable by their standards. In 1996, the average age of a member of one of the top-ten rock-concert bands in the United States was 41.[8] To repeat an earlier quotation from H. Stephen Glenn, "teenagers, left to their own devices, will always gravitate to the oldest person they can find who will take them seriously and treat them with dignity and respect."

The fourth most powerful influence on teenagers is the peer group—same-age friends. While peer influence is rather conspicuous, it is relatively short-term. Peers have a lot of influence, for example, on how to act, dress, and talk like a

PARENTS

EXTENDED FAMILY

ADULTS OUTSIDE THE HOME

THE PEER GROUP

THE MEDIA

teenager. When you watch teenagers, it's easy to see how peers influence what they wear, how they fix their hair, and what music they listen to. But peers have much less influence on substantive, long-term issues—how they choose their career, how they develop life skills, how they determine right from wrong, how they decide on values, political views, and religious beliefs. Teens look to adults for guidance in those areas.

Bringing up the rear, in terms of influence, is *the media*—television, movies, music, magazines, and so on.[9] Interestingly enough we sometimes worry most about what has the least potential for significant influence. There can be no denying that the media has influence,[10] but it has less influence than parents, family members, and friends.

So why are peers so influential today? If what I have written is true, what gives the peer group such power? The reason for this is simple. In today's world, the peer group has become influential *by default*. It has become the primary influence on today's youth because—for too many kids—parents are no longer there for them. They are either nonexistent or absent most of the time. Likewise, the extended family has vanished. Further, few teenagers today have significant adult role models, mentors, and friends. Take away parents, extended family, and adults outside the home, and that leaves the peer group and the media as primary influencer of youth. Yes, the peer group—and the media—are powerful influencers of today's kids, but it is only influence by default. Their power has been usurped from parents, family members, and adults who are no longer there.

The bridge to adulthood is a relational bridge. As junior highers are separating from their parents, they seek out other people who will affirm them and help them get a better understanding of who they are and what they

THE PEER GROUP

THE MEDIA

will become. They need friends—peer friends, yes, but also adult friends. Most junior highers I know are thrilled when adults pay attention to them and want to become their friends. Adults like that are especially influential today because they are so rare.

Later in this book, we will look at ways to encourage and involve parents in junior high ministry and to provide adult mentors for all our junior highers. If we are serious about helping kids to grow "in wisdom and in stature and in favor with God and man," then we must not fail to surround kids with the best influences we can.

How Junior Highers Can Choose Friends That Are Good for Them

One of the great fears parents have is that their early adolescent children will become part of the wrong crowd. Their fears are justified. It is very easy for junior highers to choose friends who do not hold Christian values and who may exert a negative influence on them. There are many junior highers who smoke, drink, use drugs, or involve themselves in other kinds of harmful behaviors. It is natural to want to discourage this kind of behavior, if possible, and to encourage our kids to choose the right kinds of friends.

One thing is certain: we cannot choose friends for our kids. They must have the freedom to make their own friendship choices. We can and should offer guidance, but it is usually counterproductive in the long run to criticize or to put down the friends our junior highers have. To do so is to attack their judgment and to show that we have little or no faith in them. When it is apparent that there are some dangers inherent in a particular relationship, then it should certainly be discussed, but we must never assume that antisocial behavior is always contagious.

I sometimes remind parents that when they were teenagers, they probably had some friends they wouldn't want their own kids to have as friends. Remembering this helps us to relax a little bit. We survived a few bad friends; chances are pretty good our kids will, too. Psychologist Eda Le Shan advises:

> There are times when it is a necessary part of growing up to live
> through a particular relationship. Much growth and learning about
> oneself can take place, even in some of the most ill-advised
> friendships. . . . The only real protection against poor friendship
> choices is whatever help we can give our children in respecting
> themselves so much that they are unlikely to choose relationships
> that will hurt or demean them. . . . [11]

Most adolescents choose friends from the group they feel most comfortable being a part of. If youngsters choose friends from a group of kids who have low self-esteem and no sense of self-respect, there are two possibilities: either (a) they are experimenting to see how it feels to be part of this particular group; or (b) they identify with this group. Young people who have no self-respect tend to seek out other kids who have no self-respect. They will stick together and reinforce their collective outlook on life. Conversely highly motivated kids who have a healthy sense of self-respect don't feel comfortable being part of that group. Instead they tend to choose friends who are like themselves and who have higher aspirations.

We must remember that young adolescents generally get a sense of who they are (their self-image) from the feedback they get from other people. They get it from their parents, their family members, and from other adults who interact with them, as well as from their peer friends and the media. If the primary message a young person hears is *You will never amount to anything, You are so stupid, You are a troublemaker*, etc., it should not surprise us when she chooses friends who have low self esteem. Dr. Le Shan is correct: the best way to help kids to choose good friends is to give them a high view of themselves. The best strategy we can take to help kids choose good friends is to affirm them and let them know that we like them, believe in them, and expect the best from them.

Another way we can help kids choose the right friends is to create a place where they can find the right friends. That's one of the primary goals of an effective junior high ministry. A junior high group should be a place where kids are able to socialize, to have fun together, to get to know each other, and to make friends with others who share their faith and values. Research has proven that if a young person has just one friend who will stand with him against the crowd, he will be much less likely to give in to negative peer pressure and much more likely to take a stand for Christ.[12] I have attended many junior high conferences and watched kids stand together committing themselves to be witnesses for Christ, or to abstain from sexual immorality, or to say no to drugs and alcohol. Obviously it would be very hard for kids to do that all by themselves. But positive peer pressure is just as powerful as negative peer pressure. That's why it's important to help junior highers find friends in the family of faith.

Choosing between Friends and Faith

Junior high ministry can be very rewarding. Early adolescents, who are trying to think for themselves and make meaningful commitments on their own, are often very open and responsive to the message of the gospel. Unlike older teens and adults, junior highers have not become rigid, skeptical, or hardened toward spiritual things. This makes them very reachable without manipulation or coercion. I have seen hundreds of junior highers choose freely to follow Christ.

But junior highers, young Christians that they are, are rarely able to put much of their faith into practice right away, especially if it means putting their friendships in jeopardy. They are not ready to sacrifice their friends for their faith. As we have seen, friends are the lifeblood of adolescence, and hardly anything is more important to a junior higher. I sometimes tell people that the three most important things to a junior higher are (1) their friends, (2) their friends, and (3) their friends. What this means is that if a choice has to be made between friends and faith, they will usually choose their friends every time. In their view, faith can come later. "When I'm an adult, then it will be easy. But right now, I gotta have friends."

If we understand that this is true, we can be sensitive to the social needs of a junior higher. I don't believe that it is necessary to force kids at this age to make a choice between having friends and having faith in Christ. Many times we communicate this to kids inadvertently. For example, when we ask them to make certain kinds of public stands (like witnessing), we are indirectly asking them to make a decision. The junior higher tends to think: *If I do this, my friends will think I'm some kind of a nut—a Jesus freak!*

I led weekly Bible clubs at several junior high schools when I was a Youth for Christ staff member early in my youth ministry career. Most of these clubs met after school, usually at a church or home within walking distance of the school, and they were reasonably well attended. But there was one club that did not have a convenient meeting place near the school. I had to use a church bus to pick up the kids after school.

Each week when the school day was over, that old red and white bus (with "First Baptist Church" painted all over it) would be parked in front of the school. At the time, I had no idea why only two or three kids would show up. Dozens of kids at the school had said they wanted the club, but when it came time to get on that bus, they were nowhere to be found. In retrospect I know I was asking for the impossible. To get on that funny-looking church bus in plain view of all their friends would have taken a lot more courage than even a lot of adults are able to muster.

> **Even though they wanted to attend the Bible club, no way were they getting on an old red and white bus with FIRST BAPTIST CHURCH written all over it.**

It takes a great deal of boldness to be able to stand apart from the pressure of the crowd. And boldness takes time to acquire. Junior highers should not be made to feel they are less than fully Christian because they fear being different. They will have many opportunities during their lives to stand up for their faith and to move against the flow of group pressure, but these opportunities should come as a natural result of their growing Christian commitment. As junior high workers, we are better off helping kids to understand the meaning of their faith rather than forcing them to make impossible choices. When we know why we believe, we are able to make wise decisions.

On the other hand, junior highers can be encouraged to share Christ with their friends, invite these friends to church or to the youth group meeting, get involved in service projects, and make all kinds of public stands, so long as they feel reasonably secure doing so. It's not an all-or-nothing proposition. Every group and every individual is different, and you as the junior high worker must be sensitive to each person's needs and level of maturity. Generally it's best to avoid situations that might be excessively threatening to the early adolescent. There is no need to push them so hard that they become frustrated and defeated.

Cliques

The clique is probably the most prevalent social structure of early adolescence. A clique is defined by Webster as "a narrow exclusive circle or group of persons." Eric Johnson defines it as "a small group of friends who stick together and shut others out."[13] While cliques are certainly not limited to junior highers, they do seem to take on great importance during the early adolescent years and cause a great deal of concern for middle school and junior high workers and teachers. Ideally we want to foster a feeling of unity within the group, with each person expressing openness and friendliness toward everyone else, but that is very seldom attained in junior high groups. Even though most junior highers themselves regard cliques as unfair and wrong, they can't seem to avoid them. They are a major part of the social life of the adolescent; they help in the transition from dependency on the family to the many upcoming associations outside the family. A junior higher would probably define the clique that he or she is a part of as "my best friends."

A common question asked by youth workers in the church is "How can I break up the cliques in my junior high group?" The question arises naturally, since it is generally acknowledged that cliques are not desirable and should be eliminated if possible. For a long time I had difficulty coming up with an answer that would satisfy me, let alone anyone else. I, like most junior high workers, have never had much success at breaking up cliques. I finally came to the conclusion that it was essentially counterproductive and perhaps even a mistake to try. Good or bad, cliques are going to exist and are part of the early adolescent landscape. It's best to work around them rather than against them.

It is possible, however, to reduce the negative impact of cliques in the junior high group. One way is to provide as many opportunities as possible for group interaction and participation. Whenever the group or class is doing something together—mixing, playing games, talking to each other—relationships between cliques and individuals are more likely to improve. But when kids come to a meeting or activity in their cliques, stay in their cliques, listen to or participate in the program in their cliques, and then leave in their cliques, there is little chance that conditions will improve. Rather than lecture on the evils of cliques, it is best to involve the kids in a variety of activity-centered learning experiences that require communication and cooperation with each other, as well as in group games, and other chances to relate to those outside their little cliques.

Most people of all ages find new friends by accident, not by design. You can't tell someone to stop liking one person and start liking someone else. You don't create community and unity by having little buzz groups and hand-holding sessions (although it *has* happened). Community and friendships develop usually as a by-product of something else. If a group puts on a play, goes on a long trip together, or participates in a service project, chances are good that kids will make new friends, cliques will become less important, and community will be encouraged almost automatically.

It's also true that small group projects or activities *in which the group is allowed to choose its own members* serve to encourage or strengthen cliques. Small groups work fine with junior highers, but it is usually best to use a random selection process to determine group members or to assign kids to groups not entirely made up of their close friends.

Creating a Sense of Belonging

An appropriate goal of junior high ministry is to create a place where every young person can feel that he or she is part of the group. This is one reason why I believe that junior high clubs—with a unique name, membership cards, caps or T-shirts, rites and responsibilities of membership, etc.—can be very effective. Many junior high groups have names like JC-DC which stands for Jesus Christ's Disciple Club, or THE CLICK, which stands for Christ Living in Christian Kids. Clubs like these can provide a sense of belonging which is very important to early adolescents.

Anything you can do to promote inclusiveness and community will be beneficial in junior high ministry. It helps to remember that junior high groups don't develop community automatically. In fact the reverse is more likely. If you don't intentionally do things to build community, you will more than likely see it fall apart. Kids naturally get into their cliques and do as little as possible to allow new kids or kids who are different to become part of their particular group. That's why you will need to constantly be looking for ways to help kids get to know each other better and learn to accept each other as fellow members of the body of Christ.

A few years ago I wrote a book called *Up Close and Personal* which offers dozens of ideas for building community in youth groups.[14] It is based on the concept that there are some things you can do to encourage community, and there are other things you can do to destroy it. For example, when you play games that exclude those who are not athletic, or who are unable to compete, you may inadvertently undermine or destroy community. On the other hand, when you play games that allow everyone an equal chance to have fun or to win, then community is going to be enhanced. Bottom line: if you want community to happen, it's a good idea to program your junior high ministry with that in mind.

Watch Out for Loners!

Within any junior high group there are usually a few kids who just don't seem to fit in. While this is not a problem for most junior highers, there are some who have real difficulty making friends and finding acceptance from others in the group. They may be rejected because of their appearance, personality, where they live, what school they go to, what their family is like, their abilities, interests, mannerisms, language, or perhaps just because they are new. One junior high pastor told me recently of a seventh-grade boy in his youth group who had been sexually abused as a child and had a number of psychological problems that caused him to be labeled as an outcast. A group of boys caught him after school one day, beat him up, and literally set his nose on fire. I still have trouble imagining this, but when I think about that boy, my heart breaks for him.

The list of reasons why a person might be excluded from the group can be endless, and they are undeniably insensitive from an adult perspective. Even though junior highers may seem cruel to each other, they are merely being typically junior highish. They have discovered that one way to satisfy their own need to feel accepted or superior is to find someone else whom they can look down upon, ridicule, pick on or simply ignore. If a junior higher can identify someone else in the group as a nerd or a loser, then that makes him look superior by comparison. It's a rather sinister, although not unusual, way for a young person to build his own self-esteem. It can also be extremely painful to the young person who is the object of this kind of discrimination—as most junior highers are at one time or another.

> **Junior highers' cruelty to each other is often an attempt to satisfy their need to feel accepted or superior.**

No junior high group should allow a situation like this to exist unchecked. It is wise for junior high workers to stay on the lookout for those in the group who appear to be rejected and try to help them find their place in the group. While you can't force people into being well-adjusted and having friends, doing nothing is usually not the best alternative. Kids should be made aware that one of the things that sets the Christian community apart from the non-Christian community is that no one is shut out. Everyone is accepted, regardless of how the world sees things. That has always been an identifying mark of the Christian.

Some junior highers who are rejected are quite capable of living with the situation without any negative impact, and they may appear to accept their roles as loners with ease. We should, of course, be supportive and thankful for them. But that is usually not the case. Most young adolescents who have no real friends in the group and who are unhappy will, given the opportunity, simply leave and seek acceptance elsewhere. Those who, for whatever reason, must stick it out will more than likely have a hard time and experience some long-term negative impact. We should do whatever we can to find out why a person is being rejected and, whenever possible, provide help.

A few years ago in one of my junior high groups, an eighth-grade girl was being shunned by the other girls (and boys) in the group. It was having a negative effect on her, so we youth workers decided to see if we could help. We discovered that her parents had been divorced for some time and that she lived with her father, who had never remarried. One result of this was an apparent lack of guidance in personal hygiene and other social graces that are important for young ladies emerging into womanhood. One of our female counselors was able to spend quite a bit of time with this girl and helped her considerably. Of course, acceptance did not instantly occur just because she smelled or looked better, but gradually she did grow more comfortable as barriers between her and the others in the group were broken down. Her self-image began to improve as well.

There are no easy answers here, of course, but the sensitive junior high worker will give special attention to kids who need it and will find creative ways to discourage the natural tendency for junior highers to discriminate against those who may be a little bit different. We can help by getting kids involved with each other more and by allowing needy kids to get more recognition by being allowed to do the things they do well. Sometimes it just means that we must be an especially good friend to every person in the group, thus becoming a common link between them all. Perhaps in us they can see Christ, the one who is able to make us all one.

Notes

1. David Elkind, *All Grown Up and No Place to Go*, (Addison Wesley Longman, 1984), p. 24.

2. Joan Lipsitz, "The Age Group," in *Toward Adolescence: The Middle School Years*, ed. Mauritz Johnson (The National Society for the Study of Education), p. 14.

3. Alvin W. Howard and George C. Stoumbis, *The Junior High and Middle School: Issues and Practices* (Intext Educational Publishers, 1970), p. 34. Used by permission of Harper & Row Publishers, Inc.

4. Jerome Kagan, "A Conception of Early Adolescence," *Twelve to Sixteen: Early Adolescence*, Robert Coles and others (eds.) (W.W. Norton, 1972), p. 103.

5. R. D. Enright, D. K. Lapsley, and L. M. Olsen, "Early Adolescent Labor," *The Journal of Early Adolescence*, vol. 5, no. 4 (Winter, 1985), pp. 402-403.

6. Elkind, *All Grown Up and No Place to Go*, pp. 4-5.

7. Search Institute, "Young Adolescents and Their Parents," *Project Report* (Search Institute, 1984), pp. 50-55.

8. "Harper's Index," *Harper's Magazine* (March, 1997), p. 13.

9. From a poll of 758 children and adolescents between the ages of 10 and 17, along with their parents, commissioned by *Newsweek* and the Children's Defense Fund and published in *Newsweek*, November 22, 1993, p. 53. Respondents were asked who had a "very important" influence on them (or, for parents, who influenced them when they were their children's age.) Children and adolescent responses: parents—86 percent; grandparents—56 percent; place of worship—55 percent; teachers— 50 percent; peers—41 percent; community organizations—23 percent; media—22 percent. Parent responses: parents—81 percent; grandparents—47 percent; place of worship—55 percent; teachers—48 percent; peers—37 percent; community organizations—17 percent; media—20 percent. Also, from research conducted in 1996 by the University of Minnesota and the University of North Carolina with 12,118 students in 134 schools nationwide, grades seven through 12, and reported in *The Wall Street Journal*, September 10, 1997, p. B9. This study found that "the closer teenagers were to their parents and the more connected they felt to teachers at school, the less likely they were to smoke, drink alcohol, engage in violence, commit suicide, or have sex at a young age."

10. With increasing frequency, we hear about youth who imitate what they observe or hear on television, movies, or music videos. Some teenagers, for example, have

committed suicide after listening to rock songs glorifying suicide or death. While such incidents do happen, they are rare and certainly not the norm.

11. Eda J. Le Shan, *Sex and Your Teenager: A Guide for Parents* (David McKay Co., 1969), p. 51. Used by permission.

12. James Dobson, *Preparing for Adolescence* (Vision House Publishers, 1978), pp. 46-49.

13. Eric W. Johnson, *How to Live through Junior High School* (J. B. Lippincott, 1975), p. 199.

14. Wayne Rice, *Up Close and Personal* (Youth Specialties/Zondervan, 1989).

• S I X •

INTELLECTUAL DEVELOPMENT IN JUNIOR HIGHERS

When I was a child, I talked like a child, I thought like a child, I reasoned like a child. When I became a man, I put childish ways behind me.

—St. Paul, in his first letter to the Corinthians (13:11)

Junior highers are not only changing from children into adults physically and socially, but intellectually as well. There are basic structural differences between the way a child thinks and the way an adult thinks (as the apostle Paul makes clear in the passage quoted above), and once again, we find that it is during the junior high years when most young people pass through an exciting period of intellectual change. The brain shifts gears, so to speak, and a whole new world emerges, much more complicated than before, yet wonderfully exciting.

Prior to the age of 11 or 12, a child's understanding of reality is largely tied to what he or she can experience. But a qualitative change occurs coinciding with the onset of puberty, something greater than simply becoming more intelligent or learning more. Junior highers develop the ability to reason more logically, to conceptualize, to think abstractly, and to move from one abstraction to another. A junior higher can speculate on the many possible effects of something he wants to do. He can keep a lot of "ifs" in his head at one time and yet come up with an answer. These are all things he was unable to do when he thought like a child.

Meet Jean Piaget

In recent years many different theories have been proposed about intellectual development in children and adolescents.[1] Not all of them have survived close scrutiny, however. For example, in the late 1970s, a theory called *brain growth periodization* was getting a lot of attention by educators and psychologists. This theory held that brain growth increases during certain periods of life and decreases (stops growing) during other periods of life. During the periods when the brain is growing, it can absorb new information. When it is not growing, no new information can be absorbed. Interestingly enough, this theory identified early adolescence (12 to 14) as one of the "no growth" periods.[2] This theory certainly offered a good reason why junior highers were bored with algebra and American history, but it didn't help us understand the inquisitiveness and seemingly unquenchable curiosity of this age group. While a few people still believe this theory is credible, it has been discarded by most developmental psychologists as having little or no substance.[3]

The most widely accepted research in the field of cognitive development (how the mind develops) has been done by the late Jean Piaget, a Swiss psychologist.[4] He conducted numerous studies over a period of several decades and made brilliant observations of the thought processes of children, especially of their ability to think logically. He noted that intelligence, whatever that may be, does not increase at a steady rate, but in spurts. Therefore, the conventional IQ score often is not an accurate measure of intelligence because people shift from one stage of thinking to a higher stage at different ages.

Piaget's stages of cognitive development are levels of thought, each one more sophisticated than the one before. People move from one stage to the next, never backward, as they mature. Piaget called the first stage the *sensori-motor* period. It is best characterized by infants who do little or no organized thinking. They merely respond. Their perception of the world is obtained directly through their physical senses. By about age two, the child has learned that actions have physical consequences and that he and his environment are not the same.

The second stage is called the period of *prelogical or pre-operational* thought and lasts typically from ages two to five. The thinking of children during this stage contains a magical element—they are not able to distinguish well between events or objects they experience and those they imagine. Although things are beginning to make sense, their point of view is still that everything in the world revolves around them. Language and other symbols develop at this stage.

Piaget's third stage is called the period of *concrete operations*.

(An *operation* is defined as a logical thought process.) Here children are not as ego centered, but they still relate most things to themselves. Children and young adolescents between the ages of five and 12 are usually in this group. At this stage kids learn to observe, count, organize, memorize, and reorganize concrete objects and information. They can figure things out for themselves and solve problems. But they need concrete reference points. They have a hard time visualizing things they can't see. For example, a child at this stage would have a hard time imagining something that is 12 feet wide and 40 feet long. They must see it in front of them to visualize it. Concrete thinkers need direct contact with ideas, things, events, situations, and people in order for these things to be represented in their minds. The mind is much like a computer at this stage, processing information and making conclusions based on concrete data. It is during the stage of concrete operations when children attend grammar school and are given many opportunities to use this ability. They learn facts and figures, the parts of speech, the names of all the presidents, how to read and write, multiply and divide, and so on. Their education is limited primarily to the realm of the "here and now" as they are not yet able to visualize and project alternatives and possibilities into the future. When a young adolescent is beginning puberty, he or she is more likely than not to be a stage-three (concrete) thinker.

The fourth (and final) stage is called the period of *formal operations*. This is adultlike thinking. Most people enter this stage between the ages of 11 and 15—if they are going to enter it at all. Piaget found that some people never do. But when a person *does* reach stage four, he or she is able for the first time to deal with abstractions—to reason, to understand and construct complex systems of thought, to formulate philosophies, to struggle with contradictions, to think about the future, and to appreciate the beauty of a metaphor. A stage-four thinker can perform operations on operations, classify classifications, combine combinations, and relate relationships. Formal thinkers can think about thought and acquire knowledge that is very complex, while also having an awareness that knowledge is extremely limited and fragmentary. This incredible new power to think is usually acquired

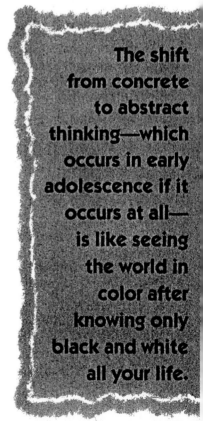

The shift from concrete to abstract thinking—which occurs in early adolescence if it occurs at all—is like seeing the world in color after knowing only black and white all your life.

during early adolescence—the junior high years. Junior high and middle school teachers report that they get a lot of pleasure from seeing young adolescents experience the "sudden comprehension of content" when, as one teacher put it, "the light goes on."[5]

The shift from stage-three to stage-four thinking is much like seeing things in color after having only known black and white all your life. A brand new dimension is added to a person's ability to think. Children have a very limited understanding of concepts like *love* and *hate* for example, because they are quite abstract. When they reach early adolescence and acquire formal thinking abilities, new depth is added to their understanding and experience of them. David Elkind calls this "thinking in a new key" and he reminds us that it doesn't happen overnight. As he puts it:

> It is important to remember that young people are as unfamiliar with their new thinking abilities as they are with their newly configured bodies. Moreover, thinking on a higher plane takes time to get used to. Teenagers need to become accustomed to living in a new body. And just as they are often awkward in the use of their transformed bodies, they are sometimes equally awkward in the use of their new thinking abilities. As adults we have to be careful not to mistake their awkwardness in thinking, which may sometimes manifest itself in the form of insensitive remarks, for anything more sinister than inexperience.[6]

Graphically Piaget's stages of cognitive development might look like this:

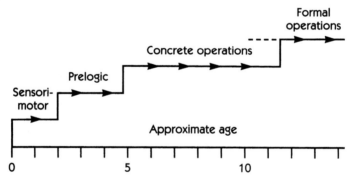

While theories about intellectual development are no more than that—*theories,* they do give us a framework for understanding how kids process information and how we can help them to learn. Piaget's theory in particular has some important implications for doing junior high ministry. For example, we need to remember that some junior highers are at stage three in their thinking and others are at stage four. If you have sixth-graders in your junior high ministry, then you have quite a few stage-three thinkers. Some of your eighth- or ninth-graders will possess much more advanced thinking abilities. But most junior highers are in-between. Early adolescent minds are in a transitional and fluctuating state, sometimes thinking like a child, sometimes thinking like an adult. In his later writings, Piaget concluded that most people don't fully acquire stage-four thinking abilities until *late* adolescence.[7]

I am reminded of an incident at a junior high retreat a few years ago when the camp director asked all the kids to climb what was called the Pamper Pole. It was so named because some people needed to put on Pampers when they climbed up. After the kids climbed the pole, they were to jump off with a cable tied to their harness, and this cable would carry them safely to the ground, some 100 feet below. The camp director explained that this was an example of faith. When you become a Christian, he said, you "jump off" into the arms of Christ and you trust him to carry you to heaven. Later that day, one of the counselors reported that an 11-year-old girl came to her in tears, extremely distraught because she had come to the conclusion that she could not be a Christian. She thought that in order to become one, you had to jump off the Pamper Pole, and she was terrified of it.

That young adolescent girl misunderstood because she was unable to make the leap—not from the Pamper Pole—but from stage-three thinking to stage-four thinking. She took the camp director literally rather than figuratively, which requires formal operational thinking. We have to remember that we have young people like that in our junior high groups.

One thing you don't want to do as a junior high worker is to put individual students into an intellectual box. It would not be a good idea to group kids into the stage-three group and the stage-four group. It's almost impossible to pinpoint when a youth makes the shift from concrete to formal operations, although many believe that age does play a major role. In fact it has been said that the thinking of a 12-year-old German is closer to that of a 12-year-old American than to that of his 15-year-old brother.[8] But while this may be generally true, there are, of course, slow developers, fast developers, and those who don't develop at all. We need to keep in mind that junior highers are in transition and that *variability* is the operative word. It is likely that there will be, within the same age group, kids who are radically different from each other in their intellectual abilities.

Junior high teacher Eric Johnson offers this example:

> If you asked a committee of fifth-graders to go out and count how many gravestones there were in the nearby cemetery . . . and how many of the people there died between 1800 and 1900, they'd rush right out, bright-eyed, pencil in hand, to do the research. They'd

return breathless, eager to report the results of their counting. The class might well whip out their notebooks and conscientiously write down the figures and have the feeling they were doing something important. Ask some seventh-graders to do the same thing and they'd groan, object and, if necessary, procrastinate, but probably not bother to formulate the reasons why such an activity would be worthless. But ask ninth-graders to do it, and their first reaction would be (unless they thought you were joking) to inquire why the job should be done and what relation it might have to the purposes of the course.[9]

In a single group of junior high kids, you will have some who think more like fifth-graders and others who think more like ninth-graders, and everywhere in-between. This is another reason why junior high ministry has to be very personal and adds weight to the importance of building relationships with individual kids. This doesn't mean that junior highers must be individually tutored, nor does it mean that they cannot be challenged with levels of thinking they are unaccustomed to. It does mean, however, that we will be aware of kids who are having difficulty understanding certain concepts or who show an apparent lack of interest or seem bored.

Booorrring!

Most children have a hard time listening to a sermon because sermons are boring. But they are not boring because the pastor is necessarily a boring speaker. Usually it's because a sermon consists primarily of stage-four (abstract) concepts—which only those who have made the shift from concrete to formal operations can understand. Even if a child—or anyone who had not made the shift to formal operations—were listening closely, he or she would probably not comprehend the meaning of what was being said.

It's common for pastors to include a children's sermon somewhere in the church service to alleviate this problem. It is intended to communicate with children on their level—the level of concrete operations. Unfortunately, a common mistake that is made in children's sermons is the use of object lessons and parables that require formal operational thinking to understand. Object lessons and parables, while they are very concrete, are metaphorical in nature. They represent an abstract idea. For someone to make the leap from the object to what it represents requires the ability to think on an abstract level. It is ironic that we commonly use object lessons with children (who haven't yet developed the ability to appreciate them), and we stop using them just when people *have* developed the ability to understand them—at adulthood. We assume that they are too juvenile for older people.

But that is not the case. Most adults enjoy and prefer sermons that are well-illustrated with stories and concrete examples. Jesus used parables and object lessons continually in his teaching. Junior highers, especially, love object lessons and stories because they begin with the familiar (concrete operations) and move them into the realm of their new thinking abilities—the abstract.

It is also important to recognize that a person who has reached the stage of formal operations may become bored when she is forced to limit herself to concrete thinking. No real intellectual challenge is offered when stage-four thinkers are asked to memorize religious facts or to accept everything they are taught without questioning. While it is always good to begin with some concrete learning, it is important to allow junior highers to do some abstract thinking as well. Junior highers are ready to ask questions and to "learn about their learning."

> **It's ironic that we stop using object lessons about the time that children acquire abstract-thinking skills. Adolescents are too old for juvenile object lessons, we wrongly reason.**

In many mainline denominations, junior highers are given the opportunity to go through the process of confirmation, a series of classes (often taught by the pastor or a priest) that instruct students in the basics of the Christian faith. While these classes are beneficial as a traditional rite of passage, they frequently become tedious and counterproductive because they limit students to the memorization of religious facts and dogma. While young adolescents do need to learn *what* we believe as Christians, they also need to explore their faith, ask questions, and discover *why* we believe what we do. Unless kids are given the opportunity to do this kind of thinking, they will not only find their Christian education boring and irrelevant, but they will be unlikely to embrace their faith as their own.

Questions, Questions, and More Questions

As adolescents move from stage-three to stage-four thinking, they commonly begin to question much of what they have been taught in the past. This can make them seem argumentative at times. They will disagree just to disagree. They may actually have valid points to make from time to time, but often, young adolescents will argue a position simply to understand themselves and their thinking better. As one author put it, "Sometimes they appear to be figuring out what they believe—at least for the moment—by listening to themselves talk about themselves."[10]

But many of the questions and arguments stay below the surface. Junior highers don't always verbalize what they are thinking. Still, their new thinking capabilities require them to reaffirm the learning they previously acquired from their parents, teachers, and peers. They want assurance that it is really true. They will often spot inconsistencies and contradictions that they hadn't seen before, or that, at least, didn't bother them before.

Jerome Kagan cites the following example:

> The 14-year-old broods about the inconsistency among the following three propositions:
> 1. God loves man.
> 2. The world contains many unhappy people.
> 3. If God loved man, he would not make so many people unhappy.
> The adolescent is troubled by the incompatibility that is immediately sensed when he examines these statements together. He notes the contradictions and has at least four choices. He can deny the second premise that man is ever unhappy; this is unlikely for the factual basis is too overwhelming. He can deny that God loves man; this is avoided for love of man is one of the definitional qualities of God. He can assume that the unhappiness serves an ulterior purpose God has for man; this possibility is sometimes chosen. Finally, he can simply deny the hypothesis of God.[11]

Despite the oversimplification this example is typical of how early adolescents privately work out their own set of values and beliefs. When they were younger, they listened to Bible stories like "Jonah and the Whale" and accepted them without question. But junior highers will commonly find this harder to do. They will want answers to questions like "How could a person be swallowed by a whale and survive? What about stomach acid? If he was underwater all that time, how could he breathe in the whale's belly? And how did the whale puke him up on dry land? Did the whale come on shore?" And so on. You can see why young adolescents sometimes begin to wonder if all they have heard before is true.

Another example: Junior highers have been told that sex (for them) is wrong, yet they find pleasure through sexual experiences. Is pleasure therefore wrong? They have been told that God answers prayers, yet they prayed and nothing happened. Why? Many junior highers are dismayed to find themselves facing an endless stream of problems like these that force them to make some adjustments regarding beliefs they hold at the moment. Left alone, the adolescent grows more and more skeptical, assuming that all religious truth is nothing more than wishful thinking. Sometimes this leaves the adolescent temporarily without a commitment to any belief at all.

By the way, don't worry if you can't answer all their questions. Sometimes the best approach is simply to encourage their questions and let them know that questions are good. The best way to grow as a Christian is to ask questions and to seek the truth. No one wants to believe something that is not true. If you can't answer a question, you might say, "That's a great question. I wish I had the answer to that one!" Then invite students to do a little research on their own, or join you in finding satisfactory answers to their questions. You can also teach kids a lot about faith when questions come up. Faith is believing even when we don't have all the answers.

Idealism and Pseudo-Stupidity

As junior highers develop new ways of thinking, they typically become very idealistic. Because they can now think in terms of *possibilities*, anything imaginable to early adolescents seems possible. And they tend to imagine things in terms of perfection. They have a hard time being realistic. They will offer ideal solutions to complex problems and perfect outcomes and alternatives to every situation. This characteristic of early adolescent thinking is very strong because their thought processes lack the ability to make the connection between what they think and what is reality.

Psychologist David Elkind calls this idealism *pseudo-stupidity*.[12] It looks like stupidity when in fact it is not. It's just that the obvious or the realistic seems to elude them. For example, when a junior higher loses a sock or a shoe or a book, he may look in the least obvious places. Instead of looking under his bed or the bottom of his locker, he will come up with mysterious conspiracy theories involving fellow students or even aliens from outer space. A junior higher may approach subjects in school at a much too complex level and fail, not because the assignments are too difficult but because they are too simple.

When young adolescents make the shift to formal operational thinking, they need time to learn how to use their new thinking abilities. They don't always have them under control. The ability to weigh many different alternatives is not yet coupled with the ability to assign priorities and to decide which choice is most

> **"Pseudo-stupidity" explains why some junior highers can't see the obvious or realistic—why, when he loses a sock, he'll look everyplace *but* under his bed or at the bottom of his locker.**

appropriate. Consequently, they often appear to be stupid when, in fact, they are too bright.

It is typical for junior highers to suspect complex, devious motives in the behavior of their friends, teachers, parents, brothers, and sisters for the simplest or most accidental occurrences. A simple discussion with a junior higher can become extremely complicated and sidetracked by the young adolescent's overeager intellectualization of the issue at hand. This can result in miscommunication, misunder- standing, frustration, and, more often than not, hurt feelings.

Delia Ephron offers an example of this in her book *Teenage Romance*. What follows is a conversation between a mother and her teenage daughter. The situation: It's Saturday night and the girl's mother is insisting that she be home by midnight.

> "Oh, Mom, come on. Nobody gets home that early, nobody! Do you want me to be the only kid in the entire group that has to leave early? The only one who can't stay out? Do you? Do you want me to ruin everybody else's time because I have to leave because my mom doesn't trust me while everyone else's mom does? Is that what you want? Is it? Great, just great. You're really getting impossible, you know that? You've changed, Mom, you have. You never listen, you never try to understand. You just give orders—do this, do that. . . . You never let me do anything I want. Never. If you had your way, I'd be in jail. You know, you're ruining my life. Probably no one will ever invite me anywhere again as long as I live. I'll probably never have another date. I'll spend the rest of my life in my room."[13]

It is helpful to remember that junior highers may sometimes think this way. They may say things that sound stupid and unreas- onable when in fact they are being as reasonable as they can at this point in their development. As junior high workers, we should be as understanding and as patient as possible when confronted with the idealism of young adolescents. We can help them learn to be realistic and mature in their thinking by being realistic and mature in our responses.

The idealistic nature of junior high thinking can also be one of the endearing qualities of early adolescence. Sometimes their idealism translates into the kind of enthusiasm that is hard to find with other age groups, especially adults. For example, when you tell junior highers that God wants to use them to change the world, they get excited. They believe it! They see all kinds of possibilities and are ready to go change the world. Our challenge is to help channel some of that idealism into real opportunities for service so they don't become cynical and discouraged.

The Lie of the Personal Fable

Sometimes the idealistic nature of early adolescent thinking causes junior highers to temporarily hold an unrealistic view of themselves. Elkind has labeled this view the *personal fable*. It is a form of self-centeredness that says, "I am a special case. I am unique." Indeed, young people are special and unique, but the personal fable distorts reality to the point that the young person sees himself as immune or invulnerable to the things that happen to other people. "Others will grow old and die, but not me. Others will get pregnant, but not me. Others will get hooked on drugs, but not me." The personal fable is an untrue story that young people tell themselves about themselves.

> It's generally futile warning junior highers of the consequences of their behavior: they'll be the exception, they figure.

It is often futile to talk to junior highers about the consequences of their behavior, because they don't believe those consequences will actually happen to them. They believe they will always be the exception. When kids get into accidents, get pregnant, or get involved with drugs, they do these things not because they have chosen to accept the consequences of their actions, but because they never believed those consequences would happen to them. In the perfect world of early adolescence, things that happen to other people don't happen to them.

Despite the widely publicized health risks associated with smoking cigarettes, early adolescents continue to smoke at an alarming rate. When the American Cancer Society created a series of anti-smoking posters aimed at young teens, they discovered that the most effective poster featured a celebrity with cigarettes stuck in her ears. The headline read, "Smoking spoils your looks." This poster was so effective because it emphasized smoking's effect on "how others see you" (the here and now) rather than "what might happen to you" in the future. Similarly, many junior highers express their fear of getting AIDS in terms of what others would think of them rather than in terms of the health risks.

Another example of the personal fable is the junior higher who says, "You don't understand me. You just don't know what it feels like!" The young adolescent perceives that his feelings and needs are so unique that they are beyond the realm of anyone else's understanding, especially that of adults. Sometimes this can make communication with a junior higher difficult, particularly when you are trying to let him know that you *do* understand.

It is usually unwise to argue with a young adolescent about this. Instead, accept her point of view and encourage her to check her version of reality against that of others. Rather than trying to persuade a junior higher that his perception of himself is wrong, you can help him see that other people are just as special and unique as he is. If we try to understand others better, then that opens the possibility that others can also understand us better.

While the personal fable does affect the thinking of many junior highers, recent studies caution us to avoid overgeneralizing on this point. Researchers studied 86 low-risk adolescents (kids who were living at home with their parents and succeeding in school) and compared them with 95 high-risk adolescents (kids who were in group homes or treatment centers.) They found that belief in the personal fable (a sense of invulnerability) was high for high-risk kids, but not so high with the low-risk group. Their conclusion: "there is very little empirical support for the claim that perceived invulnerability is particularly large during adolescence."[14]

"Everybody's Thinking about Me, Right?"

Another characteristic of young adolescence made possible by the advent of formal operations is what Elkind has called the *imaginary audience*. It is this characteristic that accounts for the junior higher's extreme self-consciousness. Formal operations enable young people to think about other people's thinking. This new ability to think about other people's thoughts, however, is coupled with the inability to distinguish between what is of interest to others and what is of interest to the self. Since junior highers are primarily preoccupied with themselves, they assume that everyone else has the same concern. Young adolescents believe that everyone in their vicinity is thinking about what they themselves are thinking about, namely "me." They feel like they are constantly on stage and that everyone is as concerned with their appearance and behavior as they are. They surround themselves with an imaginary audience.

This is another reason why young teenagers will spend so much time in the bathroom bathing and combing their hair. When they stand in front of the mirror, they imagine how everyone else will see them and what they will think. Everyone does this to some extent, but with junior highers, it is commonly obsessive.

The imaginary audience also helps to explain why junior highers feel such a need to show off or to engage in disruptive or destructive behavior. In many respects such behavior is really a performance. When a young person commits an act of vandalism, for example, he is probably thinking more about the reaction of the audience than he is about destroying property.

Fortunately imaginary-audience behavior tends to decline with age as young people come to realize that other people have their own problems and concerns. But until then the imaginary audience is very real indeed. Elkind suggests that we can help kids learn to differentiate between their own concerns and the concerns of others by taking a middle-ground position.[15] If a junior higher says that nobody likes him, for example, it would do no good to tell him that people do like him. Instead, it would be better to say, "Well, I like you. And frankly I can't understand why others wouldn't like you, too. What do others say or do that makes you feel that way?" This approach helps kids to test their feelings against reality and to see the world as it really is.

Adolescent Relapse

It would seem logical that with newly acquired mental capabilities, junior highers would be anxious to excel academically and to put their improved brain power to work, but the opposite is often true. For many junior highers, the quality of schoolwork goes down, not up, during their early adolescent years. Kids who may have excelled academically during their prejunior high years often do quite poorly when they reach adolescence, much to the dismay of parents and teachers alike. Junior highers seem intellectually lazy and bored with learning. This is sometimes called *adolescent relapse* and it poses a frustrating problem for both school teachers and junior high workers in the church.

As I wrote earlier, some people have attributed this development to a decrease in brain growth which occurs during early adolescence, but such an explanation is not only dubious but overly simplistic. There are other good reasons why adolescent relapse is normal and to be expected.

First, one has to keep in mind that early adolescence is a time of rapid growth and enormous change. Kids are growing and changing in every area of their lives and this results in some major distractions. There are what I call *other urgencies* that take priority over academics at this time in a young person's life. Getting good grades simply becomes less important than making friends, falling in love, separating from parents, looking good, fitting in with the right group, and becoming popular. There is a lot going on in the life of the early adolescent, to say the least. To expect a junior higher to be a good student at this time in his life is not always realistic. It's not easy for school teachers (or junior high workers in the church) to make history lessons (or Bible lessons) interesting enough to prevail over these "other urgencies." It is often not until the 10th, 11th, or even the 12th grades that young people develop a

They are motivated neither to please their parents nor to prepare for adulthood.

driving intellectual curiosity and a pleasure from dealing with ideas. This makes designing junior high curriculum a real challenge for everyone involved.

A second reason for adolescent relapse, closely related to the first, is the newness of not only their new thinking abilities, but the educational setting in which they must learn. Most junior high and middle schools require early adolescents to adjust quickly to an entirely new way of relating to their teachers and their curricula. Students often have difficulty getting themselves organized for each class and being responsible for their assignments without a teacher watching and guiding them every step of the way, as is usually the case in elementary school. For a time the disorientation that early adolescents experience can negatively affect their school work.

Thirdly, because of all the internal changes they are experiencing, junior highers have shorter attention spans and shorter concentration levels than other age groups. This is a handicap that forces them to work twice as hard to learn about the same as they did in elementary school. This can be discouraging for young people who are doing their best but doing worse. Teachers can help students by reassuring them that they are doing fine and that eventually all their hard effort will pay off.

Another cause of adolescent relapse has to do with motivation. Junior highers are not sufficiently motivated to perform at a high level academically. They are actually between motivations. When they were younger they were motivated to do well in school because it pleased their parents. They would bring their papers home from school (with good grades on them) and their parents would proudly display them on the refrigerator door. This motivated them to continue to get good grades. When they get older, they will again be highly motivated by a desire to be better equipped for adulthood, to get a good job, or to expand their knowledge on a particular subject. But during the early adolescent years, they are caught between these two motivations. They are motivated neither to please their parents nor to prepare themselves for adulthood.

Motivating Junior Highers to Learn

So in light of all this, how do we motivate junior highers to become good learners? There are no easy answers, but what follows are some suggestions that may increase the *chances* that the junior highers in your group will be more interested in learning what you are teaching.

• **Make other urgencies part of the curriculum.** Since other urgencies can be significant distractions to learning, use them to your advantage.

In other words, make your teaching relevant to their life experience. Kids will always be more interested in things that relate to their world, their concerns, what they are experiencing, and so on. If the subject matter has no practical application, it may be a complete waste of time.

• **Use variety in your teaching.** Active, growing minds become bored easily. Use a variety of approaches and methods to cover a variety of topics. Don't use the same approach week after week after week. Surprise the kids once in a while. Give them something to look forward to.

• **Involve kids in the learning process.** Use as many activity-centered learning experiences as you can. Avoid lecturing when teaching can be done some other way.

• **Create a warm, friendly atmosphere in which learning can take place.** If kids feel right away that they are accepted and that they are in a place that is fun, exciting, and happy, then motivation to learn isn't far behind.

• **Keep it personal.** If each junior higher realizes her importance—that she is special and cared for, and if you are a friend, she will be motivated to please you, not disappoint you. It is usually the kids who feel left out who are least motivated to participate and to learn.

Notes

1. See Karen Bartsch, "Adolescents' Theoretical Thinking," *Early Adolescence: Perspectives on Research, Policy and Intervention*, Richard M. Lerner (ed.) (Lawrence Erlbaum Associates, 1993), pp. 143-157.

2. Herman Epstein, "Growth Spurts During Brain Development: Implications for Educational Policy" (chapter 10), *Education and the Brain*, J. Chall (ed.) (National Society for the Study of Education Yearbook, University of Chicago Press, 1979) and Conrad F. Toepfer, Jr., "Brain Growth Periodization: A New Dogma for Education?" *The Middle School Journal* (August, 1979).

3. Hershel Thornburg, editor of *The Journal of Early Adolescence* wrote in a letter to the author (April 13, 1983): "Developmental psychologists as a whole believe that brain growth periodization has no validity at all. . . . In short, I believe the theory has little or nothing to offer our understanding of adolescent thought."

4. Jean Piaget, *The Psychology of Intelligence* (Routledge and Kegan Paul, 1950).

5. Peter Scales, *Boxed In and Bored*, (Search Institute, 1996), p. 26.

6. David Elkind, *All Grown Up and No Place to Go*, (Addison Wesley Longman, 1984), p. 24.

7. Jean Piaget, "Intellectual Evolution from Adoelscence to Adulthood," *Human Development*, 15 (1972), pp. 1-12.

8. Joan Lipsitz, *Growing Up Forgotten* (Lexington Books, 1977), p. 47.

9. Eric W. Johnson, *How to Live through Junior High School* (J. B. Lippencott, 1975), p. 59.

10. Chris Stevenson, *Teaching Ten to Fourteen-Year-Olds* (Longman Press, 1992), p. 84.

11. Jerome Kagan, "A Conception of Early Adolescence," *Twelve to Sixteen: Early Adolescence*, Robert Coles, et al. (eds.) (W.W. Norton, 1972), pp. 93-94.

12. David Elkind, "Understanding the Young Adolescent," *Adolescence*, XIII, No. 49 (Spring 1978): pp. 127-134.

13. Delia Ephron, *Teenage Romance* (Viking Press, 1981), p. 37.

14. Marily Quadrel, Baruch Fischoff, and Wendy Davis, 1993, *American Psychologist*, Volume 48, Number 2, pp. 102-16. Quoted in Peter Scales, *Boxed In and Bored* (Search Institute, 1996), p. 24.

15. Elkind, *All Grown Up and No Place to Go*, p. 38.

• S E V E N •

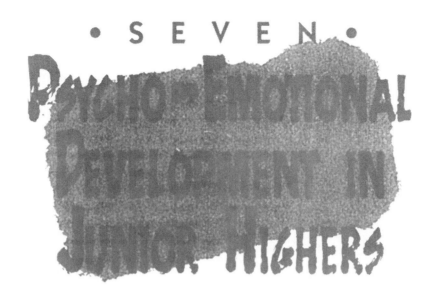

PSYCHO-EMOTIONAL DEVELOPMENT IN JUNIOR HIGHERS

I don't know why I cry so much and why I get so upset over things. Sometimes I think I'm getting younger, not older.

—Lauren, age 13

By adult standards junior highers are very emotional people. Because they have acquired the ability to think in a new way, they have also acquired the ability to feel in a new way. They have brand new emotions that are often very intense and completely unpredictable. Junior highers have been known to giggle uncontrollably during the first part of a youth meeting and then become angry or despondent during the second half. And this can occur for no apparent reason. While such behavior is typical, it is important to understand that there really is no such thing as a "typical junior higher" when it comes to emotions. In one junior high youth group you can have kids who are alternately boisterous and loud, quiet and shy, rebellious and mean, outgoing and confident, loving and kind—and they are all normal.

Like the other areas of life that we have discussed earlier in this book, psycho-emotional development has much to do with the transition from childhood to adulthood that is taking place during the early adolescent years. More accurately, psycho-emotional changes are the *result of* changes taking place in all of the other areas. The child approaches the early adolescent years depending on the same mind, body, and social structures that have supported him for 11 or 12 years. Then, as if by magic, much that he has come to depend upon begins to

> **They don't hide their emotions well. If they feel lousy, they'll let you know—and probably in a disruptively creative way, too.**

change. His body begins to grow and develop. His friends and interests outside the home begin to compete with the security previously found in his family. His view of the world begins to change as his mind devel-ops. And then he finds that his emotions begin to flip-flop like Mexican jumping beans, due largely to the release of hormones into the body at uneven rates causing temporary chemical imbalances. The young ado-lescent's once stable world suddenly feels like it's made out of Jell-O.

Junior highers are emotional people, but we need to remember that most emotions are positive and not very spectacular. When we think of emotions, we usually think of agitation and excitement. A person who is classified as emotional is sometimes regarded as unstable—as if emotions were strange forces mysteriously arising from the depths to seize the person and place him at their mercy. This extreme view exaggerates the dramatic and disturbing aspects of emotions and fails to acknowledge that much of an individual's emotional life is calm and constructive. A person can be quite emotional without flying into a rage, crying hysterically, or being silly. Emotions are always present in one form or another, no matter what behavior we are displaying at the moment. All of this is true for junior highers as well as other human beings.

If junior highers experience emotional turmoil, it is the result of turmoil in the physical, social, or intellectual areas of their lives which are changing and growing. Emotions are not foreign intrusions; they are more or less a reflection of what is going on generally in one's life, as well as a reflection of one's maturity. They hardly exist apart from these contexts. This is why it is practically impossible to make predictions about how a group of people will integrate their emotions with their behavior (especially junior highers), since people respond to situations and circumstances in their own way. One person may go through a great deal of emotional stress in a given situation, while another person may have no difficulty at all. Such is the case with junior highers. There are some early adolescents who seem to be sitting on an emotional powder keg, while others are able to take most everything in stride and show an unusual amount of emotional stability and maturity.

Even though emotional development is actually a secondary characteristic of junior highers, their emotional inconsistency and unpredictability cause a good deal of concern and frustration for parents, teachers, and youth workers because a junior higher's emotions are likely to be translated into some kind of action. In other words, they don't hide their emotions very well, even though they may try to. If a junior higher is feeling lousy, he will more than likely let you know in some disruptively creative way, and perhaps he will attempt to make everyone else around him feel lousy, too. One of the real challenges of junior high ministry is learning to understand and respond appropriately to the sometimes erratic and bizarre behavior that junior highers demonstrate from time to time.

Emotional Roller Coaster

One of the most common emotional characteristics of junior highers is their moodiness. They can run the gamut of emotions in a very short period of time. It is not uncommon to hear a distraught and angry junior higher say, "I absolutely hate you!" this minute, and then five minutes later smile and say, "You're not mad at me, are you?"

This roller coaster ride of emotions is usually attributed to hormonal changes that accompany puberty. As the body attempts to adjust to the presence of increasing amounts of hormones, the uneven secretions affect the emotions of early adolescents, causing them to be unstable.[1] Kids who seem happy one hour can be miserable the next, sometimes because of some seemingly insignificant event, and at other times for no reason at all.

It is important to remember that junior highers are not very skilled at dealing with their emotional ups and downs. They often overreact to them, and display behaviors that can seem rude, insensitive, sarcastic, and hurtful. While there will be times when these behaviors are intentional, most of the time they are not. Junior highers are so focused on themselves and their own needs they don't always realize they are being rude or that they are hurting other people's feelings. When a junior higher says "I didn't mean anything by it," he is probably telling the truth. It's not always helpful to attribute bad motives to every bad behavior. As kids react to the emotion they are feeling at the time, they often act before they think. As they mature they will hopefully learn to keep their emotional outbursts under control. This kind of behavior is not limited to junior highers, of course. We all know people who continue to struggle with this well into their adult years.

How can we help junior highers deal with their emotional ups

> **Don't always attribute bad motives to bad behavior. When she says, "I didn't mean anything by it," she's probably telling the truth.**

and downs? One way is by remaining calm. Junior high workers are well advised to keep an even keel in the midst of the storm. Adults who work with junior highers need to provide a semblance of stability when junior highers are exhibiting distressing behavior.[2] Junior highers are not helped when their adult leaders respond to them with emotional outbursts of their own.

We can also assure junior highers that their faith in God is not dependent upon how they are feeling at the moment. They may be on a roller-coaster ride, but God is always the same—he loves them and stays close to them even though they *feel* far away from him. We'll discuss this more in chapter eight.

Emotional Extremes

The emotions of early adolescents are also very intense. With junior highers there really is no middle ground, no halfway mark. Everything is one extreme or the other—the best there is or the absolute worst. The highs of a junior higher are very high and the lows are very low. People are either totally awesome (the best) or they are complete nobodies (the worst). Events and problems take on an importance out of all proportion to their actual significance. A seemingly insignificant event can bring an outburst of anger or a fountain of tears. A broken romance, failure to make the team, or poor grades can result in depression so great as to make a young adolescent feel suicidal. Suicide, by the way, does happen among 10-to-14-year-olds, but it is relatively rare. According to the National Center for Health Statistics, in 1991 there were only 1.5 suicides per 100,000 10-to-14-year-olds, compared with 14.4 per 100,000 for all age groups combined.[3] Other common symptoms of emotional distress in adolescents include eating disorders (bulimia, anorexia), insomnia, truancy, delinquency, drug or alcohol abuse, and complete withdrawal.

Emotions are intense during early adolescence primarily because they are new. As a junior higher acquires an adultlike way of thinking, he also acquires adultlike emotions, which are unlike those he had as a child. It takes him awhile to get used to them or to control them. That's why, when a junior higher is feeling good about some-thing, he is very often ecstatic about it. When in love, it is greater love than anyone could possibly understand. As an eighth-grader in love, I remember plastering my bedroom walls from floor to ceiling with my girl friend's name, and writing her name over every square inch of my schoolbooks, homework papers, desk tops, tennis shoes, ball gloves, and anything else with space enough to write. Of course, when we broke up, I was heartbroken and wept bitterly—but it didn't take too long for someone else to take her place.

So it goes with the emotions of junior highers. Unlike older, more mature teenagers, they fail to cope with their feelings realistically or consistently. Instead they tend to surrender to them.

The emotions of junior highers can be explosive as well as deep. At times, their discontent with themselves and others will express itself in anger—anger likely to be expressed physically rather than with the verbal expression manifested by older adolescents. If something happens that the junior higher doesn't like—a person bumps into her or calls her a derogatory name—she may lash out and throw a punch. Junior high and middle schools deal with considerable fighting between students, with the girls often being just as violent as the boys. Anger against adults often expresses itself in outbursts that end in tears. It is not as focused as it is in high school students. The anger of the junior higher is highly charged and usually short-lived. It is also quite difficult to deal with. You can't reason with an angry, tearful junior higher. It's best just to be understanding and wait it out.

In *Reviving Ophelia,* psychologist Mary Pipher describes the emotional state of some adolescent girls:

> A friend once told me that the best way to understand teenagers was to think of them as constantly on LSD. It was good advice. . . . Emotions are extreme and changeable. Small events can trigger enormous reactions. A negative comment about appearance or a bad mark on a test can hurl a teenager into despair. Not only are feelings chaotic, but girls often lose perspective. Girls have tried to kill themselves because they were grounded for a weekend or didn't get asked to the prom. A snowstorm or a new dress can produce bliss. There's still a childlike capacity to be swept away. . . . The feeling of the moment is all that exists.[4]

Because of the intensity of their emotions, we need to remember that early adolescents are highly susceptible to emotional appeals. They are fascinated by whatever triggers a deep emotional response. Of course this makes them a prime audience for TV shows and films that play on emotions. They like listening to music that is highly emotional and are also vulnerable to drug abuse and mysticism because of the emotional power.

It is tempting for junior high workers in the church to want to take full advantage of this when attempting to produce desired results. You can get junior highers to do almost anything if you can get to their emotions. If you can make them feel guilty, afraid, excited, ecstatic, angry, or whatever—you can usually elicit the desired response. But like emotions themselves, these responses are usually very shallow and temporary. Emotions are not only intense at this age, they are also rather fleeting, and anything based on them will likewise be fleeting.

This is not to say that emotions are wrong or that they should be discouraged or restrained in the church. On the contrary young adolescents need to have positive emotional experiences that come from personally encountering God. Emotions will always enter into the picture whenever a young person responds to the gospel, but it is neither fair nor wise for us to manipulate them emotionally. Be careful that invitations to accept Christ as Savior, to dedicate one's life to Christ, and to volunteer for Christian service are presented without undue emotional pressure that may lead to only surface commitments.

Personality Development by Trial and Error

Perhaps the most accurate generalization we can make about the emotions of a junior higher is: you can't make many generalizations about the emotions of a junior higher. They are completely unpredictable. This helps to set junior highers apart from the rest of the human race. Adults and little children can normally be put into categories without too much difficulty: "She's such a pleasant little girl," or "Mr. Jones is a real happy-go-lucky sort of guy." Junior highers, on the other hand, may be pleasant today and holy terrors tomorrow. I have had kids in my junior high groups who were unusually cooperative and enthusiastic one week and unexplainably belligerent and disruptive the next. I've also observed aggressive hostility and childlike submissiveness in the same meeting from the same kid. The young person who is talkative and open one moment could suddenly clam up altogether. It's easy to conclude that these might be victims of some strange form of schizophrenia—but they are just being junior highers.

These strange shifts in mood and behavior are not limited to individuals; they are also found in groups. It is not uncommon for the dynamics in a group of junior highers to change drastically from one week to the next. A particular lesson plan or program idea may be a smashing success on a given date with a given group of junior highers, but it could have been a complete flop if you had used it a week or a month earlier. It all depends on the mood of the group. In my own ministry with junior highers I have always had more concern (before a meeting, class, or social event) with the emotional condition of the group (how the kids would respond) than with how many would show up or with how good the program or lesson plan might be. There was always the fear that the group might be wired (wild and crazy) or on a real downer (uncooperative or just plain nasty).

Is there a reasonable explanation for such unreasonable behavior? As it turns out, there is one that makes a lot of sense. It

> They're talkative one minute, and they clam up the next. It's not schizophrenia—they're just junior highers.

certainly helps us understand what is going on, even if it doesn't alter the situation much. Some psychologists have concluded that early adolescents are essentially "trying on" different personalities for size to see which ones fit them best. They will express a variety of emotions, feelings, attitudes, and temperaments to discover the range of reactions they get from others, especially their peers. If the reaction is favorable, the behavior may be repeated; if it is not, the behavior may be discontinued. This may be an oversimplification, but it does help us get a handle on what's happening. It is consistent with what we know about the primary tasks of early adolescence. Young people are making a transition from childhood to adulthood, and each one is trying to come up with an identity of his or her own. The personality, like the body and the mind, is being shaped during the junior high years, and it is probably in its most unstable period.

This is why it is not at all unusual for early adolescents to be extroverts one day and introverts the next. They are experimenting in order to discover the personality type they will be most comfortable with as adults. Junior highers may try all sorts of personalities—the class clown, the tough guy, the brain, the teacher's pet, the quiet type, the spoiled brat, the flirt—before their own distinctive personality traits begin to dominate. They don't commit themselves to a particular pattern, that comes in a few years. If junior highers get positive feedback from others by acting a certain way, this behavior will no doubt be continued. Conversely, negative feedback will usually act as a deterrent. Keep in mind, however, that negative feedback from an adult may very well be interpreted as positive feedback to junior highers. Obviously, this tends to complicate things when you are trying to encourage or discourage particular kinds of behavior.

Keep in mind that all of this is quite involuntary. Junior highers aren't actually aware of the subconscious trial-and-error personality-shaping process they are engaged in. A young adolescent doesn't wake up in the morning and say to himself, "Yesterday I tried my warm and friendly personality; today I'll see how my mean and nasty one goes over." On the contrary, this happens as part of the natural process of growing up. It's normal and even necessary.

Self-Esteem and the Early Adolescent

With all the changes that are taking place in the life of early adolescents, it's not surprising that they struggle with feelings of insecurity and self-doubt. Psychologists say that a person's self-esteem reaches its lowest point during early adolescence, particularly between the ages of 12 and 15.[5]

Self-esteem (sometimes used interchangeably with *self-concept* or *self-image*) is basically what or how people think about themselves.

There are many factors that contribute to a person's self-esteem (hundreds of books have been written on this subject), but chief among them is how other people relate to them. As I wrote earlier, other people are like mirrors who reflect back to the young adolescent his or her self-image. If others treat them with respect, they will be more likely to treat themselves with respect. On the other hand, if others mistreat them, they will be more likely to mistreat themselves. Youth who develop a positive self-image are more confident, more successful at school, better problem solvers, better able to cope with stress, and less vulnerable to negative peer pressure. They are also less likely to become discipline problems. Conversely youth with low self-esteem are generally more vulnerable to negative peer pressure and self-destructive behaviors.

Family therapist and former junior high worker Bill Wennerholm has identified a number of steps that young people must take to build self-esteem and to become healthy adults. They are part of a gradual process that usually takes several years:

1. The establishment of emotional and psychological independence from parents.

2. The achievement of a separate personal identity.

3. An ability to motivate oneself and set one's own goals and direction.

4. The development of one's own values and beliefs.

5. The ability to be in intimate reciprocal relationships.

6. The establishment of an appropriate sexual identity, which includes accepting and appreciating one's own unique body.

7. The ability to function in a work capacity.[6]

Each of these steps takes time and requires the cooperation and feedback of others, especially parents and adults who interact with early adolescents. Notice that none of these steps are directly related to self-esteem. Just as happiness can't be achieved by acting happy, so a positive self-esteem is not achieved by thinking positive thoughts about yourself. True self-esteem is not contrived or pumped up. It is a by-product of healthy development and healthy relationships. Self-esteem comes, as the old TV commercial used to say, the old-fashioned way: it has to be earned.

H. Stephen Glenn and Jane Nelson, in their book *Raising Self-Reliant Children in a Self-Indulgent World* offer another list they call The Significant Seven. It includes three perceptions and four skills that all children must acquire in order to develop a healthy self-concept and to function in the world as capable, self-reliant adults.

PERCEPTIONS

1. A strong perception of personal capability. ("I am capable. I can do things for myself.")

2. A strong perception of personal significance. ("I contribute in meaningful ways and I am genuinely needed.")

3. A strong perception of personal power. ("I can influence or control what happens to me. I am not just a victim of circumstances that happen to me.")

SKILLS

4. Strong intrapersonal skills. The ability to understand personal emotions and use that understanding to develop self-discipline and self-control and to learn from experience.

5. Strong interpersonal skills. The ability to work with others and develop friendships through communication, cooperation, negotiation, sharing, empathizing, and listening.

6. Strong systemic skills. The ability to respond to the limits and consequences of everyday life with responsibility, adaptability, flexibility, and integrity.

7. Strong judgment skills. The ability to use wisdom and evaluate situations according to appropriate values.[7]

Glenn and Nelson make a strong argument that children of the past were at a distinct advantage over modern youth in developing these perceptions and skills simply because they were surrounded by caring adults who helped them grow up successfully. They were given a place in society where they could naturally acquire a positive self-image as a result of the opportunities they had to interact with adults and contribute to their family and their world. As we have already pointed out, today's kids do not have such a place and are therefore hard pressed to develop The Significant Seven on their own.

Building self-esteem is a multifaceted task. It involves having opportunities and tools to feel competent and successful at doing things. It involves learning what your strengths are and how you can build on them. In involves learning how to make good decisions, how to solve problems and how to overcome mistakes. It involves getting recognition, encouragement, praise, and unconditional love from others—especially from parents and significant adults.

Catch Junior Highers in the Act of Doing Something Good

You can't control how junior highers feel about themselves, but you can control how you respond to them. You can impact their self-image significantly by letting them know that you do indeed like them and want to be around them. This is another reason why relationships in youth ministry are so important—they help young people build self-esteem. You give junior highers some very important information about themselves when you let them know you believe in them and take them seriously. And as we discussed in chapter two, a good way to do this is to listen to them. When you give a junior higher your attention by being a good listener, you let her know that what she has to say is important and that you value her as a person.

Another excellent way to help early adolescents build self-esteem is to say something positive to them whenever you can and conversely, to avoid putting them down or making fun of them. Be liberal with praise. Catch them doing something good and let them know that you noticed. Most junior highers I know are so used to being scolded, nagged, criticized, and ridiculed that they think they have a sign on their back that says, "Kick me, I'm a junior high kid!" Compliment your junior highers whenever you have the opportunity. Mark Twain once said, "I can live two months on one good compliment."

Junior highers, of course, need to be complimented more often than that. And when you do compliment them, it's best to emphasize positive character traits rather than possessions or appearance. "I really appreciated the way you helped out last night," rather than "That's a great-looking shirt!" And don't hesitate to compliment them in front of other people, especially their parents. Even though they may act uneasy and embarrassed, down deep inside they are taking their bows and basking in the glory of it all.

Giving Them Opportunities to Succeed

We can also help young adolescents build self-esteem by giving them meaningful responsibilities and opportunities for success. The second most important value to junior highers (the first is "to make my own decisions") is "to do something important with my life."[8] Idealistic junior highers have a keen desire to do something important with their lives, but they have few opportunities to do so. As a result they become discouraged and begin to believe that they are, in fact, incompetent and useless.

Most adults consider junior highers too immature and too irresponsible to do meaningful work. This is why there is virtually no job market for them. Interestingly enough, junior highers are the nation's baby-sitters. Almost every 11-to-14-year-old earns extra money by baby-sitting. The irony of this is that often the people who consider junior highers to be so immature and irresponsible are the same people who entrust their most prized possessions—their babies—into the care and safekeeping of junior highers. Either junior highers are in fact responsible, or adults are acting irresponsibly by leaving them alone with their babies. I think we know the truth. Junior highers are capable of accepting responsibility and they should be given every opportunity to "do something important with their lives." The same junior higher who won't pick up his dirty clothes off the bedroom floor will often jump at the chance to do something for someone else who needs work done.

There are literally millions of junior highers all over America who have nothing to do after school except to hang out, watch television, or get into trouble. Some of them are the "latchkey kids" who come home to empty houses because of working parents or parents who are absent. These young people represent a tremendous mission field for junior high workers who want to reach junior highers for Christ and make a significant difference in their lives. Churches could provide all kinds of meaningful after-school activities, such as mission and service projects, apprenticeships, volunteer work, and the arts, such as drama and music. The after-school hours remain a tremendous opportunity for ministry to junior highers.[9]

The Value of Patience

The unpredictability of junior highers predictably generates a good deal of anxiety for people who work with this age group. It is no easy task to adapt to the emotional ups and downs of junior highers week by week. It requires a considerable amount of patience, particularly when the behavior of the group is more negative than positive. The temptation in such situations is to respond in anger, to punish them in some way, to give them a tongue-lashing, to call in their parents, or to threaten them with whatever might seem appropriate. In my experience as a junior high worker, I can recall times of panic, despair, or anger, and my impulsive actions at such times did more damage than good. If you lose your temper, or overreact in a negative way, it rarely accomplishes much. It only reveals an area of weakness that can be exploited by the kids at some later date. There is nothing wrong with being firm and strict and honest about your feelings, but young adolescents need to see maturity and consistency in their adult leaders as much as possible. Junior highers demand almost superhuman standards from the adults around them.

Rather than losing control, it's best to try to be as understanding as possible and relatively good-natured through it all, even when the kids are not cooperating with you. The best advice is to have patience, make as few demands on them as possible, and wait it out. Sometimes it's a good idea to punt—switch gears and move the program or the activity in a new direction. For this reason, it's wise always to have a backup plan.

To be patient with junior highers also requires resilience. When young adolescents are angry or distressed, they are prone to attack you verbally. They may tell you off, call you names, or tell you that you're stupid, or old, or ugly. If you are insecure about yourself or get hurt easily, you could be in trouble. Experienced junior high workers recognize that kids don't usually mean what they say when they are emotionally upset. If you can remain calm and refrain from responding in like manner, they will often come back with their apologies, asking for forgiveness. Be sure to give it to them.

When Discipline Is Necessary

The emotional ups and downs of junior highers will often create a real dilemma for the adult worker who is trying to be patient and understanding, yet at the same time remain firm and in control. How does a person maintain order and exercise discipline in a junior high group without being tyrannical or without alienating, humiliating, or hurting the kids? Obviously, there is nothing to be gained by passively allowing complete chaos to exist in a youth group meeting or other activity. It is not usually in the best interest of the group to permit a few high-strung, disruptive kids to destroy a meeting or ruin a learning experience for others. A certain amount of discipline that is effective without being oppressive or counterproductive is necessary.

The question of discipline—how much, how often, and how to go about it—is usually a nagging problem for people who work with junior highers. Again there are no easy answers, since every situation will require a little different approach. Each youth worker needs to have his own style, consistent with his personality and the personality of the group. When discipline is necessary, the important thing is to do it with consistency or with a predetermined standard that is fair, just, and understood by everyone from the very beginning. It should not seem arbitrary or impulsive. If kids have a good idea in advance that certain types of behavior will result in some corresponding consequence, they will not only try to avoid it, but also their dislike for the disciplinary action will be transferred to the "system" rather than to you personally.

This may mean that some basic rules should be established and everyone made aware of them in some way. For example, whenever I allow junior highers to participate in a discussion, I first lay down a few ground rules:

- Only one person talks at a time.
- Raise your hand if you want to speak.
- If someone says something that you don't agree with, don't yell or laugh or put that person down. Just raise your hand and you'll get your chance to express your opinion.

It's not advisable to have too many rules. Rules tend to sound negative, and they put a damper on things. In fact, the more rules you have, the more rules get broken, and the more discipline problems you have when you try to enforce all the rules!

One of the best ways to establish a few basic rules is to allow the kids to help create them. You might consider creating a "youth group contract" with the kids. At one of your meetings, announce or pass out a list of proposed rules that you have chosen in advance (the more the better). It's good to include a few that border on the ridiculous, like "No spitting tobacco juice on the floor." Ask the kids for their suggestions as well. When the list is complete, divide the group into smaller units and have them decide which rules they want to keep and which they want to eliminate. They should keep those that they feel are fair, just, and necessary for the smooth running of the youth group.

Then have a discussion with the entire group, with each smaller group sharing its conclusions along with its reasons. If you find that the kids have eliminated some useful rules or have kept some undesirable ones, you may express your feelings also. But the final decision should be left to a vote of the group. Usually they will do a very good job of selecting or modifying the rules they consider essential and will be willing to honor. When all the discussion is completed, then the rules can be listed on a sheet of poster paper or parchment (like the Bill of Rights) and signed at the bottom by everyone in the group. It can be posted on the wall as a reminder that you now have a contract.

Of course it may be necessary to add amendments as you go along, adding or dropping rules when the group agrees. Some rules may be more important than others. The idea is simply to predetermine standards for group behavior in advance, so that you are never accused of being a dictator when you must administer some disciplinary or corrective action. Usually this procedure is more appropriate with larger groups than smaller ones. Again you should do what is best for your own group and what is consistent with your style of ministry.

> **Rule breakers are given Ugly Cards—like traffic tickets—that carry specific penalties, like cleanup with you after the meeting.**

Obviously the next problem is what to do when someone is guilty of disruptive conduct or compromising the rules. Do you make them stand in the corner or do 50 push-ups? Do you report them to their parents or kick them out of the meeting? Do you embarrass them or put them down in front of the other kids? Do you hang them by their thumbs?

As a rule I have found it best to handle these problems individually with kids who consistently cause problems. This is where some personal counseling and honest sharing is extremely worthwhile. I have rarely had problems with kids I have a good relationship with and have spent a lot of time with on a one-to-one basis. Because they value my friendship, they are less apt to disappoint me and put that friendship in jeopardy.

One group has what it calls the Ugly Card system. It works this way: Whenever someone breaks the rules or creates a problem, he is given one or more Ugly Cards, depending on the offense. These cards are much like traffic tickets, with predetermined penalties attached. One or two cards is usually a warning, while a third, fourth, or fifth might result in some form of punishment. A person might have to stay and clean up after the meeting or be sent to the Ugly Room (use your imagination) while the youth meeting is going on. On the other hand, there may be ways for kids to get rid of their Ugly Cards by doing some positive things rather than being punished.

> **If you make a big deal out of everything, you won't be heard when you need to be heard. Save your energy for things that matter.**

You might want to try the opposite approach and reward kids for good behavior rather than penalizing them for bad behavior. I know a youth group that gives every junior higher three tickets (the kind used in drawings) when they enter the room for a meeting. These tickets are used for a door prize drawing to be held at the end of the meeting. Prizes usually include Christian music tapes, free hamburger coupons and the like. The tickets are given to all the kids based on their assumed good behavior. But if they misbehave during the meeting (clearly violate the rules), they are fined one or more tickets, depending on the offense. They have to give up one or more of their tickets. Kids really hate it when they discover that the winning tickets are held by the adult leaders.

Here's yet another idea: When I ran junior high camps at Forest Home Christian Conference Center (in southern California), we sometimes employed a discipline system that worked nicely to deal with serious offenses by campers. At the beginning of camp, the basic rules were usually announced (usually only two or three) and campers were informed that if anyone could not abide by these simple rules, we would arrange for them to be taken home. They would have to be expelled from the camp.

When we did have a serious violation of the rules, someone in authority (usually the camp dean) would sit down with the problem camper and his counselor and tell him there was no alternative but to send him home. By now the camper would realize that he was in serious trouble and would beg to stay, all to no avail. Zero tolerance.

But wait! At that point, the camper's counselor would become the camper's advocate and request that the camper be given a second chance—assuring the camp dean that the camper would change his ways. After some consideration, the camp dean would relent and the camper would be allowed to stay—if he changed his ways. Usually this resulted in an immediately improved relationship between the camper and the counselor and almost always a positive change in the camper's behavior. I was involved in more than 30 camps with close to 5,000 kids; to my knowledge, we never sent anyone home.

Regardless of whether or not you use a system like those above, there are some basic principles and guidelines that all junior high workers should remember to follow to reduce the chances of student misbehavior. Here's a Top 20 list on discipline:

1. Know the kids. If you know the kids' names, and have a good relationship with them, they will be less likely to misbehave. Kids will always be more respectful of the rules if they have a good relationship with the rule maker. They will want to protect that relationship.

2. Use praise liberally with your kids. If they notice that you reward positive behavior, they'll be less likely to try out negative behaviors. Praise individual students when it's appropriate and praise the group as a whole. Tell them how great they are. They'll start to believe it.

3. Pay attention. If you are with a group of junior highers, be alert to what's going on in the room. Kids are less likely to misbehave when they know they are being watched.

4. Don't try to maintain order all by yourself. If you have a good ratio of adults to junior highers, kids will act in a more "adult" manner. But if there are only kids in the room, they will act more like kids. I'm not suggesting that you employ "narcs" (chaperons who are only there to maintain discipline). You want adults who like kids and are willing to get involved with them.

5. Don't expect perfection from your junior highers. In other words, let kids be kids. Don't expect the same standards from them that you would expect from a group of adults. It's normal for junior highers to sometimes be energetic, loud, silly, inconsiderate, annoying, disrespectful, . . . well, you get the picture.

6. Pick your battles wisely (or you'll be battling all the time). Prioritize the issues you feel are important enough to warrant strict disciplinary measures. Using foul language or lying, for example, is worse than giggling inappropriately. If you treat giggling the same as swearing, you send the wrong message to kids. If you make a big deal out of everything, you won't be heard when you need to be heard. Save your energy for things that matter. Don't sweat the small stuff.

7. Be clear with rules and expectations. Don't expect junior highers to read your mind. Don't assume that they know what's expected of them. You can have high expectations and high standards (in fact, you *should* have high expectations and high standards), but if those expectations are not clear, and if the boundary lines are fuzzy, they will simply ignore them.

8. When you discipline a student, make sure they know exactly *why* they are being disciplined. If they aren't clear about that, they will say, "He doesn't like me," or "He's always picking on me. I didn't do anything wrong."

9. Avoid disciplining students in front of their peers. While the temptation is great to make an example out of wrongdoers, the results are usually counterproductive. You don't want to embarrass or humiliate the young people so much that you destroy them, nor do you want to give them the attention that they were probably trying to get in the first place.

10. Allow kids to retain their dignity when you have to reprimand them for bad behavior. Regardless of what they have done, they are still human beings. While they don't always show it, junior highers have fragile egos. Make it clear to the kid who is being disciplined that his *behavior* is unacceptable, not him personally. He is okay; his behavior is not.

11. Look beyond behavior to what is at the cause of the behavior. Perhaps the junior higher needs attention (give it to her in a positive way), has a low self-image (build her up), or just needs something to do (get her involved). Some kids are just bored. Boredom is not really a discipline problem; it's really more of a programming problem.

12. Remember the Boy Scout motto: Be prepared. Have a plan. In meeting situations, when junior highers notice that you are "winging it" and don't know what to do next, they'll improvise real quick. This is especially important with transitions—moving from one activity to the next. Make your transitions quickly and smoothly, without a lot of dead time. Have all your props and materials ready and let your kids know you are in control of the program at all times.

13. Avoid raising your voice or yelling. Don't get mad and lose your cool, pout, threaten the kids, make them feel guilty, or call their spirituality into question. Remain calm and try to keep *your* emotions under control. Even in the midst of chaos, kids need to know that *someone* is in control. They need stability.

14. Avoid making threats you don't intend to (or can't) carry out. A threat made but not carried out will only reinforce bad behavior.

15. Give your junior highers plenty of opportunities to blow off steam. Because of rapid bone growth and muscle development, they can't sit still for long periods of time. They get fidgety and restless rather quickly. Give them a chance to talk, yell, run, be with friends, or goof off, so that when it's time to settle down, they will be ready to do that. They need opportunities to burn off some of their physical and emotional energy.

16. Keep your sense of humor. If someone does something funny, at least try to smile (if you can't laugh). Learn to enjoy the humor in some of the things they do rather than get mad because it distracts from what you had planned. Some discipline problems are really immature attempts to be funny (granted, they usually aren't) and it is sometimes best to play along until you have their attention once again.

17. Learn to roll with the flow. If kids aren't responding as you had planned, wait it out or switch to plan B. If the emotions of a junior high group seem like the waves of an ocean, learn to surf.

18. Be consistent in your disciplinary measures. Apply the same rules and consequences to all students. Lack of consistency will result in students trying to get away with things more often. For example, if a student is inconsistently punished for a particular behavior, she will take a chance of misbehaving more often on the chance that she will get away with it this time. Multiply this by a group of 30 students and you've got some real problems.

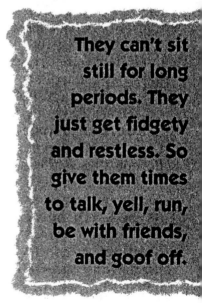

They can't sit still for long periods. They just get fidgety and restless. So give them times to talk, yell, run, be with friends, and goof off.

19. Be fair in your disciplinary measures. Fairness is a big deal to junior highers. They become extremely frustrated and angry when they feel they are not being treated fairly or equally. This means you don't play favorites, or treat particular kinds of kids differently from the others.

20. Don't always be looking for trouble. If you expect something bad to happen, it probably will. Kids will usually live up or down to whatever expectations we have of them. I have found that junior high workers who are overly concerned about discipline problems are usually the ones who get more than their share of discipline problems. It's kind of a chicken-and-egg situation. People who don't worry all that much about discipline generally have fewer discipline problems.

Remember that discipline depends a lot more on attitude than on rules, systems, punishments, and enforcement. There is much more to be concerned about in junior high ministry than enforcing rules and maintaining order. You can spend all your time doing that. It is wise to know what you will do when a problem arises, but it is never helpful to dwell on the negative when working with kids. Keep it in the background. When a junior higher needs to be disciplined, try to be as understanding and as helpful as possible. Punishment or revenge is strong medicine for most early adolescent misbehavior. Try to interpret the cause of the behavior and then decide (calmly) the action that you should take—if any.

And remember that every pearl got its start irritating an oyster.

Behavior That Hides More Than It Reveals

People always wonder how an experienced junior high worker is able to function in what appears to be a state of total confusion. I can remember times when I would invite the pastor of our church to speak briefly to the junior high group, and invariably he would stand before the group and try to quiet the kids down and achieve total silence—unsuccessfully. Frustrated, he would look over in my direction and expect me (plead with me) to *do* something, when really there was not much that I or anyone else could do. What he needed to do was to proceed and to ignore the ever-present stirring of the crowd. Despite all the noise, he would be heard, even though he might wonder how in the world that might be possible. Rarely can you tell how well you are communicating with a group of junior highers simply by noting the decibel level or by waiting to get positive feedback from the group.

Then there was the time I had spent several weeks studying and discussing the concept of Christian love with my junior high group. We particularly concentrated on what it meant to be the body of Christ and how as Christians we should care for and love each other, to strive for unity and harmony, and so forth. The kids were really into it, and I was confident that the way the group had responded to this material meant that our group was going to be the most loving, harmonious collection of junior highers in town. Unfortunately it wasn't to be. Less than a week later, two of the dominant cliques in the group were at each other's throats again, so one half wouldn't even speak to the other half. It was all I could do to prevent an all-out war. Apparently our study about love didn't make a very deep impression on them, I concluded.

Naturally when things like this happen, you begin to wonder whether you are getting anywhere as a junior high worker or teacher. Normally, you hope that you see results reflected in some kind of positive behavior, but with junior high kids, you just can't count on it. And it rarely has anything to do with how well or how poorly you are doing your job. Learning and growth in junior highers will be taking place even when their behavior seems to indicate otherwise. A junior higher's behavior will many times hide more than it reveals, so you can't really depend on positive behavior to measure your success, failure, or results. You will be disappointed when you do.

Again, this is one of the reasons why junior high workers need patience. I have been involved in youth ministry now for over 30 years, and every now and then someone will approach me with a statement like "You probably don't remember me, but. . . . " And they are usually right until they refresh my memory. It often turns out that this person was in one of my junior high groups many years ago, when I was convinced beyond a shadow of a doubt that my efforts were a total waste of time. I am still humbled and amazed when one of these people expresses his or her gratitude for my ministry way back then and in some cases informs me that it was while in my junior high group that he or she made a commitment to Christ that is still meaningful today.

Notes

1. Gail Caissy, *Early Adolescence: Understanding the 10 to 15-Year-Old* (Insight Books 1994), p. 33.

2. Joan Lipsitz makes a helpful distinction between distressed (disturbed) and distressing (irritating) behavior. Few early adolescents are distressed, that is, experiencing serious pathological behavior that requires intervention or professional attention. But almost all early adolescents can be distressing at times—causing frustration for parents, teachers and other adults who have to be around them. See Lipsitz, "The Age Group," in *Toward Adolescence: The Middle School Years* (University of Chicago Press, 1980), p. 22.

3. National Center for Health Statistics, *Vital Statistics of the United States 1991. Mortality,* Volume 1, Part B. (U.S. Department of Health and Human Services, 1995.) Table 8-5.

4. Mary Pipher, *Reviving Ophelia* (Ballantine Books, 1994), p. 57.

5. Caissy, p. 42.

6. Bill Wennerholm, "Adolescence, the Bridge from Self-Esteem to Self-Esteem," *Changes*, Vol. 1, No. 1 (Spring 1982), p. 3.

7. H. Stephen Glenn and Jane Nelson, *Raising Self-Reliant Children in a Self-Indulgent World* (Prima, 1989), p. 49.

8. Search Institute, "Young Adolescents and Their Parents," *Project Report* (Search Institute, 1984), p. 129.

9. See Leah M. Lefstein and William Kerewsky, *3:00 to 6:00 p.m.: Young Adolescents at Home and in the Community* (The Center for Early Adolescence, 1982).

• E I G H T •

FAITH DEVELOPMENT IN JUNIOR HIGHERS

I used to be religious, but I lost a lot of faith. I think I go to church just to waste time. I'm not really into it. But I do believe in God.
                                                           —Jean, age 14

No one is quite sure how it all started, but everyone thinks they know who started it. It happened during the morning worship service, shortly after the pastor invited the congregation to pause for a few moments of silent prayer and meditation. The organ was playing softly. Heads were bowed and eyes were closed. Suddenly there was heard a sort of muffled, choking noise, like someone trying to contain a cough. This was immediately followed by giggles, then snorts, and within a few seconds, like a wave, the first three rows of the church, occupied primarily by junior highers, were laughing hysterically.

According to one 14-year-old eyewitness, it started when "somebody cut the cheese," although he declined to identify the guilty party. Some believe that it was the same elder who tried to introduce a resolution at the next church board meeting to ban junior highers from all worship services where adults are present. "These children are not capable of understanding the things of God," he said. "They are not only irreverent, but they are spiritually incompetent."

There are quite a few today who hold the view that *junior high spirituality* is something of an oxymoron. They don't believe it is possible to be both a junior higher *and* a spiritual person. They are wrong, of course. Junior highers are exploring their spiritual yearnings and they are fully capable of making lasting faith commitments.

Significantly the only glimpse we have of the young man Jesus before he began his public ministry is in Luke 2, in the temple. Jesus was 12 years old and like many junior highers, he was very interested in spiritual matters. It's not surprising that the elders were amazed by Jesus' questions and his grasp of spiritual things. If we would take more time to listen to today's kids—allowing them to ask their questions and to share their spiritual journeys with us—we would also be amazed.

It's never easy to make generalizations about spiritual development, but whenever we talk about the faith of a junior higher, the first thing we need to remember is that it is *junior high* faith. It is not adult faith. Nor is it childish faith. Junior high faith has distinct characteristics of its own—appropriate for an early adolescent.

Roberta Hestenes, when she was serving as president of Eastern College, was asked in an interview, "What exactly is spiritual maturity? What does it look like?" Her response:

> Maturity is engaging in behavior that is appropriate to the stage in which you are. A four-year-old is mature when he or she does everything that is reasonable for a four-year-old to do. We don't consider a four-year-old immature because he can't do what a 12-year-old does. But if he doesn't do the things four-year-olds are capable of, then he's immature. So one definition of maturity is living up to the capacities God has made possible for you.[1]

This means that we need to ask: What can we reasonably expect from a junior higher in terms of faith development? On the next few pages we will try to describe a few characteristics of early adolescent faith.

Junior High Faith Is Transitional

When we talk about the spiritual dimension of life, we really can't set it apart from the rest of life as if it were an entity unto itself. It is not. One's faith touches every area of life—the physical, intellectual, social, and emotional. This is why we have devoted so much space to these other areas so far. The "whole gospel" affects the whole person, not just the soul.

As we have seen, junior highers are changing a great deal during early adolescence in every area of life. They are, in many different and important ways, making a once-in-a-lifetime transition from childhood to adulthood.

And they are making the same transition in the spiritual area of life as well.

When we talk about spirituality, we are talking about one's relationship to God. And like most other relationships (a marriage, for example) spirituality has both an intellectual and an emotional component. Intellectually it is necessary to understand what the relationship is all about—who the relationship is with, why it's important—and there must be a commitment to that relationship. But a relationship needs emotional validation, too. Such emotions can be described with words like *love, passion, affection, romance, infatuation, adoration, devotion,* and *joy.* Most marriages require that a couple feel romantic love at least once in a while to be successful, but they also need a healthy dose of intel-lectual commitment to each other and to the concept of marriage itself. Likewise, one's spiritual life is both an emotional experience (feelings) and an act of the will (beliefs).

To assess spiritual development in junior highers, then, it is helpful to pay particular attention to how junior highers think (intellectual development) and how junior highers feel (emotional development). If we understand that junior highers are in the process of making a transition in life both intellectually and emotionally, then we will have a better understanding of early adolescent spiritual development. Junior highers are indeed making a spiritual transition that parallels the changes that are taking place in these other areas.

Junior High Faith Is Skeptical

When junior highers were younger, they had a faith that was simple, almost mythical—one that provided clear-cut answers to life's most difficult questions. It provided them with invincible heroes of the faith to admire and to emulate. They believed primarily because their parents and their teachers believed. But now, with the advent of adulthood and the ability to think on an adult level (Piaget's stage of *formal operations*), they sense that the faith of their childhood will no longer suffice. They don't want to be embarrassed by what they believe. Instead, they need to develop a more mature kind of faith, one that is personal and makes the transition from childhood to adulthood along with them.

Unless the church is willing to help junior highers discover this faith, it is in danger of losing them. Many junior highers reject their faith and lose interest in the church because they are still being asked to believe in a God whom they have literally outgrown. It is important, therefore, to help junior highers begin to experience God in completely new ways and to see how their faith in Christ relates to the new world that is opening up before them.

With their newly acquired ability to think, junior highers will naturally begin to doubt and question the faith of their childhood. Some youth find it necessary to discard this old faith alto-gether, rather than modify it or try to live it long enough to understand it more fully.

For others, faith in God is weakened by a growing mind and a newly acquired world view that discredits anything that cannot be empirically proven or that doesn't make good sense. Some kids begin to think of their religion as a world of make-believe, and like many once

143

cherished childhood myths, it is temporarily cast aside. They may continue to believe in God, but they aren't real sure about anything else. The quote by 14-year-old Jean at the beginning of this chapter is typical.

Of course there are always a certain number of junior highers who will have no doubts whatsoever (no serious ones anyway) and will remain absolutely faithful throughout their early adolescent years, and for them we can be thankful. These young people will simply build upon the foundation of their childhood faith. Still they will need to modify their old beliefs and to increase their understanding of them. There will also be quite a few who have nagging doubts about their faith but are afraid to express them. Early adolescents generally lack the self-confidence necessary to express these feelings openly, so they tend to keep them locked inside.

Doubting increases during early adolescence, and it helps to remember that it is normal, even necessary at times. There is really no need to discourage doubt or to eliminate it. We can help junior highers by letting them know their doubts and questions are permitted, they are normal, and God approves of them. Doubt is a necessary part of one's spiritual development. As Frederick Buechner once wrote, "Doubts are the ants in the pants of faith; they keep it alive and moving."[2] Even John the Baptist expressed doubts about Jesus when he was imprisoned for his faith (Matthew 11:3). Kids need to know that while they may doubt God and find him confusing and distant at times, God never doubts them. Sensitive youth workers will try to provide an environment of safety where junior highers have the freedom to be open, to ask questions, and to mine their faith for answers that make sense to them.

This is another reason why relationships are so important in junior high ministry. Junior highers need a person, not a program, to whom they can turn with many of the questions and problems they are struggling with in their lives. They need someone in whom they can confide—an adult friend who understands and cares enough to listen. They need someone who will take their questions and ideas seriously without criticism. In most cases parents are unable to fill this role. The solution to doubt is not necessarily better curriculum, more weekend retreats, confirmation classes, or a special youth commitment service. You can get a lot more mileage out of just being a mentor and friend.

Junior High Faith Is Personal

Psychologist David Elkind observed that religion changes for the early adolescent from being *institutional* to *personal*. It becomes more of a personal relationship with God. For a child religion is tied very closely to the church or to religious activities (institutional). But for the young adolescent who has acquired new ways of thinking, religion is tied much more closely to a belief system, which is more personal and private.

> Teenagers, who value their privacy—now that they have discovered that they can live in secret in their heads—and who are afraid that their secrets might be found out, discover that a personal God is a most trustworthy confidant. He won't squeal.[3]

The upshot of this is that some young adolescents become turned off by institutional religion. They may want to stop attending church or participating in religious activities they enjoyed as a child. This causes alarm for parents and church leaders who fear that the youth is in danger of losing her faith. While such fears may be justified, there is a strong chance that the junior higher is turning her back on the church simply as a way of expressing her need for autonomy. In a way she is saying, "I'm not a kid anymore. I don't believe in that stuff anymore." It's part of the process of breaking free from parental and religious authority and the baggage

such a good idea. Due to his penchant for showing off and drawing attention to himself, he was having a negative impact on the other Junior High Disciples. But after a few weeks, I began to notice a slight change. He started bringing his Bible to class. He started to participate in the singing and the discussions. Almost miraculously, his attitude seemed different. Six months into the program, he was quoting Scripture in class and leading the group in prayer. Tim's parents came to me and said they were amazed at the progress we had made with Tim. Now he was doing his household chores, getting good grades at school, and spending a little time every day in personal devotions.

But the greatest moment of all for me was when Tim, after having been involved in Junior High Disciples for only 14 months, came to me and said that God had called him to the mission field. I began literally jumping up and down for joy!

Then my wife woke me up and told me I was shaking the bed.

that goes along with it. Junior highers who lose their enthusiasm for church rarely feel that way because they have examined their faith and found it wanting. They aren't rejecting God so much as they are rejecting an old way of thinking about God. Young adolescents simply want to be able to make their own decisions about spiritual things, so they may temporarily hang up entirely the faith they inherited from their parents.

This does not mean that they don't have a personal belief in God; they just don't see a need for the institutional part of it or the outward expression of it. In fact, research has confirmed that 95 percent of early adolescents believe in God, and that 75 percent pray every day.[4] There is no need to panic. Elkind recommends patience: "In general, most young people return to the faith of their parents once they become young adults and particularly when they become parents."[5] Scripture puts it another way: "Train a child in the way he should go, and when he is old, he will not turn from it" (Proverbs 22:6).

I like to compare the transition that junior highers are making in their faith with the circus acrobat on the flying trapeze. Just as the trapeze artist lets go of one trapeze and sails through the air, temporarily without any support, and then grabs safely onto another trapeze—much like the one he left behind, so the junior higher lets go of his childhood faith in order to grab onto a newer, more mature, version of it. It will look a lot like the one left behind, but this one will be more personal, more secure. Meanwhile, like the spectators at the circus, we gasp and hold our breath, hoping and praying that the trapeze artist—the junior higher—doesn't fall. And just as the trapeze artist "flies through the air with the greatest of ease," knowing that a safety net is in place, so our kids need to know that we are there for them.

We can be that safety net for young adolescents who have temporarily let go of their faith by loving them and taking their need for a sabbatical from institutional religion seriously. That doesn't mean that we encourage them to stay home from church, however. I generally tell parents that it's okay to force your kids to attend church. Staying home from church is not a good habit to start in early adolescence. But you can't force junior highers to *like* church or to participate in every activity. One of the purposes of a good junior high ministry is to

> Leaving church does not mean they're rejecting God as much as they're rejecting a way of thinking about God. They just want to make their own decisions about spiritual things.

provide for kids a place where they can be themselves and explore their faith in new ways. Sometimes it helps to take kids away from the church—to a home or a park or some strange location—and there discuss spiritual things with them. This approach is less institutional and much more personal. Young adolescents will respond positively to an atmosphere of acceptance and friendship with opportunities to discover Christ in a fresh, new way.

Junior High Faith Is Emotional

As we discussed in chapter seven, junior highers are experiencing adultlike emotions and feelings for the first time in their lives. And because these emotions are new, they are also surprising in their intensity and are very unpredictable. These emotions will stabilize as the years pass, but these early emotional experiences will be very formative.

It is important therefore to give junior highers religious experiences that will allow them to "feel" God's presence and to sense his love. They need the kind of positive emotional experiences that will validate their understanding of the Christian faith. Joy, wonder, sorrow, guilt, compassion, praise, peace—these are just a few of the emotions that are an important part of the Christian faith, and junior highers are now capable of understanding them in a new way. They need to feel deeply sorry for their sins and they also need to experience the joy of salvation. When junior highers shed tears, they are real tears representing real feelings that will have a significant impact on their lives.

Junior highers will enjoy worship when it is an emotional experience for them. In most cases, however, worship is anything but emotional. Listening to boring sermons, reciting creeds, and singing hard-to-understand hymns usually carry little emotional weight for junior highers. This is why there is real value in taking kids to camps, retreats, and other places where they can worship God and receive the kind of mountaintop experience that may not last forever but will never be forgotten. These experiences are formative in the spiritual development of young people. We must never play on the emotions of junior highers, nor manipulate them emotionally, but we can give them opportunities to experience God's presence very deeply.

While junior highers need to feel emotional about their faith, they also need to know that faith is not *dependent* on those emotions. Faith in Christ sometimes makes a person feel euphoric or peaceful or confident, but faith in Christ is *not* the result of these feelings. The emotions of junior highers fluctuate a great deal. They need to be assured that Christ is always with them, even when they are despondent, ashamed, afraid, angry, or upset. They are just as much a Christian at these times as when they are feeling happy and good about themselves. God is constant; we change. We are the ones on the roller coaster, sometimes up and sometimes down. Junior highers are going to experience a variety of feelings—some good and some bad—and they need to know that Christ is always there and understands all of them.

It helps to remember that junior highers are full of conflicting feelings at times. If they seem restless, bored, distracted, or full of giggles during a worship service or when they are expected to pay attention, it's not necessarily because they are unspiritual. They are just junior highers, with a faith that is "under construction." Just as they are learning how to solve the mysteries of algebra and to handle the disappointment of a broken friendship, so they are trying to fully grasp what it means to call themselves a *Christian*. As junior high workers, we need to take their journey seriously, have patience with them, and give them every opportunity to grow and mature as fellow members of the body of Christ.

Junior High Faith Is Inconsistent

One of the most frustrating aspects of junior high ministry is that young adolescents are not very good at connecting what they believe (or say they believe) with what they do. They don't practice what they preach. David Elkind uses the term *apparent hypocrisy* to describe this characteristic of early adolescence. "Young adolescents are able to con-ceptualize fairly abstract rules of behavior, but they lack the experience to see their relevance to concrete behavior. [They] believe that if they can conceive and express high moral principles, then they have in effect attained them and nothing more in a concrete way need be done."[6]

In other words, it is normal for junior highers to say one thing and to behave completely differently. What appears to be hypocritical to us is actually a step forward for them. It's good that they can now "conceive and express" their beliefs and ideals. But sometimes that's as far as it goes. They haven't yet learned to carry out the actions that would seem to follow logically from the beliefs and ideals that they now profess to have. Unfortunately this makes them look like hypocrites.

But they are not being hypocritical in the same way we would think an adult hypocritical. Ordinarily when adults show hypocritical behavior, we assume that they have the maturity to understand that you should not say one thing and do something else that is obviously contradictory. Junior highers are beginning to understand how that works (and they are often quick to point out hypocrisy in others), but they haven't learned how to apply it to themselves. This is why a junior higher can express very strong views about fairness and then—without a moment's hesitation—be very unfair to someone else. We shouldn't be surprised when junior highers criticize their parents for being selfish and materialistic and then demand from them more money to buy the most expensive sneakers and the latest CDs. It's not unusual for junior highers to express strong feelings about saying no to negative behaviors of all kinds, and then engaging in those same behaviors the very next day. This is one reason why junior highers sometimes live two lives—the one that attends church and the one that goes to school and hangs out with friends. Those two lives may be completely different from each other and very inconsistent, but the junior higher living them will not perceive that there is a problem—or at least not a serious one.

Praxis means distributing food, visiting shut-ins, doing yard work— instead of merely having Bible studies about serving others.

Obviously the Christian life requires that there be a connection between faith and everyday life. It's not enough just to believe. Faith must be acted out and lived for it to have validity. But while this is true, we must not expect too much from our junior highers too soon. We must be patient with them and recognize that they are doing well just to express their values and beliefs verbally (if they do). In time they will discover the need to back up those beliefs with their actions. And we as adults still continue to struggle with it. In Romans 7 the apostle Paul expressed frustration with his repeated failures to live consistently with what he believed. Junior highers are just beginning to experience all of that.

We can also help junior highers practice putting their faith into action by giving them opportunities to be doers of the Word. They will understand the connection between faith and works much better if they can experience it for themselves. This kind of experiential learning is sometimes called *praxis,* a term taken from the Greek word for *action.* It is one of the best ways to teach junior highers. For example, if you want your junior highers to understand the scriptural idea that we serve Christ by serving others, then do something more than have a Bible study about it. Take them somewhere where they can actually serve. Have them distribute food at a rescue mission, or visit people in a convalescent home, or do yard work for shut-ins. Help them to see firsthand how their beliefs translate into actions.

And in the classroom we need to emphasize the practical aspects of the Christian faith. Young adolescents are not going to be helped a great deal by studying a history of the 12 tribes of Israel. But they will be helped by discussing how the Christian faith impacts their friendships, their family life, their sexuality, their TV viewing habits, and so on.

If we want the gospel to make a difference in the lives of junior highers, we must be careful to show them how the Christian faith impacts their lives in the here and now. Junior highers need to see that the gospel has practical applications. We can't assume that they already know this. If we can demonstrate to them a few of the ways in which Christ can enrich their lives and meet their needs, they will soon realize that Christianity is much more than a private set of beliefs and doctrines that only exist in your head. It can change the way you live.

Junior highers not only struggle with inconsistency, they sometimes stuggle with outright failure. When I was a junior higher, my biggest problem with the Christian life was not so much *not knowing what to do* as *being unable to do it*. I was taught that good Christians do not sin, or at least they don't sin very much. If they did sin, they were extremely minor sins, more like little mistakes that were forgiven instantly or hardly worth forgiving at all. But I was a sinner, sinning big sins instead of little ones, and as a result, I was constantly losing my faith. In my church we called it *backsliding*. For me it was usually more than a slide backward—it was more like a crash landing.

Many junior highers experience this. They hear again and again that the Christian life is keeping the 10 Commandments, obeying your parents, loving your neighbor, sitting quietly in church, keeping a smile on your face, acting like an adult, and so on. And they find such a life impossible to live—so they just give up on it.

Certainly all of us need to be challenged to have high standards and to live according to the commands and principles that are set forth in Scripture. But we must be careful not to discourage junior high kids by misleading them. None of us are successful at doing the right thing 100 percent of the time. We need to let kids know that they can fail and still be a growing Christian, loved by God. Almost by definition, junior highers' lives are full of failure, and they need to know that Christ will be with them even in the midst of failure. God does not expect perfection from junior highers. Their perfection, after all, was purchased on the cross and given to them as a free gift through Jesus Christ. That's all they need.

In this regard junior highers can begin to understand the true meaning of

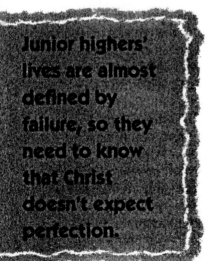

Junior highers' lives are almost defined by failure, so they need to know that Christ doesn't expect perfection.

commitment. Commitment is often misunderstood by today's kids. It really has more to do with failure than it does with success. If you are committed to something, then you hang in there and keep going even when things aren't going too well. Historians claim that the inventor Thomas Edison made over 900 light bulbs before he finally made one that actually worked. In other words, he failed 900 times. Although he must have been discouraged at times, he stayed with it simply because he was committed to inventing a light bulb. He didn't give up.

The Christian life is a lot like that. You don't get it right the first time or even the second. Every time Edison made a light bulb that didn't work, he learned one more way *not* to make a light bulb. It was actually a positive experience. Maybe what we need to do is help our junior highers learn from their mistakes, rather than be defeated by them. Let junior highers be junior highers. They are not going to act like adults. Spiritual growth takes time.

Junior High Faith Is Idealistic

It is part of the early adolescent paradox that even in the midst of struggle, failure, and doubt, junior highers are extremely idealistic. They have a strong desire to be committed to something and make their lives count. It is not uncommon for junior highers to list as career choices occupations relating to service, such as doctor, nurse, missionary, and teacher.

For this reason it is important they be given many opportunities to serve and use the gifts God has given them. Their idealism, while it may be strong during their early adolescent years, will diminish over the years if not given expression. Junior high workers in the church should find as many ways as possible to channel the energies and enthusiasm of junior highers into positive activities that allow them to give of themselves and see the results of their efforts. They need to feel the significance and affirmation that comes from doing things that are worthwhile and that benefit others.

Junior highers need to know that they are important and that God can use them right now. They are not the future high school group. Neither are they the "church of tomorrow," as they are often called. I heard a seventh-grade girl once respond to that description of the youth group with this question: "Don't they know I'm alive right now?" We need to include junior highers in the church of today.

Some kids may feel that they were hopelessly shortchanged when God was distributing the talents, gifts, and abilities necessary for becoming a somebody in God's scheme of things. A certain degree of discouragement might set in when they compare themselves with biblical or historical heroes of the faith, popular Christian celebrities of today, or adult Christians they know, such as the pastor or the youth director. Despite a genuine desire to accomplish much and to serve in some way, there is often the overriding fear that they are miserably unqualified and illequipped.

We can help junior highers to know that God can and will use them just the way they are—like the little girl who wanted to become a great pianist, but all she could play on the piano was the simple little tune "Chopsticks." No matter how hard she tried, that was the best she could do. Her parents decided after some time to arrange for a great maestro to teach her to play properly. And of course, the little girl was delighted.

When the little girl and her parents arrived at the maestro's mansion for the first lesson, she climbed up onto the piano bench in front of the maestro's grand concert piano and immediately began playing "Chopsticks." Her embarrassed parents told her to stop, but the maestro encouraged her to continue. He then took a seat on the bench next to the little girl and began to play along with her, adding chords, runs, and arpeggios. The little girl continued to play "Chopsticks." The parents couldn't believe their ears. What they heard was a beautiful piano duet, played by their daughter and the maestro, and amazingly enough the central theme of it was "Chopsticks."

Junior highers may only have "Chopsticks" to offer to God right now, but God sits on the piano bench beside them. He can take their little and turn it into much. We just need to encourage them to keep on playing.

Junior High Faith Is Relational

James Fowler of Duke University conducted research in the field of faith development and discovered—as Piaget did in the field of cognitive development—that there are progressive stages of faith common to almost everyone.[7] He identified six stages of faith in all, including one that applies specifically to junior highers. This is his third stage—which he calls the *synthetic* or *conventional* stage—beginning at around age 11 or 12 and ending (usually) at late adolescence, around 16 or 17. He found that young adolescents at stage three base their faith largely on what others say or think—according to popular convention (hence the word *conventional*). In Fowler's view, junior high faith "is anxious to respond faithfully to the expectations and judgment of significant others. As yet the person is without a sufficient grasp of his or her own identity to make autonomous judgments

> It's not easy for junior highers to feel secure in their faith without friends who share that faith.

from an independent perspective."[8]

What this means is that the faith of a junior higher is extremely dependent on relationships. Junior highers need to have their faith validated by significant others in their lives. And since they are in the process of pulling away from their parents, those significant others are more often than not peer friends and unrelated adults. It's not easy for a junior higher to feel secure in his or her faith without friends who share the same faith. On the other hand, if they have friends who believe as they do, they will feel rather courageous about standing up for their convictions. In that sense we can say that junior high faith is very relational. God communicates best to junior highers through relationships.

This understanding underscores the importance of doing junior high ministry. One of our goals is to provide kids with a place where they will feel affirmed and validated as a follower of Jesus Christ. Junior highers need to know that they are not alone. In a sense we want to provide some "positive peer pressure" to encourage kids to stand firm in their faith.

Likewise, we need to provide junior highers with positive role models—older youth and adults who are people of faith. So much of what junior highers learn about faith and values comes not from words but by example. It is vitally important that we surround junior highers with people they can look up to and who will inspire them to follow their example and to follow Jesus Christ, the ultimate model for all of us.

Junior highers are incurable hero-worshipers. They are easily led (or misled) by anyone able to capture their admiration and allegiance. In many cases, this amounts to near worship of teen idols, singers, actors, and other celebrities who are marketed directly to this age group. Howard and Stoumbis emphasize the importance of role models:

> This is the time for admiration and imitation of the hero figure, which makes it important that the proper figures for emulation are presented to the adolescent. While their parents and teachers are no longer likely to be the persons to be imitated and admired, partly because of their fallibility, familiarity, and authority symbols, the early adolescent will still seek an older model to emulate—preferably one who is competent and successful by his adolescent standards.[9]

One of the most effective ways to reach junior highers for Christ, or to encourage junior highers to remain strong in their faith, is to point them toward models who are willing to identify themselves with Jesus Christ. They don't have to be famous or talented, although I am thankful for the Christian recording artists and Christian sports figures who have become successful and accepted by the adolescent crowd.

We need more of those kinds of people.

But even more important than celebrity Christians are those adult role models who really care about them. As we discussed in chapter five, early adolescents need and want adult friends who are willing to walk with them across the bridge from childhood to adulthood. Rather than isolate our young people from adults in the church by creating a "youth ghetto," we need to find ways to encourage interaction between the young and the old.

Like it or not, we who work with junior highers are more often than not thrust into the position of model, simply because we are one of the few adults who have regular contact with the kids. They watch us, and we show them what adult Christians are like. We should not be intimidated by this; we do not have to be perfect and give kids the wrong impression. That's why it's a good idea to let kids see you in different settings, not just at church when you are on your best behavior. They need to see you at home, with your family, on the job, at play, and whenever you are just being yourself. This is a tremendous responsibility. We should strive to set as good an example for our junior highers as we can. We shouldn't let our lives contradict the gospel that we represent.

Most importantly, we need to love our junior highers. They will follow us and become disciples of Jesus not because of what we teach or say, but because of our love for them. The renowned psychologist Bruno Bettelheim recently made this observation about Christ's ministry to his disciples:

> Most of us, when hearing or using the word disciple are likely to be reminded of the biblical apostles. Their deepest wish was to emulate Christ. They made him their guide not just because they believed in his teachings but because of their love for him and his love for them. Without such mutual love the Master's teaching and example, convincing though they were, would never have persuaded the disciples to change their lives and beliefs as radically as they did.[10]

Notes

1. Roberta Hestenes, "Can Spiritual Maturity Be Taught?" *Leadership Journal* (Christianity Today, Inc., Volume IX, Number 4, 1988), p. 14.

2. Frederick Buechner, *Wishful Thinking* (Harper & Row, 1973), p. 20.

3. David Elkind, *All Grown Up and No Place to Go*, (Addison Wesley Longman, 1984), p. 42.

4. Search Institute, "Young Adolescents and Their Parents," *Project Report* (Search Institute, 1984), p. 160.

5. Elkind, *All Grown Up and No Place to Go*, p. 43.

6. David Elkind, "Understanding the Young Adolescent," *Adolescence*, Vol. XIII, No. 49, Spring 1978, p. 133.

7. James W. Fowler, "Toward a Developmental Perspective on Faith," *Religious Education* 69:2 (March-April 1974), pp. 207-219.

8. Cited in Thomas H. Groome, *Christian Religious Education* (Harper & Row, 1980), p. 70.

9. Alvin W. Howard and George C. Stoumbis, *The Junior High and Middle School: Issues and Practices*, p. 34.

10. Bruno Bettelheim, quoted in "Reflections," *Christianity Today*, Vol. 25, No. 5, p. 6.

PROGRAMMING FOR JUNIOR HIGHERS

I would hope to be known as one who loved and built up people—not programs. It was for people, not programs, that Jesus lived, died and rose. My legacy must be in lives. Anything less would amount to very little.

—Doug Burleigh

What does a successful junior high program look like? How many meetings per week should there be? How many adults should be involved? Should junior highers and senior highers meet together or separately? Which curriculum is best? Are today's kids too sophisticated to play games? What about confirmation classes? How do I get my junior highers excited about Bible study? What about sixth-graders—should they be included in the junior high ministry or remain in the children's department? Should junior highers participate in service projects? How do I motivate them to come? And, what is the meaning of the universe?

Tough questions, all of them. Unfortunately there are no easy answers that will hold true for everyone in all situations. A good answer here might be a bad answer there. It's like telling someone that water is good. That statement is true if you are thirsty, but not if you are drowning. Likewise it's difficult to be specific about programming for junior high groups. What works for one group may not work at all for another. People sometimes ask me, "What should my junior high program look like?" My best answer is usually something like this: "Do whatever it takes to meet the needs of your kids." That could mean lots of meetings or no meetings at all, lots of activities or none at all. Lest this sound like a complete evasion of the question, let me remind you that junior high ministry is first of all relational. The key is *people*, not *programs*. If you love junior highers and are able to relate to them well, just about any program will probably do the job.

Having said that, it's obvious that most junior high ministries won't survive without programs. In this chapter I want to give you some guidelines on how to go about creating a junior high ministry program that will meet the needs of your kids and realize your ministry objectives. I won't be describing for you the perfect junior high ministry program (as if one existed), nor will I give you a list of program ideas that are guaranteed to work with your junior high group. By the way, if you ever see an advertisement for a junior high program that is "guaranteed to work," be careful. "Guaranteed to work" is probably pure marketing hype, especially when it comes to junior high ministry. I've seen some of my favorite youth ministry ideas go down in flames with particular groups of kids—and been amazed to watch what I thought were the dumbest ideas in the world work great with the same group. Go figure.

Still if you are brave enough to use them, I have included some of my favorite ideas for junior high ministry in chapter 12, and I've also listed in the back of this book some outstanding resources that contain a lot more.

The Purpose of Programs

Programs are tools that we use to make junior high ministry possible. It's important to remember that they are not ends in themselves. They simply provide opportunities to do ministry—to be with kids, to talk with kids, to laugh and play with kids, to share Christ with kids. Programs are the disposable part of youth ministry. It's best to "use 'em and lose 'em." It's always dangerous to let programs determine what the ministry will look like. It's the ministry that should instead determine what the programs look like.

It's like the young couple who were preparing dinner. The husband asked his wife, "Why did you just cut both ends off the ham before cooking it?"

"Well, that's the way my mother always did it," she replied.

Later she asked her mother, "Mom, why *did* you cut both ends off a ham before you cook it?"

Replied Mom, "Well, that's the way *my* mother did it." So mother and daughter visited Grandma to ask her the same question.

"It was the only way I could get it into my pan," Grandma said.

The story illustrates how we sometimes keep on doing the same thing in the church over and over—sometimes for generations— without asking the question, "Why are we doing this?" I sometimes suggest to youth workers that they consider throwing *all* their programs out the window and starting over from scratch. (This is easier said than done, of course, especially in a traditional church environment.) You may find out that you don't really need Sunday school classes, or those weekly youth group meetings, or that week at Camp Fun-N-Games. Those programs may have been perfect at some time in the past, but this is not your parents' junior high ministry.

To answer the question, "Why are we doing this?" it's helpful to remember that the purpose of programming is essentially fourfold:

1. Programs help meet the needs of kids.

As we discussed in chapter three, programs for junior highers need to be designed around an informed understanding of the needs of early adolescents. We can't make the mistake of "drawing targets around our arrows." Using what we know to be true about junior highers as a guide, we can create programs that will not only be creative or fun or entertaining, but programs that will do something worthwhile.

There are all kinds of needs. In this book we have spent a lot of time looking at the *developmental* needs of junior highers. These are the needs that most all junior highers have. We can say that they are common to the age group. If we have a good understanding of the needs of early adolescents, we will create programs that are developmentally appropriate for them. Unfortunately some junior high programs are only discarded or warmed-over high school programs. The vast majority of junior high schools are nothing more than miniature high schools—which is why middle schools were created. The big idea behind the middle school movement has been to develop a new kind of school—one that takes seriously the developmental needs of early adolescent youth.[1] We will look at some characteristics of a junior high ministry program that is developmentally appropriate below.

> **Consider throwing *all* your programs out the window and starting from scratch. Just maybe you don't need that week at camp Fun-N-Games, or weekly youth meetings, or even Sunday school.**

There are other needs that will be specific to the junior highers you are working with. Some needs will be determined by a particular environment or ethnic background. Kids in Los Angeles have different needs from those in Sioux Falls. The needs of urban Hispanic youth will be different from those of suburban white kids. Needs will also be impacted by news events of the day, popular culture, or individual life experiences of kids and families in your church. If your youths have experienced the death of a friend, or have been victims of a crime, or have lived through a natural disaster, they will have specific needs which will dictate the kinds of programs you choose.

The best way to determine needs is to spend time with kids. You can learn a lot by reading books (like this one) and taking advantage of other helpful resources specifically designed to keep you informed.[2] But there is no substitute for just being with students, finding out firsthand their worries, concerns, fears, problems, likes and dislikes, opinions and ideas. Find out how they are feeling and what is important to them. Take surveys and conduct interviews with your kids or with parents. Visit them in their homes, meet their parents, discover their life situations. The more you know about your kids, the more successful your programming will be.

2. Programs provide a place where relationships happen.

In junior high ministry, this reason alone can justify any program you do. If you and other adult leaders are there, and if the kids are there, then there is a good chance that some relationship building can take place and that makes it worth doing. Adults will come to a Bible study simply to learn about the Bible, but junior highers won't. They will, however, come for the relationships. For this reason every junior high program needs to have a strong relational emphasis.

Youth ministry expert Dave Stone tells a funny story about a dog food company that boasted the most nutritious dog food in America, the best advertising, the best employee-benefit program, the best production facilities, the best and highest-paid executives in the dog food industry, and so on. But sales of this company's dog food were slipping. They couldn't figure out why. Finally, they did some market research to find out the answer: "The dogs don't like it."

Sometimes we boast about all the programs we have in the church—the large budgets, the great facilities, the incredible high-tech gadgets and gizmos—but even with all that, the kids sometimes stay away by the thousands simply because "they don't like it." If the programs provide a place where their friends are—where they can enjoy relationships—they will usually like it. The big question kids usually ask about programs is not "what are we going to do," but "who's going to be there." That's what matters most to junior highers.

3. Programs give junior highers something to do.

By this I mean that programs get them involved. One of the primary reasons we plan programs is because we want to give our junior highers opportunities to use their gifts, talents, and skills to be participants with us in the life and ministry of the church. Some youth workers, I think, see programs as something to keep themselves busy, rather than something to involve the kids. But we don't plan programs because they are in our job descriptions, because we have time to kill, or because we like to entertain kids. As we will discuss later, kids want to be involved, and programs are ways to make their involvement a reality.

4. Programs attract kids and create interest.
Sometimes programs are used simply to draw kids to something that they would not otherwise attend, or to motivate kids to learn about something that they would otherwise ignore. It is helpful to remember that there we must make the distinction between what kids want and what they need. Some-times they don't *want* what they *need*. Programs can be used to turn their needs into wants. For example, most junior highers don't automatically gravitate toward Bible memorization. But if you were to organize Bible quiz teams or play games that require memorizing Bible facts, you'd find junior highers doing something they wouldn't otherwise do.

One of the reasons we have to be creative with our junior high ministry programming is because our goal is to meet kids' needs, not their wants. Programs help to create interest and attract kids so that those needs can be met. A rock music concert will attract kids to hear the gospel. A Sunday morning pizza breakfast will attract kids to come to a worship service. A mission trip to an exotic location can help kids realize, perhaps for the first time, that they can serve God and make a positive difference in the world. While we need to be careful to avoid "bait and switch" tactics that promise kids one thing and deliver something else, we can use programs very effectively to heighten interest and motivate kids to come.

Characteristics of an Effective Junior High Program
So—to return to our first question—what does a successful junior high program look like? While I can't give you a one-size-fits-all program, I can give you some key characteristics that are common to highly effective junior high programs and that respond well to the developmental needs of this age group. Some of them were first brought to my attention by Joan Lipsitz and Gayle Dorman, founders of the Center for Early Adolescence (now a part of Search Institute in Minneapolis).[2] Most of these characteristics are grounded solidly in research, and I believe they can be very helpful in both planning and evaluating junior high programs in the church.

Variety and diversity
Because junior highers are growing and changing very rapidly, and at a variety of rates, an appropriate activity for one young person might be

completely inappropriate for another. So when programming for *groups* of junior highers, it is best to provide a wide variety of experiences and activities. This could mean providing different kinds of programs from one week to the next, or perhaps a variety of choices or "electives" each week. Remember that it is possible to have two junior highers in the same group who are light years apart developmentally. Take that into consideration and provide more than one way for kids to learn and to be involved.

For example, if you are doing a study about the concept of "Christian love," try approaching it from a number of different angles. You might have a "Bible Word Search," which appeals to those who enjoy that sort of thing and an essay-writing exercise for those who are capable of thinking about the subject on a deeper level. You could allow some of the group to create a collage or a mural that describes Christian love, while others brainstorm a list of "things to do" that would demonstrate Christian love in the family. Provide enough variety so that everyone has an opportunity to learn and to enjoy the experience equally.

Exploration and discovery

Rapidly changing bodies and minds require new ways of thinking, new experiences, and new reactions from others. Junior highers need opportunities to get a new window on life as they move from childhood into adulthood, and they need time to reflect on how they fit into their new world. They need adventure—field trips, service projects, environments, and experiences they have never had before—and time to discover for themselves who they are and the kind of person they want to be.

This is one reason why the junior high years are the perfect time to get kids out of the classroom and into the real world as often as possible. The Tour of Your Life activity in chapter 12 is a good example of this. I know a youth worker who takes his youth group to an incredible assortment of places around town for their regular weekly meetings, and the kids love it. One week the group meets at a local securities firm, and there they discuss the topic of money. Another week they meet inside the county jail, and there they discuss the topic of law. The next week the group might visit a local slum, and there they discuss the subject of Christ's concern for the poor. Experiences like this leave an indelible imprint on the lives of junior highers.

Experience and participation

At a Youth Specialties National Youth Workers Convention a few years ago, author and psychologist David Elkind made a statement to the effect that "if we really wanted to be responsive to the developmental needs of early adolescents, we would close down all the junior high schools and allow those students to go somewhere and build a boat." I laughed when I heard him say that, not so much because it was funny, but because I knew he was right. Junior highers learn best experientially. If they are given something to do like building a boat, they not only learn how to build a boat, but they learn important life skills like responsibility, how to follow directions, how to cooperate with others, how to set and accomplish goals, and how to delay gratification. They learn skills that in reality can only be learned by experience.

But not only do kids learn *best* experientially; in some cases, it's the *only* way they learn. I have never met a junior higher, for example, who took time to read the directions for a video game they've never played before. They just put in their quarters or load the software and figure it out as they go along. I have tried to explain to junior highers the rules of a game, or how to use a word processor, or the point of a passage of Scripture—only to watch kids roll their eyes and act like they are being tortured. They just want to dive in and figure it out for themselves. Most of the learning strategies suggested in chapter 12 are experiential in nature. If we want kids to learn, we need to provide them with experiences from which they can learn.

As junior highers develop more mature social, physical, and intellectual skills, they need opportunities to use them. There is a tremendous amount of untapped potential waiting for youth workers who will take the time to adapt responsibilities and tasks to match the skills and abilities of junior highers. You don't want to give them more responsibility than they can handle (so they don't become frustrated and quit) but they do need to feel that they have a contribution to make that is important and appreciated. Junior highers need to be involved—to be active participants rather than passive spectators. This is also one of the ways to eliminate the discipline problem common in many junior high groups. Kids who are involved are much less likely to become discipline problems.

One junior high worker who was taking a group of kids on a long bus trip came up with a great idea that illustrates this point. He assigned everyone on the bus a job. His list of jobs was titled In-Transit

> Some kids learn *only* experientially. I've met few kids who actually read the instructions to a new video game. They just load the software and figure it out as they play.

Occupation Opportunities and included such positions as Sound Technician (operates the tape deck), Navigator (tracks progress on map), Interior Recreation Assistant (helps with games), Secretary (writes down everything that happens on the bus), and Bus Attendant #1 (checks oil, tires, lights, and so on at each stop). The result was not only a much better behaved group of kids on the bus, but a lot less work for the driver and adult leaders.

Positive interaction with peers and adults

No junior high program will succeed without positive relationships between junior highers and between junior highers and the adults who work with them. As we discussed earlier, junior highers are in the process of pulling away from parents and they are seeking support, affirmation, and feedback from friends and adults outside the home. A successful youth program will take advantage of this new focus and will foster a sense of community and belonging among the kids. It will also provide adults who will take time to build relationships with each young person.

This is one reason why I believe that effective junior high ministry is easier in smaller groups. It is difficult to build relationships and community in a group so large that some kids are missed. If your junior high group is large, then it would be wise to break it down into smaller units that have identities of their own. One method I have used is to break the group down into teams with coaches (adult sponsors) who work exclusively with their small group of kids. Of course there are times when the entire group needs to be together, but most of the time, in classes and in discussion, the smaller group works best.

Positive interaction can take many forms. For example, whenever a group is playing together, talking to each other, working together, or serving together, positive interaction is likely to take place. It is important to understand that certain kinds of things foster good interaction and community, and other things prevent or undermine it. Meetings in which the kids are mere spectators do not allow for much positive interaction. Games and activities that exclude kids who are not skilled or athletically inclined do not encourage positive interaction. We have to be careful to choose activities that promote community and help all kids feel liked and part of the group.[4]

Physical activity

Junior highers are well known for their bursts of energy as well as their periods of laziness. They need plenty of opportunities to stretch, wiggle, and exercise their rapidly growing bodies. This is one reason their attention spans are relatively short. I recommend that activities be divided into short segments that provide a change of pace every 10 to

15 minutes. The timely insertion of a game, an audio visual, a walk, a discussion, or a rest period will do wonders to keep kids interested and involved. Competitive games that include physical activity are very popular with junior highers, so long as they take into consideration the diversity in size, coordination, and athletic skill of the age group.

Competence and achievement

Junior highers have an overwhelming desire to do something well and to receive recognition for what they have done. They hunger for chances to prove themselves, especially in ways that receive praise from others if they succeed (and won't be too humiliating if they fail.) They are often afraid to take great risks, but when there is a good chance for success and when help is provided, they are anxious to try. Youth workers can greatly increase their junior highers' sense of self-esteem and self-confidence by providing opportunities from an activity as simple as successfully participating in a game, or an achievement as difficult as playing a musical instrument in front of a large group. Junior highers can do service projects, participate in a worship service, help plan a Vacation Bible School, or teach a Sunday school class with good results.

Structure and clear limits

Young adolescents are keenly aware that they live in a society governed by rules, and they want to understand their limits within that system. They want freedom, but they also want to know the boundaries of that freedom. They need to be given well-defined rules and limits, but unlike younger children, they are capable of helping to formulate those rules and limits. They also require that those rules be fair and equitable. If discipline is an ongoing problem in your youth group, it could be that the rules are not clear, or that the young people have been deprived of a significant role in the formation and discussion of the rules.

Fun and laughter

I have added this characteristic to Lipsitz and Dorman's list because young adolescents, like other human beings, enjoy participating in activities and programs that are fun. But this doesn't mean programs have to be silly or shallow. Even serious times can be fun when they are done with friends and adults who are fun to be around, or when the program includes a touch of creativity. I know one group of junior highers, for example, who meet for a Bible study in a tree house. For them, Bible study is indeed fun.

Fun doesn't necessarily mean funny. Some people think that to make something fun, you have to have everyone rolling in the aisles with laughter. That is not true at all. Fun is simply the opposite of dull and boring. Junior highers are famous for calling everything "Boooorring!" And usually they are not being overly critical; they are just being honest. Too often we get into a real rut with our programming and resort to the same old things again and again. Someone once said that a rut is nothing more than a grave with both ends kicked out, and that is definitely true in junior high ministry. If you want to make your junior high group fun, just try something brand new once in a while. Your kids will love it.

So What Do You Cut, What Do You Keep?

Even though we understand and appreciate the characteristics of an effective junior high ministry program, we still have the problem of deciding what to do. We know that we will have to plan a certain number of meetings and activities, but how many, what kind, who with, and when? Two things are certain: (1) there will never be a shortage of things to do, and (2) there's no way you can do everything. One of the problems with going to youth ministry conferences is that you usually come home with a very long "to do" list. Every seminar leader gives you a list of great ideas that he or she believes is absolutely essential for effective youth ministry. As wonderful as these ideas are, the reality is— if you try to do them all, you'll end up exhausted and your kids will end up at somebody else's junior high group.

If you want to make good decisions about your junior high ministry program, the following steps may prove to be helpful:

Develop a philosophy of junior high ministry that will guide everything you do.

Some people refer to this as developing a vision statement or a mission statement. The main idea here is to know why you are doing what you do. You may want to base your philosophy on a key verse of Scripture, such as Luke 2:52, Colossians 1:28, or Ephesians 4:11-13. You might adopt a philosophy or mission statement like, "Following the pattern of Jesus in Luke 2:52, the junior high ministry of [our church] is committed to providing both the people and the programs to help students grow strong in four key areas of life: the physical, the intellectual, the social, and the spiritual." With a single, simple philosophy such as this, you can evaluate everything you do in light of it. Decisions regarding programs and activities can be based on to what extent it contributes to or detracts from the mission or philosophy statement.

Set some priorities.

Even with a philosophy or mission statement, there will still be a need to prioritize. Some things are simply more important than others. You will need to decide for yourself (or with your junior high ministry team) where your priorities are. You may want to give evangelism and outreach the highest priority. But what about community building? Worship? Discipleship? Mission and service? While all of these are equally important, most junior high ministries (indeed most *churches*) find it impossible to commit the same amount of time and resources to all of them. You will need to set some priorities, based on the needs of your junior highers, the giftedness of the leaders, and where you feel God is leading. After reading this book, you may catch the vision for beginning a ministry to parents, or developing a mentoring program. If you want to give these a high priority, you will probably need to let a few other things go.

In addition you will need to set some personal priorities. You may have family or career responsibilities that will impact what you are able to do. In my own ministry, I have tried to remember a bit of wisdom I heard many years ago: "You must be first a person, then a partner, then a parent, and lastly a professional, whatever your profession might be." That means I must take care of myself first (especially in my spiritual life), then my marriage, then my children, then the ministry that God has called me to do. With an understanding of priorities such as these, you will be able to make better decisions about how you use your time and energy.

Set some goals.

Once you have decided what the important things are, you can set some goals. Some may be long range; others can be short range. For example, if one of your priorities is to involve your students in mission and service, then a long-range goal might be to conduct at least one mission project per year. A short-term goal might be to have the specific details of the project for the coming year decided by a certain date—that is, what the project will be, when it will be done, etc. This process of goal setting can be done with every area of ministry that you have made a priority.

Make some specific plans.

Next comes the planning stage, at which time you decide how you will accomplish

> **Early adolescents enjoy being on a leadership team and helping plan their group's activities. This gives them some ownership of the programs and helps develop their leadership skills.**

the goals you have set. You can begin to fill in the calendar with specific program elements. Once you have a general plan, you can involve your junior highers in the planning of the specific details. I have found that early adolescents really do enjoy being part of a leadership team and helping out with the planning of their group activities. This will give them a degree of ownership of the program and help them to develop their leadership skills.

A word of caution, however. Junior highers are rarely capable of deciding what needs to be done. They have a rather limited view of their own needs and are better off serving in an apprenticeship role—learning how to think creatively, what it takes to make things happen, how to get things done, etc. Junior highers need to be given some responsibility a little at a time. Whatever responsibilities we give kids, we want them to be successful. This will build their confidence and develop the skills they need to take on more responsibility next time. Remember that junior highers should only help with the details of the programs that you have already decided to do. If you allow junior highers to decide what the programs or activities will be, they will more than likely choose only fun things (10 trips to Disneyland), or things they have done before (because that's all they are familiar with). That's why it's best for you as the adult leader to decide *what* will be done, and then allow the junior highers to help make it happen.

A Word about Balance

When you are planning your junior high program, it's a good idea to keep in mind that balance is sometimes required, even when you have set some priorities that get more attention. Veteran junior high worker Darrel Pearson has identified six areas that are easy to get out of balance:

• **Fun versus serious.** Even though most junior high programming should include an element of fun, it's important to remember that we are not just trying to give kids a good time.

• **High energy versus low energy.** Most junior highers have a lot of energy to burn, so it's usually a good idea to provide opportunities for that. If you start your meetings and activities with some high energy games or crowd breakers, you'll usually have more successful quiet times, when kids can sit, think, and relax.

• **Large group versus small group.** If you have a large group, remember that it's important to break them into smaller, more intimate units for community building, discussion, and sharing. If you have a small group, it's a good idea to find ways to give your kids the opportunity to be with a larger group as well. Take them to citywide events, denominational youth gatherings, or combine with some other youth groups to do some things you can't do on your own.

• **Scheduled versus spontaneous.** While it is important to do advance planning, it's also a good idea to leave enough time on the calendar to allow for spontaneous activities that can be inserted from time to time. It's also wise to remember that "the best laid plans" sometimes need to be changed at the last minute. Junior high ministry requires a good amount of flexibility and spontaneity.

• **Basics versus in-depth.** It's not unusual to have junior highers in your group who are totally unfamiliar with the Bible, the stories of faith, or other knowledge that would be considered basic. On the other hand, you will have other students who have been raised in the church and need to go deeper. Our programs need to reflect a balance that will meet the needs of both groups.

• **Intellectual versus emotional.** While junior highers are ready to begin thinking through their faith, asking questions, and learning about theological issues, they are also very emotional and have a need to feel their faith, not just understand it. That's why it's important for us to keep a balance between the intellectual (objective) and the emotional (subjective.)[5]

Obviously we can't have perfect balance in everything we do, but it's helpful to remember that most of us are unbalanced personally, which makes our programming become unbalanced. If you are more of a thinker than a feeler, your tendency will be to program accordingly. That's why it's helpful to remember to at least try to achieve some balance in what we do.

Thinking Creatively

One of the characteristics of junior high ministry programming is *creativity*—sometimes a euphemism for "you've got to be kidding!" After all where else but in junior high ministry would anyone come up with a game like Snoot Shoot—which involves blowing breakfast cereal out your nose for distance? There are lots of books and program resources containing ideas for junior high ministry, but it is still important for junior high workers to develop their creative thinking skills. There will be times when the right idea for your group can't be found in a book and you will need to know how to think creatively. Resources are wonderful, but knowing how to be creative is even better. As the old saying goes, "Give a man a fish (an idea) and you've fed him for a day, but teach him how to fish (to be creative) and you've fed him for lifetime."

Here are a few tips to help you develop your creative skills:

Creativity is taking something old and making it new.

The essence of creativity is the ability to copy well. That may surprise you, but most creative people I know (myself included) rarely invent things out of the blue. Creative people take what has already been done, and simply adapt it or change it slightly to fit their own style or purpose. Musicians do this, artists do this, and youth workers do this as well. We learn from those who have gone before us. Whenever you look at an old idea, you can make it new by changing it a little bit. For example, volleyball is an old game. But you can make it brand new by changing the rules, changing the equipment, changing the net, changing the size or shape of the court, adding elements like a slick playing surface, arming certain players with Super Soaker guns, or making players wear roller skates. Any idea can become new with a few changes here and there.

Creativity is looking at things a second time.

The first time you look at something you only see what's there on the surface. The second look is when you ask the question, "How can I use this in my ministry? What else is here that I'm not seeing?" Creativity is making the assumption that there's more here than meets the eye. For example, let's say you read an article in the newspaper about a man who wins a fortune in the state lottery. Your "second look" at that article might suggest a lesson plan for your next junior high meeting. Perhaps you could bring the article in as a discussion starter on money and Christian values. The main idea here is simply: *keep your eyes open.* There are all kinds of things all around us that can be creatively used in junior high ministry programming if we are willing to take a second look.

Creativity is a willingness to risk failure.

You can't be creative if you are afraid of making mistakes. If you always have to play it safe and go with the sure thing, you'll never be creative. Creativity is risky business—and that means a willingness to watch your good ideas go down in flames. Creative junior high workers look pretty foolish at times. But take heart—junior highers are much more forgiving than other age groups. If you work with adults, for example—and make a mistake—they will probably question your leadership skills, call a committee meeting, and put someone else in charge next time. But junior highers understand risk taking and failure. It happens to them all the time. While they will undoubtedly go out of their way to make you feel like a failure, they'll usually forgive and forget—and come back for more.

Creativity requires effort.

As the old saying goes, "Creativity is 10 percent inspiration and 90 percent perspiration." Most creative people aren't *born* creative. They have to work at it. Great ideas don't just pop into people's heads. They come from learning how to think creatively, doing some research, talking to other people, getting out of the comfort zone, reading books, and making lists. You may not think you are very creative, but with a little effort, you can become a lot more creative than you are right now.

Creativity loves company.

Most creative people are much more creative in groups. As iron sharpens iron, creativity happens whenever people get together and start bouncing ideas off each other. There's nothing like a brainstorming session for generating new ideas. Next time you need a great idea for a meeting or activity, get some of your adult leaders (or some of your junior highers) together and give them permission to come up with as many ideas as they can—no matter how outrageous. You'll end up with more ideas than you can use—and a few that should *never* be used—but chances are good you'll find a true diamond in the rough.

You don't have to be creative in order to have creative programs. You only have to make old ideas new, take a few risks, look a second time, put forth some effort, and brainstorm a little. Before you know it, you'll have everything you need to put together the perfect program.

Notes

1. Unfortunately the middle school movement has not been entirely successful in that regard. *In Boxed In and Bored: How Middle Schools Continue to Fail Adolescents— and What Some Middle Schools Do Right*, Peter Scales comments that "Too many young adolescents are lectured to just when they need to explore and interact in small groups. Too many are left without effective guidance and connections with caring adults just at the time when their physical, emotional, social, spiritual and cognitive selves are undergoing great change. Too many are given curriculum that is less challenging and rules that are more strict than they experienced in elementary school, just when they need more academic challenge and a greater sense of participation in developing and enforcing the rules that regulate their behavior." (Search Institute, 1996), p. 13.

2. Highly recommended: "Youth Culture Update," a regular department in the bimonthly journal *Youthworker.* Call 800-769-7624 for subscription information.

3. Gayle Dorman and Joan Lipsitz, "Early Adolescent Development," *Middle Grades Assessment Program: User's Manual* (Center for Early Adolescence, 1981), pp. 6-8.

4. For more information on community-building in youth ministry, see Wayne Rice, *Up Close and Personal* (Youth Specialties/Zondervan, 1989).

5. Darrell Pearson and Steve Dickie, *Creative Programming Ideas for Junior High Ministry*, (Youth Specialties/Zondervan, 1992), pp. 32-34.

• T E N •
INVOLVING PARENTS IN JUNIOR HIGH MINISTRY

Parents play a role second only to that of the Holy Spirit in building the spiritual foundation of their children's lives.
—Mark DeVries

One of the rewards of long-term junior high ministry is occasionally watching one of your kids grow up to become an adult leader in the church. A few months ago, I received a very thoughtful phone call from a former student of mine whose name is Doug. Several years ago he became the associate pastor of a large church in Southern California. He called to tell me about a celebration dinner and "roast" that his church had put on in his honor the night before—to show appreciation for his years of faithful service. It was a big night for him, and he wanted to thank me for having had such a big influence on him when he was a kid. "I just thought you'd like a little encouragement," he said. "Your efforts way back then were not in vain."

It was a wonderful phone call—the kind all youth workers pray they'll get some day. It made my day. But I also had this nagging feeling that I didn't deserve nearly as much credit as Doug was so graciously willing to give me. You see, I knew Doug's parents. They were godly people who served faithfully in the church and modeled exemplary values in front of their son for years before I ever met him. I only knew Doug for three years. He was a great kid—a leader in the youth group—and probably influenced me as much as I influenced him. I'm pretty sure Doug would have ended up serving God whether I had been there or not.

But his call made me think. How often do I feel this way? When I run down my list of personal youth ministry success stories, I am humbled by how many of them involved parents who were there for their kids. There are exceptions, of course, but so often the good kids were the ones with good parents. The youth who fell through the cracks, on the other hand, usually did so because they came from homes without much parental support. I have noticed a growing awareness among all of us who work with youth in the church that while we play an important role in the lives of kids, we are extremely limited in what we can do. Over the long haul it is difficult, if not impossible, to turn a young person into something or someone their parents are not.

> "Unless parents are involved in the Christian education of their children," concluded Search Institute, "it is unlikely to happen at all."

In recent years a great deal of research has been done to evaluate the effectiveness of Christian education programs in the church, particularly those aimed at children and adolescents. One such study, conducted by Search Institute, found that "unless parents are involved in the Christian education of their children, it is unlikely to happen at all."[1] They concluded that the only Christian education that consistently produces long-term results is that which is done by parents.

In his excellent book, *Family-Based Youth Ministry*, veteran youth pastor Mark DeVries writes, "Our isolated youth programs cannot compete with the formative power of the family. Over and over again, I have seen the pattern. Young people may pull away from their parents' influence during their teenage years, but as a general rule, as adults, they return to the tracks that were laid by their parents."[2]

Scripture says basically the same thing: "Train up a child in the way he should go, and when he is old, he will not depart from it" (Proverbs 22:6). What many parents don't realize, however, is that this training continues right on through adolescence. When the children become junior highers, they may not listen to their parents as much, but they sure do watch. They are paying attention. In his book *The Moral Intelligence of Children*, Robert Coles notes that the best moral teaching we do is by example:

> The witness of our lives, our ways of being with others and
> speaking to them and getting on with them—all of that is taken in
> slowly, cumulatively, by our sons and daughters, our students. To be

sure, other sources can count a great deal. . . . But in the long run of a child's life, the unself-conscious moments that are what we think of simply as the unfolding events of the day and the week turn out to be the really powerful and persuasive times, morally.[3]

I don't want to underestimate the significance of our junior high youth group meetings, lessons, activities, and programs, nor do I want to give the impression that in the long run, we really don't matter much after all. On the contrary we who work with junior highers play a very important role in the lives of kids and their families. We are often the first line of defense between junior highers and the slippery slope of negative peer pressure and the enticements of modern culture. Junior highers not only need their parents, but they need adult friends and mentors outside the home who will help them make a safe and smooth transition into adulthood. Yes, parents need us—but we need parents even more. It would be safe to say that good parents could produce good kids without our help. But it would be highly unlikely that we could produce good kids without their help.

If you want to be effective in junior high ministry, then you need to team up with parents—for many reasons. They not only influence their children more than you do, they *care* about their children more than you do. You simply are unable to care about kids the way parents can. Unfortunately parents sometimes point that out to you. They may think you should care about their kid as much as they do; that is, to care more about their kid than anyone else's—and of course you can't do that. But their caring too much is not wrong. That's what parents are supposed to do. Their caring just needs to be channeled in the right direction. A good junior high ministry should be rich in *caring*, and parents have a lot of that. They often just don't know what to do with it.

Parents also *know* a lot more about their kids than you do. Most junior high workers spend an hour or two a week with kids but parents are with them every day. They can be a tremendous resource to you. When you get to know the parents of your junior highers, you will get to know your junior highers. You'll get a better understanding of who they really are and why they act the way they do. My friend Jim Burns tells a funny story about a visit he made to the parents of a hyperactive, extremely annoying kid in his youth group. He wanted to find out if the youngster's parents were aware of the boy's behavior. When he met the parents, he quickly learned why the boy acted the way he did. The boy's parents were louder and even more annoying than their son.

Understanding the Needs of Parents

Unless you have raised your own children, you may find it difficult to relate to the parents of your junior highers. Just as you might find it hard to relate to junior highers because you don't remember your own early adolescence, so you might find it hard to relate to parents of young adolescents because you've never been one (a parent, that is) yourself.

I remember when our son Nathan was going into junior high school. Even though I was supposedly an expert on junior high kids, I couldn't help but feel a certain amount of anxiety about the transition that was taking place in the life of my son. In fact, it reminded me a lot of how I felt when he was born. When my wife Marci was pregnant with Nathan, I looked forward to the day he would be born, but I was still a little worried about all those things that were out of my control. Would our new baby be a boy or girl? Would he be born with two arms and two legs? How would his arrival change our marriage? How would having a baby change our social life? Would he be an easy child or a difficult child? These and many other questions are common to prospective parents, and I discovered they are common to parents of junior highers as well. Adolescence is a kind of second birth, and parents often feel even more anxiety than they did when their children were born, perhaps because they have to go it alone. You don't have doctors and grandparents and friends standing by your bedside, cheering you on, giving you advice, and offering congratulations. Parents of junior highers often feel terribly alone.

> Adolescence is a kind of second birth, and parents easily feel more anxiety during this birth than the first—largely because, during the birth into adolescence, parents don't have professionals and relatives at bedside, cheering them on. Parents of junior highers can feel terribly alone.

Some parents unfortunately harbor fears which author Marie Wynn has called "the myth of the teenage werewolf." It's message is "no matter how pleasant and sweet and innocent your child might be as a youngster, as soon as the first hormonal surge of puberty occurs, that beautiful child will inevitably turn into an uncontrollable monster who will wreak havoc on your home and personal lives for a decade or more."[4] This is a terrible myth, of course, that is sometimes perpetuated by horror stories in the media about teenagers, and it strikes terror into the hearts of parents. The unfortunate thing is that parents who believe the myth of the teenage werewolf are in danger of allowing it to become a self-fulfilling prophecy. After all when you expect the worst from another person, that is what you sometimes get.

Too many parents just assume that when their kids reach early adolescence, their once happy home will be turned into a battle ground or a place of torment. I do a lot of speaking to parents and one of my primary objectives is to convince parents that it is indeed possible to enjoy their children *more, not less* when they become junior highers. They are great fun to be around and they are going through an awesome and sacred time of life. Adolescence is not an illness and it doesn't need a cure. Just as parents are encouraged to enjoy their newborn babies while they are infants, so parents need to be encouraged to enjoy their children while they are becoming young adults. Junior highers need parents who have a positive attitude and expect the best from them, not the worst.

Researcher Merton Strommen wrote a helpful book about parents of young adolescents a few years ago based on a study he conducted with more than 8,000 fifth-to-ninth-graders and their parents. From that research he identified five cries—or needs—of parents that often go unnoticed and therefore unmet by the church.[5] In order, those five needs are as follows:

1. They don't understand what's going on with their kids.
Most parents feel like they are totally out of touch with youth culture and they panic when their kids start getting caught up in it. They don't know much about adolescent development, so they are often blindsided when their kids behave like normal junior highers. And parents, like most adults, have repressed their own adolescence to the extent that they don't remember that they were, in most important ways, just like their kids. All of this leads to trouble as communication breaks down and parents overreact to behaviors that are a mystery to them. Many parents end up shooting themselves in the foot.

This is a need that junior high workers can help meet. We understand kids, or at least we try to. That's what we do. If you work with junior highers, you are in a prime position to help parents understand what's going on with their kids. You can be a tremendous resource to them. Sometimes all parents need to know is that their kid is normal and that they aren't alone. This can help parents relax, have patience, and be more involved in the life of their junior higher. We fear what we don't understand. We can provide understanding for parents who sometimes fear what their children are becoming.

For the past several years, I have been conducting seminars for parents of teens and preteens all over the country called Understanding

Your Teenager.[6] When I speak to parents at these seminars, I am always amazed at how responsive and appreciative they are. I spend the first half of the seminar doing nothing but helping them understand basic adolescent development—much of the same kind of material that is covered in this book. The vast majority of parents don't know about the changes their kids are experiencing, and those who do aren't sure how to respond to them. Children, after all, don't come with instruction manuals. I came to realize long ago that by helping parents to understand their kids, I am not only helping parents, but I am helping kids. I'm really doing the best junior high ministry of my life.

2. Parents are afraid of losing their kids.

This is Strommen's "Cry for Family Closeness." Parents want to feel close to their children, yet they feel their kids pulling away. They are in the process of leaving the nest, separating from their parents in order to establish an identity of their own, and this is a painful separation not only for parents, but for kids as well.

Of course the first step toward addressing this need of parents is to help them understand what's going on. Some parents may misinterpret their child's need to separate as *rebellion,* or they may take it personally and interpret it as *rejection.* Neither is true and we can assure parents that what is happening with their kids is normal and to be expected.

Unfortunately we sometimes only aggravate the situation by separating kids from their parents even more at church. We need to be careful that all of our activities and meetings don't make matters worse by intruding on our junior highers' family time. And we really do need to be looking for positive ways to bring parents and kids together in the church. While kids are doing their normal thing of pulling away, we can offer them opportunities to be with their parents in ways that allow them to be "away from them" at the same time. I have found that most junior highers actually *like* having their parents around as long as their parents aren't treating them like they do at home.

3. Parents want their kids to act morally.

This is another way of saying that parents want their kids to behave themselves, to stay out of trouble, to be "good kids." This need of parents leads to the problem we sometimes have with parents who expect too much of youth workers. They may think it's our job to teach junior highers how to live morally and to correct all their parenting mistakes before it's too late. Some parents may even blame us for the misbehavior of their children. I once had a parent come to me and say "I didn't know you were teaching our children to smoke marijuana!!" Because she expected me to teach her kid *not* to smoke marijuana, when she found marijuana in her son's bedroom, she blamed me for it.

If we are involving parents in our junior high ministry, then hopefully we can communicate to them that we are on the same team. We want their kids to act morally, too. With that understanding we can hold each other accountable. We will commit to do everything that we can to help students learn how to make good decisions about values and behaviors, and they as parents can commit themselves to modeling moral behavior in front of their children. We need to support each other and pray for each other—as well as for our junior highers.

4. Parents want their kids to believe the way they do.

Strommen calls this "The Cry for a Shared Faith." For parents who are themselves Christians, this would most certainly top the list of hopes and aspirations for their children. And for us who work with junior highers in the church, this tops the list as well. Our ultimate goal is to disciple students, to help them to decide for themselves to become faithful followers of Jesus Christ.

Again we need to take seriously the fact that the *primary* way God brings people into a relationship with himself is through families. Parents are instructed over and over again in Scripture to teach their children, to keep telling them the stories of faith, to keep on living godly lives in front of them, to bring them up "in the nurture and admonition of the Lord" (Ephesians 6:4). Our job as junior high workers is to support parents and to fan into flame the faith that has been passed on to them from their parents. We serve as something like a safety net while kids are letting go of their childhood faith—the faith of their parents— to grasp onto a meaningful faith of their own.

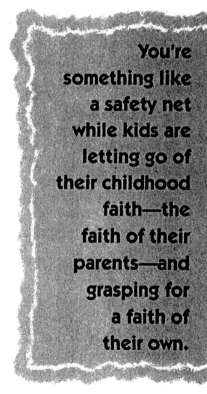

You're something like a safety net while kids are letting go of their childhood faith—the faith of their parents—and grasping for a faith of their own.

But what about those junior highers who don't have Christian parents? Is there no hope for them? Of course there is. God also uses people like us—junior high workers—to introduce young people to Christ and to make disciples of them. Our efforts to evangelize youth and to teach them how to live for Christ will not be in vain. But we need to remember that it is God who has the power to change the lives of kids, not us. He only uses us to do his work.

5. Parents want help.

"It takes a village to raise a child," says the African proverb. Unfortunately today's parents are pretty much on their own and they often are reluctant to seek help from others. To do so, they think, is to show weakness. We live in a world that values individuality, toughness, and self-sufficiency, and to admit that you need help is often perceived as a weakness. We need to remember that parents do want help, yet we shouldn't be surprised when they resist or reject the help we offer. Many youth workers who have hosted an Understanding Your Teenager seminar have been disappointed when the very parents who requested the seminar didn't show up for it. They may have been afraid of what they might hear, or they may have been afraid that others might think they were having trouble with their kids. Regardless, we can let parents know that one of the goals of our junior high ministry is to provide the kind of help they need. If we can learn to provide it, they will learn to accept it with gratitude.

Help is especially needed by single parents, parents in blended families, working parents, and parents who simply have lost control of their kids. They may come to you seeking direct intervention in the life of their junior higher. They may feel they have nowhere else to go. Obviously it's impossible for you as a junior high worker to become a surrogate parent for every kid who needs one, but this only underscores the wisdom of developing a junior high ministry team or perhaps a comprehensive mentoring program that can at least attempt to meet this need. We will discuss mentoring in some detail in chapter 11.

Keeping Communication Open

It's easy to list all the reasons why we should work with parents. The hard part is actually doing it. So let me give you a few practical ideas and suggestions for a ministry to and with parents. The lists that follow are neither exhaustive nor mandatory, but hopefully you'll find a few ideas that will inspire you to think creatively about involving parents in your junior high ministry.

The best place to start is in the area of *communication*. Too many youth workers in the church fail miserably when it comes to communicating with parents. As a result there is a lot of miscommunication and missed opportunities for ministry. Here are a few ideas:

• **Publish a newsletter for parents.** Give it a catchy title and fill it full of news, articles, cartoons, youth culture trends, quotes and excerpts from parenting books (get permission), information about upcoming events, and so on. Most word processing programs come with templates to make composing newsletters a snap. If you can't do this yourself, ask a parent to do it for you.

• **Set up a youth ministry hotline.** Dedicate a phone line at your church or home with an answering machine that provides information about coming events. You might inquire about installing a total church hotline with prompts for each department of the church ("For information about the junior high ministry, press six"). Keep it updated and use it to let parents know all those details that their kids forget to tell them.

• **Invite parents to a Junior High Ministry Open House.** Most parents feel obligated to attend open house at the beginning of every school year, to meet teachers and get a feel for what their kids will be learning. An open house for your junior high ministry could be used to introduce parents to yourself and the other adult leaders, and give them an overview of your goals and programs. You can let parents know what you'll be teaching so they can reinforce it at home. You might even want to put on a typical junior high meeting for them, allowing the parents to pretend they are junior highers all over again.

• **Visit parents in their homes.** Make a habit of visiting one junior higher's parents every week. Call ahead of time, set up an appointment, and take that opportunity to become better acquainted. Don't use this meeting to recruit them to anything or to ask them for money. You can share with them anything you would like for them to know about yourself or the junior high ministry, and you can allow them to ask questions and express concerns they might have. Above all, listen to them and take notes.

• **Use parent permission slips.** The primary purpose of permission slips is not to get a release of liability, but to inform and to show respect. This is one way you can let parents know that they are partners with you in ministry. Permission slips can carry information that parents need to know, and give parents a way of communicating with you. It's best to mail them directly to parents and to provide a self-addressed envelope and a deadline for their return.

Parents Need Encouragement, Too

It's easy for parents of junior highers to get discouraged. They are having all sorts of doubts and worries, not only about their children, but about themselves. In most cases they are desperate for a sign—any sign—that they (or their kids) are doing the right thing. For this reason, it's important for us to affirm parents and to encourage them whenever we have the opportunity. Encouragement will not only lift the spirits of parents, but it will do wonders for the relationship that you have with them. Here are a few ways you offer encouragement to parents of your junior highers:

> **Visit one parent a week, or one a month. Don't recruit them or ask to borrow their van or boat. Just share your vision for junior high ministry, answer their questions, and listen.**

• **Brag on their kids.** Don't be a constant bearer of bad news. Whenever you notice one of your junior highers doing something good, make a note of it and share that bit of good news with the parents. Too often all they hear from the adults who work with their kids is bad news—when their kids are in trouble.

• **Brag on them.** Affirm positive parenting. If you notice, for example, that a junior higher in your group has shown exceptional kindness to another person, give the parent credit for that. Next time you see that junior higher's parents, mention to them that you've noticed how well they have taught their kids to be kind to others. It's paying off! They may think you've mistaken their son or daughter for somebody else's kid, but down deep they will be very proud and extremely grateful to you. It will also encourage them to *continue* to teach their kids positive values.

• **Make phone calls and send notes to parents.** Whether you have any specific good news or positive parenting to brag about, it encourages parents when you drop them a note or make a phone call just to let them know that you are thankful for them and their son or daughter— and that you are praying for them and their family. Make it part of your weekly routine to contact two or three parents a week, just to encourage them.

• **Let them see their kids in a positive light.** Sometimes parents never get to see their kids involved in mission and service, or being a leader in the youth group, or sharing their faith with others. Invite parents to attend some of these activities, or allow your youths to participate regularly in the worship services at church. Parents love it when they can watch their kids acting in a drama, singing in a musical group, or giving a testimony. Take slides or videos of youth group activities and show them to parents and other adults. Put up a youth ministry bulletin board where you can post photos and other evidence that their kids are doing good things.

• **Remember (or attend) special family events.** It is a tremendous encouragement to parents when you remember their kids on their birthdays or when you attend their ball games, music recitals, or graduation ceremonies. Obviously this will not always be possible, especially if you have a large group of kids, but even a card or phone call shows a lot of thoughtfulness and helps to keep parents on your team.

Providing Help for Parents

Earlier we discussed the need for helping parents; now it's time to get specific. Here are some excellent ways for you to come alongside the parents of your junior highers with some practical help and support:

• **Conduct parenting seminars or classes.** Why not schedule an Understanding Your Teenager seminar at your church or purchase a video series on parenting teenagers?[7] Invite a guest speaker who can talk to parents about relationships, or sexuality, or youth culture issues. You may be able to speak to these issues yourself. Parents will appreciate opportunities to learn, and the kids will thank you for it as well. A few months ago I attended a youth event where a display was set up for our Understanding Your Teenager seminars. Dozens of kids stopped by the display to ask for material to take home to their parents. Kids really do want their parents to understand them better.

• **Organize a parents' support group.** There's a old saying that goes, "The problem with being a parent is that by the time you finally figure out what you are doing, you're out of a job." There's a lot of truth to that. Parents can benefit greatly by meeting regularly with other parents and pooling their experience. They can share common problems and offer ideas and resources that they have found helpful. And they can pray for each other's kids. I have found that the best way to encourage this type of group is to avoid making it sound like a 12-step recovery group. It's better to give it a fun name, like a P.O.T. Party (Parents of Teenagers Party) or Better Homes and Guardians, and make it a social event with a short time of discussion and prayer.

• **Facilitate dialogue between parents and junior highers.** As children become young adolescents, parents soon discover that communication becomes more difficult. We can help parents and kids keep those lines of communication open. Try scheduling junior high youth group meetings with parents as panelists, discussing issues like sexuality, careers, or "What I wish somebody had told me when I was a junior higher." Or have kids and their parents write letters to each other, expressing their feelings on subjects like peer pressure or drugs, or sharing their worries or hopes for the future. The possibilities are endless.

• **Plan fun events that bring parents and junior highers together.**
Unfortunately some families just don't have many fun times together
after the children reach adolescence. Social events, retreats, banquets,
game nights, trips to amusement parks, ball games, mountaineering
trips, fishing trips—there are all kinds of experiences that could be
shared by parents and their kids together. And they don't all have to be
events just for fun. Try planning a mission trip that requires at least one
parent to accompany every junior higher. This gives families a chance
to serve together.

• **Help junior highers understand their parents better.** I've had quite a
few kids ask me, "Hey, do you have an Understanding Your *Parents*
seminar?" Understanding goes both ways, and sometimes kids are just
as clueless as they think their parents are. I have in fact conducted
many seminars for kids to help them understand their parents, and
whenever I do, parents are grateful. It helps if kids know that their
parents have feelings just like they do, and that when they say no to
something, it has little to do with wanting to ruin their lives. If a third
party (you) can explain some of these things to kids, it may sound more
credible than coming from their parents.[8]

• **Establish a parenting resource library at the church.** There are
dozens of excellent books, videos, and cassettes on parenting teenagers
that can be purchased (or donated by parents who have them sitting on
their shelves) and placed in the church library. Let the parents know
that these materials are available free of charge (on loan). This is a
simple idea that can reap huge dividends.

• **Provide counseling when it's needed.** You will from time to time have
parents (or kids) coming to you with serious family or personal
problems. Unless you are a licensed therapist, you may not know what
to say or do. It's important for you to find out the names of counselors
in your area, along with some information about their specialty or
experience. Keep this information handy for referral purposes. If your
church can provide counseling this may not be necessary, but most
parents don't know where to go when a crisis occurs in their family. If
you will communicate to parents that it's okay to seek counseling when
needed, and that you can point them in the right direction (and
perhaps even go with them), you will be providing more help than you
realize.

• **Establish a mentoring program.** We will discuss this in the next
chapter, but it's worth mentioning again. Every parent wants an adult
mentor for their son or daughter who will have a positive influence on

them while they are teenagers. A mentoring program is one of the very best ways we can provide help for parents in today's world.

Involving Parents in Junior High Ministry

So far in this chapter, we haven't really addressed the issue of parents as junior high workers, or parents as volunteers who participate in the junior high ministry in some way. We did discuss this briefly in chapter two, but you may be wondering now, "Should parents be recruited as leaders in the junior high group?" I remember the days when the common wisdom among church youth workers was to make the youth ministry of the church completely off-limits for parents. In the days of the generation gap, in fact, we didn't recruit anyone over 30, simply because they "couldn't be trusted." (Some memories are frankly embarrassing.) To be sure, the first edition of this book did not encourage recruiting volunteers in youth ministry from the parent pool. Even now, the issue of parents doing youth ministry raises questions for many people. I am often asked by professional youth pastors who are highly skilled in youth ministry, "Now that my own kids are in the youth group, should I do something else?"

My answer to that question is an unequivocal no. There is no reason at all for a person who has the skills, the experience, and the desire to work with junior highers to refrain from doing so simply because they now have junior highers living in their homes.[9] True, kids need some other adults to relate to, and parents need to remember to put some of their parenting on hold until they get home, but if they have a desire to be involved in the junior high ministry, and if they seem to be qualified to do so (see chapter two), then by all means, invite parents to be involved in the junior high ministry.

But there is another reason why I believe parents should be invited to participate in the junior high ministry. Simply put, they need to hang out with some junior high kids. They need to be around junior highers other than their own kids. Most parents think there's something wrong with their kids. If they spend time around other kids, they'll realize that their kid is pretty normal. I believe that youth workers generally have a tremendous parenting advantage simply because they are not surprised by their children's behavior. Parents who never spend time around adolescents have a hard time understanding kids or communicating with them.

Here are just a few ways you can involve parents in the junior high ministry of your church:

• **Invite parents to serve as volunteer leaders.** Again, if parents have the desire and the qualifications to work with junior highers, and if their own kids don't object (ask them), then there is no reason why you can't have parents as leaders in the junior high ministry of your church. If parents are the *only* adult leaders of the junior high ministry, however, things get trickier. For example, junior highers need to be around a variety of adults—those who are both older and younger than their parents. And if parents are doing the junior high ministry, they may stop doing it when their own children are no longer in the junior high group. This means that the junior high ministry will have no long-term vision or continuity. Parents can be involved, but if they are only there because they want to keep an eye on their kids, this could spell trouble.

Sometimes it's a good idea to recruit parents to become leaders in the junior high ministry *before* their own kids become junior highers. If they can serve in the junior high ministry before their kids arrive (and then continue while their kids are there) it does two things: (1) it helps parents learn about junior highers before their kid becomes one, and (2) it reduces the chance that a junior higher will object to his or her parents being involved. Since their parents were involved before they were, it's not perceived as a problem.

• **Use parents as resource people.** If you will get to know all the parents in your junior high ministry, you can depend on them for such resources as cars, video cameras, refreshments, homes to meet in, ski-boats, and so on. Also, you can use them to drive, chaperone, coach, serve on panel discussions, etc.

• **Set up a Parents Advisory Council.** Invite the parents to serve on a committee or "board" that oversees the junior high ministry of the church. Meet with them periodically and seek their input. You can give them as much actual power as you would like, but their main function is to advise you and to help you avoid shooting yourself in the foot. A group like this can go to bat for you when you need support from the church's board of elders or other governing bodies of the church. They can provide or raise financial support for you, give you good ideas, make contacts with people who can help you, and help you to avoid mistakes. This is a good way to get parents on your team.

> By all means, parents of junior highers can be involved in their kids' youth group—but not because they want to keep an eye on them.

• **Invite parents to serve as prayer partners.** Ask a group of parents to become prayer warriors for your junior high ministry. Send them periodic updates and prayer requests, and ask them to join you in prayer for specific kids, their families, their adult leaders, and the junior high activities. You might want to organize this as a prayer chain with one parent who takes responsibility for it.

• **Recruit parents as mentors.** We will discuss mentoring in the next chapter, but keep in mind that parents of junior highers can serve as mentors for other people's kids.

Obstacles to Ministering with Parents— and How to Overcome Them

Even though it's easy to make a compelling case for a ministry to and with parents of junior highers, there are plenty of obstacles that may prevent you from doing it. I have listed some of those obstacles below, because I believe that the first step toward overcoming obstacles is to acknowledge their existence. Don't let any of the following obstacles prevent you from making a ministry to and with parents a priority:

• **"I don't know the parents."** There may be many parents of your junior highers who don't attend your church, or any church at all. Find out who they are and make an attempt to meet them. If they drop their kid off at meetings or events, make an effort to catch them and introduce yourself. You will need to take the initiative here.

• **"I don't like the parents."** You may have reasons to dislike certain parents, perhaps because their kid has revealed some rather unflattering things about them. My experience has been that in most cases, kids exaggerate quite a bit. Don't believe everything you hear. If you are hearing reports of physical or sexual abuse, of course, then you have a right to be concerned, and you should definitely intervene in appropriate ways. But don't assume that everything you hear is automatically true. Second, make sure that you are not being unfair in your attitude toward parents in general. I know some youth workers who say, "Parents are our biggest problem. If they were doing their job, kids wouldn't be in such trouble." While there is some truth to that, we need to remember that some parents are doing the best they can and their kids *still* choose to be rebellious or antisocial.[10] Don't avoid a ministry to parents because you don't have a high regard for them.

• **"The parents don't want to be involved."** Sometimes despite your best efforts, parents will reject your invitation to be involved in any way. Don't push them. Respect their right to stay uninvolved. Just keep the door wide open and continue to reach out to them.

• **"The kids don't want their parents to be involved."** Some kids may feel smothered by their parents and may need a place where they can be themselves without parents hovering over them. That is true, but not for *all* junior highers. If a kid doesn't want his or her parents around, find out why. Sometimes if you ask the youth for permission *before* you invite his or her parents to be involved, they are more likely to approve than *after*. But be positive. "Hey, Jason, I was thinking that your dad would make a great addition to our junior high ministry team. What do you think?"

• **"Parents may interfere with my plans."** If you feel threatened by parents, you may need to evaluate your own leadership style. Keep in mind that ministry in general is not about power, control, and territorial rights. Some youth workers fear involving anyone at all as part of a youth ministry team because they aren't team players. Parents, as well as other adults, are capable of understanding their role and they can be a very important resource for you.

> Intimidated by parents? They may be intimidated by you—embarrassed, perhaps, by what their kids may have confided to you about their inadequate parenting.

• **"Working with parents is out of my comfort zone."** This is a common fear of many junior high workers who are great at relating to kids, but have a difficult time relating to adults in general—perhaps because of their age or experience. Don't let your fear of working with parents rob you of this opportunity for ministry. Keep in mind that parents may also fear *you*. They may feel embarrassment because their kid has revealed to you their failures as a parent, or they may worry that you know some of their family secrets. It is unfortunate that our mutual fears often prevent us from reaching out to each other. One way to overcome your fear of parents is to spend some time with them and to listen to them. Read a book on parenting teenagers and you will gain some insights into parents that will also help you to overcome your fears. We tend to fear that which is unfamiliar or strange to us.

• **"Parents don't respect me or take me seriously."** This is often the result of negative stereotyping that is usually unfounded. Remember that the best way to get respect is to give it. If you will respect parents, they will be more likely to respect you. And keep in mind that if you are young, single, or have no adolescent children of your own, you really can't expect parents to respect your ability to tell them how to parent their children or to judge them. Recognize your limitations and give yourself enough time to earn the respect of parents.

• **"Working with parents is not in my job description."** Unfortunately some job descriptions are so narrowly defined in the church that you may find yourself "out of bounds" when you try to work with parents. For example, you might be trying to involve parents in the junior high ministry while the adult pastor is at the same time trying to involve parents in other ministries of the church. If working with parents is not in your job description, change it. Some youth workers I know have changed their job titles from "minister of youth" to "minister to families with teenagers." This gives them the permission they need to include parents in their ministries to youth.

• **"I don't have time to work with parents."** This of course is probably the greatest obstacle for the majority of junior high workers in the church. Most of us have too much to do and working with parents may feel like just one more thing to do. Mark DeVries provides a helpful perspective: "Youth ministry at its best involves a continual process of setting and adjusting priorities—deciding what we will wring our hands about and what we will let slide. For most of us, ministry to or through parents of teenagers has simply been one of the many things on our 'to do' list that we have had to 'let slide.'"[11] DeVries compares youth work with juggling balls or spinning plates. There is only so much you can do.

If you are convinced a ministry that involves parents is worth doing, you will probably have to take a close look at everything you are doing and make some adjustments. It's possible that you will need to hand off some of the less important tasks to someone else, or just drop them entirely. Again, if you are committed to the long-term goal of helping junior highers grow "in wisdom and stature and in favor with God and man," a ministry to parents is not one of the balls you want to let drop.

Notes

1. Peter L. Benson and Carolyn H. Elkin, *Effective Christian Education: A National Study of Protestant Congregations—A Summary Report on Faith, Loyalty and Congregational Life* (Search Institute, 1990), p. 4.

2. Mark DeVries, *Family-Based Youth Ministry* (InterVarsity Press, 1994), p. 65.

3. Robert Coles, *The Moral Intelligence of Children* (Random House, 1997), p. 31.

4. Marie Wynn, *Children without Childhood* (Penguin, 1983), p. 36.

5. Merton Strommen, *Five Cries of Parents* (Harper & Row, 1985).

6. For more information on how to schedule an Understanding Your Teenager seminar at your church with Wayne Rice or another member of the seminar team, contact Understanding Your Teenager, P.O. Box 420, Lakeside, CA 92040. Phone: 800-561-9309. Internet page: www.uyt.com.

7. Highly recommended: *Parenting Adolescents* video curriculum featuring Kevin Huggins (NavPress, 1990), or *Understanding Your Teenager* video curriculum featuring Wayne Rice and Ken Davis (Youth Specialties/Zondervan, 1992).

8. A good resource here would be Ken Davis's book *How to Live with Your Parents without Losing Your Mind* (Zondervan, 1989).

9. There may be other reasons for moving on, of course. Some youth workers, about the time their own kids are approaching adolescence, are beginning to feel the urge to move on to a new or different kind of ministry simply because they no longer enjoy sleeping on the floor at an all-night lock-in or they are finding it harder to keep up with the changing world of youth culture. Or they start to realize that they no longer are able to support their family on a youth pastor's paycheck. These and many other reasons may compel you to leave youth ministry at some point in your life, but keep in mind that effective youth ministry today requires a good deal more maturity and experience than it did a few years ago. More and more churches are looking for older, more experienced youth pastors who can relate not only to youth, but to their parents and the adults of the congregation who will serve as volunteers. In many ways, it's true: the older you get, the better you get. God may indeed be calling you to another ministry, but don't leave just because your own kids are now teenagers.

10. For a thorough discussion of this, I recommend Stanton Samenow, *Before It's Too Late* (Times Books, 1989). This Ph.D. warns that we must be careful not to blame parents for everything that is wrong with their kids. This is a popular thing to do nowadays. Some kids may permanently reject their parents' best (or worst) efforts to influence them in the right direction. Every person is an individual and must decide for him- or herself how he or she will live. Rather than blame parents, we need to equip them with the tools they need to respond appropriately to the developmental needs of their kids.

11. DeVries, p. 17.

12. Stanton E. Samenow, *Before It's Too Late: Why Some Kids Get into Trouble and What Parents Can Do about It* (Times Books, 1989), p. 13.

· E L E V E N ·
DEVELOPING A JUNIOR HIGH MENTORING PROGRAM

Every young person needs at least one adult who is irrationally committed to their well-being. —Rick Little

In Homer's *Odyssey*, the Greek warrior Odysseus goes off to fight in the Trojan wars, leaving his wife Penelope and his young son Telemachus at home. To make sure that his son is provided for, Odysseus appoints a teacher whose name is Mentor to tutor the boy and to act as a trusted guardian and friend while he is away. The siege of Troy lasts 10 years, and it takes Odysseus another 10 years to find his way home. When he does return, he finds that Telemachus has developed into a fine young man, thanks to the faithful tutelage of Mentor.

This 3,000-year-old story—which gives us the modern term *mentor* to describe a close, trusted, experienced counselor and guide—isn't that different from a lot of single-parent homes today. Telemachus, like many kids today, grew up in a home without a father. But he did have Mentor, an adult companion who cared about him and taught him what he needed to know.

Every young person needs someone like that. While most modern parents aren't leaving home to fight wars, they find it no less difficult today to provide for their children all that they need to become healthy, self-reliant adults. Even in families where both mother and father are present, young adolescents still look outside the home for affirmation and guidance. Unfortunately for many kids, all they find are peers, pop culture, and the exploitation of the media.

The quote at the beginning of this chapter comes from my

friend Rick Little, executive director of the International Youth Foundation, one of the finest youth-helping organizations in the world. In his words, all kids need someone who is "irrationally committed" to them. "Millions of children grow up virtually alone," he writes, "disconnected from adults. No love. No supervision. No positive role models. Yet these young people must still find their way—they still grow up to become adults. Children can endure the most miserable conditions—even thrive in the midst of them—if they have at least one adult committed to their success."[1]

Every junior higher needs an adult like that. Dr. Urie Bronfenbrenner of Cornell University has also written about the value of having "an irrational emotional attachment" to kids. What makes it irrational is that it communicates to the youth that he or she is special, wonderful, and precious, even though there is significant objective evidence to the contrary. It is, in Bronfenbrenner's words, "the illusion that comes with love."[2]

One remarkable example of how mentoring can impact kids took place at a middle school in East Harlem, New York. Most of the students at P.S. 121 had no real future to look forward to. They lived in an area known for its crime, drug abuse, absentee fathers, working mothers, and gang violence. Less than 50 percent of all P.S. 121 students graduated from high school.

But in 1981 a businessman by the name of Eugene Lang was invited to speak at the school's commencement ceremonies. Lang was a graduate of P.S. 121. He was one of the few students who not only completed high school, but also went to college and had become the president of a big Wall Street investment firm.

When Lang got up to speak at the commencement, he was deeply moved by the 61 young faces who stared back at him. Instead of reading the speech he prepared, he made the graduating class of P.S. 121 an incredible offer. "If you will stay in school and graduate from high school with good enough grades to get into college," he announced, "I will personally pick up the cost of your college education."

Lang's offer didn't fall on deaf ears. Those eighth-graders took him seriously. And it wasn't just the money that caught

> It wasn't just the money that got the kids' attention. The businessman regularly invited them to his corporate offices and persuaded other professional adults to tutor the kids to success.

their attention. Lang also offered them his personal attention. He invited them to come to his corporate offices to meet with him on a regular basis. He enlisted employees and other adults from the business community to tutor the students and to help them succeed.

And succeed they did. According to the statistics, only 30 of those students should have graduated from high school. But in fact, 52 did. Of those, 34 went on to college. The rest of the class received their high school equivalency degrees and did remarkably well in the years following graduation. Rather than getting involved in crime or gang activity, these students became productive members of society—all because one man decided to come alongside a group of kids and give them hope.[3]

Mentoring as a Ministry Model

Throughout this book I have stressed the importance of connecting junior highers with adults who understand them, like them, and are willing to spend some time with them. That, in a nutshell, is the essence of good junior high ministry. Yes, there is a place for programs, meetings, and activities, but they are secondary in importance to the adults who work with them and befriend them. My definition of youth ministry goes something like this: Youth ministry is caring Christian adults who enter the world of adolescents in order to guide them into a maturing relationship with God through Jesus Christ. The emphasis is on people, not programs, and this emphasis is especially critical when working with early adolescents.

In my early years of youth ministry, programs were definitely the main thing. The chief role of the youth worker was to create and maintain effective programs to attract kids, meet their needs and keep them coming. At the time the church was having a difficult time being relevant to young people who were becoming more and more alienated by the so-called Establishment. The traditional programs of the church were failing to connect with youth culture or to communicate in a language they could understand. In response to all this, we youth workers were given the task of devising new methods for reaching youth. And for the most part, we did a pretty good job. We created programs galore. No longer is there a shortage of ideas and resources for effective youth ministry programming.

There's nothing wrong with any of that, of course, but kids today need a whole lot more than programs. Kids who are growing up alone need more than a skit, game, video, or discussion starter. What they need is a person—an adult companion—who will be a mentor and friend.

This means that the role of the youth worker has got to change not only from being a programmer, but also from being a lone ranger. A mentor of mine, Jay Kesler, once described youth workers as light-bulbs—"bright young men and women who are employed by the church to attract teenagers like lightbulbs attract moths." It is unfortunate that many churches continue to regard youth workers this way. Youth-workers-as-lightbulbs usually last a year or two and then burn out, just like real lightbulbs do. And when that happens, the youth—just like moths—vanish. In most cases the church replaces the lightbulb, and the cycle repeats.

To deal with everything that's wrong with that picture of youth ministry would certainly require another book. But worth mentioning here is the fact that "bright young men and women" just don't attract kids like they used to. There are so many subcultures and needs that exist with today's youth, it is impossible for one person to relate effectively to more than a small slice of the youth population. Our society has become so diversified and fragmented that in any group of adolescents, the individual who is idolized and respected by one kid is likely to be ridiculed and scorned by any number of others. There really is no consensus of who or what is cool and uncool with today's kids. The era of one-size-fits-all youth ministry is over.

> Mentoring is simply intentionally connecting kids with adult friends who encourage and guide them into adulthood.

But old paradigms die hard. Even though most of us are painfully aware of the inadequacy of youth ministry models that emphasize programs over people and the youth-worker-as-lightbulb, it's difficult to make changes. We all know the value of one-on-one relationships in youth ministry, yet we are frustrated by the demands of planning endless activities and trying to meet the needs of *all* the kids in the youth group. We just don't have time. Besides, for many of us, we are comfortable doing things the old way. It's easier to just maintain the status quo.

Much has been written about the need for a new youth ministry model that will be adequate as we move into the 21st century.[4] I can't think of a better model than one which emphasizes the mentoring of youth—connecting kids with caring adults who will walk side by side with them through their adolescent years. Some churches have already begun to implement such a program, and in this chapter I want to give you some practical help on how to get a mentoring program going in your church. At the very least mentoring should be a *part* of your junior high ministry. Early adolescents are leaving their childhood behind and entering the adult world for the first time. They—more so than any other age group—need the help of adults who will show them the way.

What exactly is a mentoring program? Simply put, it is an attempt to intentionally connect as many kids as possible with as many adult friends as possible who will encourage and guide them into adulthood. In a sense, it is to undo what the world has done and continues to do. While modern culture separates the young and the old and puts enmity between them, we bring adults and kids together. To implement a mentoring program is in fact to participate in a holy act of reconciliation. Ironically many church youth ministries only reinforce the wall of division between the generations. When youth are isolated from the adults of the church, everybody loses. Not only do kids need adults, but adults need to recognize that they have a responsibility to the young. And the adults benefit as well. Bottom line: the church truly is the *family* of God. Our kids need to be introduced to their spiritual brothers and sisters, grandparents, uncles and aunts. With a mentoring program the church can become quite literally the extended family they never knew they had.[5]

Mentoring as a Rite of Passage

I have been impressed with the mentoring program that has been incorporated for years into the youth ministries of many Mennonite churches. One of the salient features of this program is that the Mennonites make mentoring a rite of passage for their young adolescents. Patterned after the example of Jesus, who was 12 years old when he left his mother and father and went to the temple to sit and learn from the elders (Luke 2:41-52), young adolescents are matched with an adult mentor on their 12th birthday. But there are other reasons why the age of 12 is appropriate for beginning a mentoring relationship. LaVon Welty, a veteran youth worker and pastor in the Mennonite Church, writes,

> "Experience has shown that there is greater willingness to be matched with a mentor at this age when there are fewer school commitments and other involvements. As the youth gets further into high school and grows more and more busy with academics, extracurricular activities, sports, community involvements and work, he or she will likely be more reluctant to enter into such a relationship."[6]

Given that modern society has robbed young adolescents of healthy rites of passage marking their entrance into the adult world, a mentoring program that serves this function makes a lot of sense. In the Mennonite church, every youth and his or her adult mentor is matched and then confirmed before the entire congregation in a ritual ceremony. The mentor and the youth both recite a pledge committing them to the mentoring relationship for a specified period of time. A mentoring covenant is signed, and the pastor prays for the two of them as they begin their journey together. The parents and other family members stand with them, and their friends and the rest of the congregation serve as witnesses.

While such an approach to mentoring may not be practical for every church and every tradition, the concept of matching every junior higher with an adult mentor at a particular age has a great deal of merit. There really is no better time to provide youth with adult mentors than on their entry into junior high or middle school.

Mentoring as Intervention

In every junior high ministry, you will have a few kids who need special attention. Some have been abused or live in single-parent homes. They may be doing poorly in school, or have no friends, or have been in trouble with the law, or are demonstrating extreme or rebellious behavior. Kids such as these can benefit greatly from the individual attention that a mentor can give. Research has proven that when youth who are considered at-risk enter into a mentoring relationship, they do better in school, have improved relationships at home, and are less likely to abuse drugs and alcohol.[7] Most community-based mentoring programs—such as Big Brothers and Big Sisters—concentrate on at-risk kids who need mentors. They understand mentoring primarily as a form of intervention.

Ideally a junior high mentoring program should provide mentors for *all* kids, whether or not they are considered at-risk. (In many respects, all kids *are* indeed at-risk.) But it may be more practical to focus first on providing mentors for junior highers who need them the most. These kids are not difficult to identify. When you start a mentoring program, you will have many parents, especially single moms, who will call you and request mentors for their children simply because they have observed behavior that worries them greatly. Hopefully you'll be able to respond to requests such as these.

Mentoring as Discipleship

Many junior high workers feel frustrated when trying to teach junior highers in group settings because *groups* of junior highers are generally not very attentive. They are likely to be restless, disruptive, or bored, and a lot of time is lost just trying to maintain order. That's why mentoring can serve as an excellent way to teach junior highers. Mentors can be trained to meet regularly with junior high students one-on-one and to use those times to teach from a selected curriculum. I've always been amazed that individually, junior highers will be quite enthusiastic about learning the Bible. In groups, however, they sometimes act as if they are being tortured.

Many churches with rigorous confirmation programs for their early adolescents have discovered the value of mentoring. Rather than having a confirmation class taught by a pastor or priest, kids are matched with a mentor who helps them learn the material on their own. Not only do students learn better, but they often develop a lasting relationship with someone who will hold them accountable for years to come.

As discussed in chapter eight, junior highers grow spiritually primarily by being around older Christians who model the Christian faith in front of them and who have a good relationship with them. If we are serious about making disciples out of junior highers (and we are if we take the Great Commission seriously), then we can't ignore the potential that a mentoring program provides. Mentors can be trained to spend time with kids praying, reading, studying, worshiping, serving, and growing together—one-on-one. There really is no better way to make disciples out of junior highers.

Your Role in a Mentoring Program

Let's assume that you are the person responsible for the junior high ministry at your church. Let's also assume that you are going to develop a mentoring program. How will that affect your role? As we discussed earlier, the lightbulb role is no longer an option for effective junior high ministry, so what will your new role be?

Actually there are three roles. The first is to be *keeper of the vision*. In a sense this is something of a prophetic role. Just as the prophets of old tried to wake up the people of God with the truth, so the youth worker with a passion for effective junior high ministry must articulate a new way of thinking about youth ministry to the church. Without a keeper of the vision—an advocate for youth who constantly reminds the church of its responsibility to the next generation—it is doubtful that anything good will happen. If a mentoring program is going to have a chance at success, someone needs to be its champion, making it a priority on the church's agenda. That someone will probably be you.

Second, your role should be that of a *trainer and encourager of mentors*. This, I

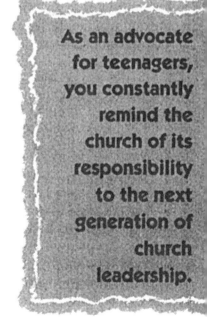

As an advocate for teenagers, you constantly remind the church of its responsibility to the next generation of church leadership.

believe, is the primary role of today's professional youth worker, whether you work with junior highers, senior highers, or some other age group. Like all leaders in the church, our first responsibility is to equip the saints. We are to pass along what we know to others, so that they can do what we do (2 Timothy 2:2). This is especially true for junior high workers. We can't do it alone. Your job is to recruit and train other adults to love kids and to mentor them in the Christian faith—and then to be a cheerleader for them. Not only do they need equipping, they need encouragement. We must encourage mentors to hang in there and to remember just how important they really are. Unless someone regularly and consistently does this, it's unlikely that mentors will last over the long haul.

Your third role is to *become a mentor yourself.* You will want to identify one or two kids you can mentor one-on-one. This may seem impossible if you were hired by the church to be a mentor for the entire youth group. But it's helpful to remember that even Jesus spent most of his time with just three disciples. Paul zeroed in on Timothy. Similarly there are limits to how many youth you can effectively mentor. If you are doing youth ministry alone, of course, you will be accused of playing favorites (as both Jesus and Paul were) which is why it is so important to have a mentoring team. You can still direct the overall program, plan meetings and activities, and relate to the entire group as their leader—but true mentoring has to be done one-on-one. This is also important because it is difficult to recruit and train others to become mentors to individual kids unless you are doing it yourself. Out of your own mentoring relationships, you will be able to lead by example and teach from experience.

Starting a Mentoring Program

Let's turn our attention now to the nuts and bolts of getting a mentoring program up and running. If you will follow the steps below, your chances of starting and maintaining an effective mentoring program will increase significantly.

1. Decide on the scope of the program.

The first thing you need to do is assess how a mentoring program will fit into the existing programs of the church. For example, will your mentoring program replace the junior high ministry program you have now, or will it be an addition to it? Will it be supported by other church staff members, particularly the senior pastor? Will there be any conflict with the adult ministries of the church, or any others that are also recruiting volunteers? All of these questions will need to be carefully answered in order to avoid frustration and failure.

2. Become a mentor yourself.

As I discussed above, it is important for you as a leader to enter into a mentoring relationship with one or more students before you try selling the program to others. Don't mentor a kid just so you'll be able to look more authentic in the eyes of other people, however. My point here is simply this: unless you yourself are a believer in mentoring, and practice what you preach, there really is little chance that you'll be able to convince others of its value. The true test of whether or not you should begin a mentoring program is whether or not you are willing to be a mentor yourself.

3. Set realistic goals.

Don't be overly ambitious, especially at first. One thing I have discovered is that mentoring is not an easy thing to sell to busy, overworked adults who already have too much to do. I have personally experienced the disappointment of seeing only five people show up for a mentor training session out of a congregation of more than a thousand members. It's easy to become discouraged and judgmental when you don't get the kind of response that you expected. But I have learned to appreciate the old adage "something is always better than nothing." I am always grateful for those five people who show up, because that's potentially five more mentors than we had before. If you set a realistic goal of recruiting and training five new mentors every six months, you'll have 50 mentors in five years. That's a wonderful outcome.

4. Define your mentoring program.

Before you begin a mentoring program in your church, you will need to be able to answer some important questions about the details of it. For example, who will administrate the program? Will it be you or someone else? In most cases, it's a good idea to have one specific person who is a "director of youth mentoring" who coordinates the program. Which students will be targeted for mentoring? Junior high? Senior high? Church kids? Nonchurched kids? What will the mentors do? The mentoring kit *One Kid at a Time: How Mentoring Can Transform Your Youth Ministry* recommends that mentors be recruited as either friendship, vocational, or support mentors.[8] *Friendship mentors* spend time with their mentees one-on-one over an extended period of time. *Vocational mentors* invite students to learn about their occupations. *Support mentors* are like spiritual grandparents who pray for individual kids and remember them on special occasions.

Some mentoring programs enlist "soft," "medium," "hard," and "hard-core" mentors. A soft mentor spends little time with his or her mentee; a hard-core mentor, on the other hand, is "an extremely caring and committed adult who basically becomes a surrogate family member—always in touch and always on call."[9] You will need to think through details such as these and decide exactly what kind of program will be best for your church.

5. Share the vision and begin recruiting mentors.

Once you have defined your program, you can begin to share the vision for mentoring with the church at large. You will want to take advantage of all the means at your disposal to do so. Make a presentation before the entire congregation. Have the students themselves invite adults to become their mentors. Put announcements in the church bulletin or church newsletter. Write letters to potential adults, or call them on the phone. You don't need to get firm commitments from people right away. Simply invite them to an initial mentor training session, at which time they can determine whether or not they want to be involved. Obviously this step is very important. Your mentoring program's success or failure will probably depend on how well you sell it to the congregation.

6. Conduct the training sessions.

Every mentor should receive training. The exact amount of training can vary depending on what you want your mentors to do, but three hours should be sufficient in most cases—at least to get them started. Martin Jacks, director of the Mentoring Center in Oakland, California, believes that mentoring programs should always be more concerned about recruiting quality mentors than about amassing large numbers of them.

"We recommend that mentoring programs make it difficult to become a mentor," he says. "Having a good heart is not enough. If someone doesn't have the patience to sit through three hours of training, he's not going to have the patience to be a mentor."[10]

You can conduct one three-hour session, or three one-hour sessions, depending on what is most convenient or practical. The *One Kid at a Time* mentoring kit offers three training sessions, with an accompanying video. The first session defines mentoring; the second session deals with the qualities of an effective mentor; and the third session answers the question, "What does a mentor do?" It is also during the training sessions when mentors are asked to fill out application forms and/or be

> If someone doesn't have the patience to sit through three hours of training, he's not going to have the patience to be a mentor.

fingerprinted (see the next section). It is also important for you to take this opportunity to get acquainted with potential mentors and learn as much as you can about them.

7. Confirm each mentor.

After mentors have completed the required training and filled out application forms, you may want to do personal interviews as well as background checks to make an assessment of the mentor's qualifications. I strongly recommend that you take this step seriously and follow through with the background checks on every mentoring candidate. You may know a person well and be very confident in their integrity and trustworthiness, but it is very important to keep complete files on everyone. In today's litigious climate, churches and organizations that fail to do background checks on the adults who work with children and youth may be found negligent if a mentor is ever accused of wrongdoing. Even though some expense is involved, it is smart to fingerprint everyone involved with youth (including yourself) and have those prints checked against the FBI's database of known sex offenders and pedophiles.

While the chances of getting a bad report on someone are slim, it reassures everyone that you have done your homework and have not assumed anything. Once you have completed this process, you can confirm your mentors and let them know that they will soon be matched with a kid.

8. Invite your junior highers to participate.

As the old saying goes, "it takes two to tango." Not only do you need to share the vision for mentoring with adults and get your mentors trained and ready to go, but you also need to share the vision with your kids and invite them to be mentored by an adult. Some kids will be reluctant to participate because they have misconceptions about mentoring. They may think that it's a plot by their parents to keep them in line. They may worry that a mentor will make them do things they don't want to do, or rob them of time with their friends. Most kids are understandably suspicious of adults and it may be a real challenge to find ways to help them realize that they need mentors.

One of the best ways to share the concept of mentoring with kids is to do it at a youth meeting or some other time when you can speak to the group and tell them about mentors in your life. You can explain to kids the advantages to having mentors (and they are many). You may want to do a Bible study on mentoring, or have some of the mentors-in-waiting come to the youth group and be introduced. I like to pass out response cards to the kids, and allow them to indicate their willingness to enter into a mentoring relationship. If you have presented mentoring in a positive light, you will undoubtedly get a good response. You will probably have more kids who want mentors than you will have mentors available for them.

9. Match mentors with individual kids.

As you might suspect, this is the trickiest part of the entire process. There is a certain amount of trial and error involved in matching junior highers with adults who are compatible with them. Sometimes the only way to find out is for mentors and kids to get together and see if they hit it off. I have planned social events for the purpose of bringing mentors and kids together informally. This allows some time to get acquainted, play games, talk, and more often than not, some pairing off happens naturally.

In other cases it might be best to simply use your best judgment and introduce the mentor to a junior higher you have chosen for him or her to mentor, and encourage them to get together a couple of times to see if they want to continue. Some mentoring programs allow junior highers to select mentors from among the adults they already know in the church. Regardless of how the matching process is done, this is a step that cannot be taken lightly. A great deal of care and thought needs to go into helping mentors get matched up with the right kids for them.

10. Provide support for your mentors.

If a mentoring program is going to succeed, it will need to provide ongoing support and encouragement for each mentor. One way to do this is to schedule regular mentor support meetings, perhaps on a monthly basis, so that mentors can get together and share experiences, get further training, and pray together for the students they are mentoring. Another way is to personally contact each mentor on a regular basis, to find out how things are going and to see if they need help. Regular phone calls, letters, or even a mentor's newsletter can be very effective. Some mentoring programs ask the mentors and their youth to write periodic reports on the mentoring relationship and turn them in to the mentoring director.

Regardless of what you do to support your mentors, the key to the long-term success of a mentoring program depends greatly on how the program is monitored and maintained. It is very easy for mentors to get discouraged or frustrated and not let you know. They may get busy and start feeling guilty because they aren't spending enough time with their junior higher. They may be having difficulties relating to their junior higher, or they may be having other problems that are interfering with their mentoring relationship. A periodic phone call or letter with a few words of encouragement can do wonders to keep mentors on the job and as effective as they can be.

Mentoring youth is not a new concept. It is simply something that we have forgotten how to do. As our lives have become busier and busier, and as we have come to depend more and more on professionals for just about everything, we have forgotten that some things are best done the old-fashioned way. Look again at Luke 2, the story of the young Jesus at age 12 who was separating from his parents and beginning his transition into adulthood. There he sits in the temple, surrounded not by kids, but by adults. Even Jesus needed mentors.

Notes

1. Rick Little, *Annual Report of the International Youth Foundation*, 1996 (34 Market Place, Suite 800, Baltimore, MD 21202), p. 1.

2. Urie Bronfenbrenner, "What Do Families Do?" *Family Affairs* (Institute for American Values, 1991), p. 3.

3. "Helping Dropouts Climb In," *New York Times*, September 13, 1986, p. 26.

4. See Mark Senter, *The Coming Revolution in Youth Ministry* (Victor Books, 1992).

5. For a more thorough treatment of mentoring, see Miles McPherson and Wayne Rice, *One Kid at a Time: How Mentoring Can Transform Your Youth Ministry*, (Youth Specialties/Cook Communications, 1994).

6. LaVon Welty, *Side by Side: Mentoring Guide for Congregational Youth Ministry* (Faith and Life Press, 1989), p. 37.

7. "Mentoring Mania Hits Oakland," *Youth Today*, March/April 1997, p. 1.

8. See note 5 above.

9. "Mentoring Mania Hits Oakland," p.13.

10. "Mentoring Mania Hits Oakland," p.13.

· T W E L V E ·
50 FUN IDEAS FOR JUNIOR HIGH GROUPS

There are literally thousands of ideas you can use with junior highers. Most of them can be found in books published by Youth Specialties, Group Publishing, and several other youth ministry publishers. But to get you started I've listed a few of my favorites here. Enjoy!

Balloon Basketball

I've used this game with junior highers for more than 30 years. It still goes over great. To play you probably need at least 40 kids and a chair for each kid. Divide into two equal teams and set up the chairs in rows, with every other row facing the opposite direction. For example, if you have 40 kids, set up eight rows of five chairs each. The first row should face in, toward the other rows, the second row faces the opposite direction, the third row faces the same as the first row, and so on. All the odd numbered rows face one way, the even numbered rows face the other way (see diagram). The two outermost rows on each side should

face in. The areas behind these rows are the two end zones. Put one team in all the chairs that face one direction, the other team in the chairs that face the other direction.

After all the players are seated, toss a balloon into the center. Using only their hands and while remaining seated, players try to bat the balloon to the end zone they are facing. As soon as the balloon drops into the end zone over the heads of the last row of people, the team facing in that direction wins two points. If the balloon goes out of bounds, just throw it back into the center. Continue the game until one team reaches 20 points or after 15 minutes of play.

Bedlam

Here's another game that is wild and fun to play. You need four teams of equal size. Each team takes one corner of the room or playing field which can be either square or rectangular. On a signal, each team attempts to move as quickly as possible to the corner directly across from them (diagonally) while doing an announced activity as they go. For example, you might announce "walking backward," or "hopping on one foot," or "doing somersaults," or "piggy back!" The first team to get all its members into the opposite corner wins that particular round. The fun part is when everybody meets in the middle, which is usually all at the same time—that's where the game gets its name.

Broom Twist Relay

This old relay game is still lots of fun with junior highers. Divide into teams and line them up in single file lines. At a point some 20 or 30 feet away, a team captain or leader stands, holding a broom. At a signal, one player from each team runs to his team leader, takes the broom, and holds it against his chest with the bristles up in the air over his head. Looking up at the broom, the player must then turn around as fast as possible 10 times, while the leader counts the number of turns. The player then hands the broom back to the leader, runs back to the team, and tags the next player. Have a video camera handy—it's hilarious!

Call In and Win!

Here's a good way to get your kids to do their daily devotions. Assign passages of Scripture for the kids to read, and then—at a certain time of the week—put a "question of the week" on your telephone answering machine. "The seventh caller with the right answer wins this week's grand prize! Give your name and the answer to this week's question when you hear the beep!" At the next meeting you can play the tape with the messages on it and award the prize to the winner!

Church Tailgate Party

Here's something a little off-the-wall, which makes it perfect for junior high ministry. Have a tailgate party in the church parking lot before Sunday school or Sunday morning services and provide plenty of food, fun, and maybe some singing. It'll get your kids "psyched up" for the morning's activities. And if you can't cook the food yourself, order pizzas, even if it's early in the morning. Kids love pizza for breakfast!

Clumps

This game is always fun, requires no skill, and can be played with almost any size group. Have all the kids stand in the center of the room and tell them to keep moving and crowding toward the center. Blow a whistle and yell out a number. If the number is four, everyone has to get into groups of four, lock arms, and sit down. Your adult leaders (referees) eliminate all those who aren't in a group of four. This is repeated, with different numbers each time, until all have been eliminated.

A couple of variations of this game: One is called Tin Pan Bang Bang. In this game no number is shouted. Instead the leader bangs on a stainless steel pot with a big metal spoon. The players must listen, count the number of bangs, then get into groups of that number. If the leader stops banging on the pot after five bangs, then the players must get into groups of five.

Another variation: Anatomy Clumps. When you yell out a number, you also yell out a part of the body, like "Five! Elbow!" which means the kids must get into groups of five and touch elbows.

Dear Abby

This is a simple yet effective way to give kids the opportunity to minister to each other. It also provides you with insight into the concerns and problems of kids in your junior high group.

Each person is given a piece of paper and pencil and instructed to write a Dear Abby letter with a question they would like to get answered. The letter can be signed "Confused," "Frustrated," or with any name they want to conceal their true identities.

After everyone has finished, collect the papers and redistribute them so that everyone has someone else's letter. Each person now pretends to be Abby and writes a helpful answer or solution to the problem. Allow plenty of time. When the answers are completed, collect the papers once again.

Now read the letters to the group, one at a time, along with the answers. Discuss them by asking the group whether or not they think the advice given was good or bad. Other solutions to the problem can be suggested by the group. There is an excellent chance that the kids will be able to give sincere, sensible, and practical help to each other.

Destination Unknown

Plan a day out with your junior high group, but don't tell your kids where you're going. Just tell them to meet at the church and you'll go from there. Take them out for a day of activities that remain a secret to everyone except the adult leaders (and the parents). You can include a picnic, a trip to an amusement park, a service project, a dinner in a restaurant, a party afterward, or whatever your time and budget will allow. Kids will enjoy the mystery.

Fast Forward Wedding Dismissal

This is a fun game when you are in an auditorium filled with junior highers, seated in rows. Have them pretend that they are at a wedding, and the wedding is now over. The ushers will dismiss them by rows, filing out the center aisle in the traditional manner. When they get out the center door, they must stay in line and circle back and up the outside aisles, taking their original seats. (If you want, you can have them go outside, through the parking lot, around the flagpole, etc. and then file back in.) The first side to get everyone back into their original seats is the winner.

The 40-Inch Dash

This quick little game is as fun to watch as it is to play. Give three or more junior highers a 40-inch piece of string with a marshmallow tied to one end. At a signal, each person puts the loose end in his or her mouth and—without using hands—"eats" his or her way to the marshmallow. The first person to reach the marshmallow is the winner.

Giant Lookie

A *lookie* is a junior high term for the gross-looking mess inside someone's mouth when they are eating something and show it to someone else. Unfortunately that's where this idea gets its name.

Everyone brings a can of their favorite condensed soup and a can of soda pop. After everyone arrives empty all the cans of soup into one large kettle, add the proper amount of water, then heat. Empty all the soft drinks into another large container. You'll be surprised to find how decent the punch and the soup taste, even when there's only one person who likes cream of asparagus.

The Giving Game

This fun game will teach junior highers about the important biblical principle of giving. To play, everyone needs a little money—just pennies and nickels. The game works best when players use real money, but you can use play money if you wish. You might want to provide some money for kids who don't have any with them. The game involves three rounds, with each round lasting approximately one minute.

When everyone is ready, announce that the object of the game is to give money away. That's the only rule. They have one minute to give away as much money as they can. Don't worry if you run out of money. Keep playing and you'll probably get some more, which you can then give away.

After this round, announce round two. Now, the rule has changed. The object of round two is to see how money you can get. This is a *getting* round. You can use any tactics you want to get as much as you can.

After a minute of round two, announce that round three is up to them. It can be another giving round, or another getting round. Let them vote with a show of hands and then do whichever they decide.

Follow up the game with some discussion. Which round did they like best? What did they learn during the game? What happens when a few people decide not to play by the rules?

Gorilla-Gangster-Gun!

This game is a variation of Rock-Paper-Scissors. Have the kids pair off and get ready to play by standing back-to-back. On the count of three each person turns around quickly and assumes the role of either the Gorilla—with arms at their sides, jumping up and down, making gorilla noises; the Gangster—by making a "mask" with fingers over the eyes; or the Gun—drawing an imaginary gun from a holster and shooting.

After doing this, one player will be the "winner" and the other is eliminated. The Gorilla always wins over the Gangster (because the Gorilla is bigger and stronger.) The Gangster always wins over the Gun (because Gangsters have all the guns.) And the Gun always wins over the Gorilla (because Gorillas don't have a chance against guns.)

The winners pair off again and the game is repeated until finally there is a grand champion. You can make this game even more fun by changing the characters to action heroes, movie stars, sports figures, members of your group, or whatever. Be creative!

Graceland

Here's an easy learning game based on Jesus' parable of the workers in the vineyard (Matthew 20:1-16). This sometimes perplexing story can become very real by allowing your junior highers to actually experience it. Tell the kids that you are going to play some games. They will have a chance to win points, and the players that accumulate a certain number of points will win a great prize. (For example, a delicious ice cream sundae with any toppings they choose.) Chances are most of the kids will get excited about this.

You can play any games you want. Set up some simple table games, or games like Ping-Pong or Horse (on the basketball court). The main idea is to give kids a chance to accumulate points. After the time limit is up, tally up all the points, and have an awards ceremony. Make a big deal out of how hard the winning players worked to get their points. They are to be congratulated. However, you've decided to give everyone the prize that was promised to the winning players. *Everybody gets a free ice cream sundae with any topping!*

Everybody will be quite happy about this, of course, except for the kids who won the most points. They will probably feel cheated. They will feel that you were unfair. "It's not fair that the other kids get ice cream sundaes when they didn't deserve them!"

This of course can lead to a great discussion of the parable. Read it to the kids and ask them if they feel anything like the workers who complained about how they were paid. Help the kids to understand that none of us deserve God's grace. That's what makes it so amazing!

The Great Button Controversy

Here's a little discussion starter about peer pressure. Put 10 or 12 buttons in a box and pass them around the group. Have each student count the buttons and remember how many were in the box. By prior arrangement, the next-to-last person removes one button from the box secretly, so that the last person's count is off by one. When you ask the kids how many they counted, everyone will agree except for that one person (hopefully). In all probability the last person will change his count to conform to the others, even though he is sure he is right. Follow up with a discussion of peer pressure and how we often make the mistake of assuming the crowd is right simply because we are outnumbered.

Group Impressions

This is a great crowd breaker for a junior high meeting, when everyone is seated in chairs, or on the floor. Divide the group down the middle and have them compete to see which side can do the best impression of a situation you will describe. They have 15 seconds to do their impression. For example, you might say, "You are in a movie theater, watching the saddest part of the saddest movie ever made. Ready, set, GO!" Appoint a panel of judges (maybe your adult leaders) who will watch and decide which side does the best impression. Other situations might include: a crowd of teens at a rock concert, an audience at a horror movie, a congregation listening to a really boring sermon, a group that has just been zapped with laughing gas, students who just ate in the school cafeteria and got food poisoning, football fans just as team scores the winning points in the big game, a warehouse full of mannequins, a '60s-style antiwar demonstration, etc. Take videos of this one.

Hang It on Your Nose

Write the names of famous celebrities on file folder labels and then stick them on the noses of the kids (up and down the ridge of the nose) so that they can't see what's written on the label. Then have everyone walk around and try to guess whose name is on their nose by asking yes or no questions of each other. Only one question per person allowed.

Hustle

This game lives up to its name. You need something that everyone can scramble through or under (like a bench, a big drain pipe, a cardboard box, or an old car). One team at a time lines up single file on one side of the bench (or whatever) and, on a signal, hustles under the object and circles back to the end of the line as quickly as possible. Each team has a counter who counts the kids as they pass under the object. The goal is to see how many kids (one at a time) can hustle under the object in one minute (or some other time limit). Give each team two tries.

Incoming!

Let the kids have a war by blowing Q-Tip missiles at each other through straws. Each team occupies the territory on its side of the room. Place an equal number of trash cans (or cardboard boxes) on each side that represent military installations. Team members must stay in their own territory and shoot into the other team's territory. When players shoot a Q-Tip into the trash can of the opposing team, they score a point—just count the number of Q-Tips in the trash cans to see who wins.

Junior High Music Critics

Here's a way to get your kids thinking critically about the music they listen to (a better alternative than record-burning). Get a few kids in your junior high group to form a "music council" who will periodically listen to the current Top 20 songs (or MTV videos) and evaluate them carefully. The songs can be taped, purchased, borrowed, or whatever. Get the lyrics (if possible) and rate the songs in areas such as musical appeal, lyrics, content, values of the song (compared to Christian values), lifestyle of the artists, and so on. The results can be shared with the rest of the group, and the kids can decide how to respond. They can decide whether they should listen to (or buy) the songs (or albums) or not. You can get a lot of mileage out of something like this in terms of discussion and interest.

Lick and Stick

For this crazy game have your kids pair off into boy-girl couples. Give the girls some Lifesaver candies, and have them first suck on the candies, then when they are ready, stick them onto the face of their boy partners. Whoever can get the whole roll of Lifesavers stuck onto their partner's face first wins.

Long John Stuff

This game is hilarious and especially fun with junior highers. You will need two pairs of large long underwear, about 100 small (six-inch round) balloons, and a straight pin. Divide your group into two teams, and have each team select one person from their team to put on a pair of long johns. It would be best for them to pick someone who isn't too big. The long johns should go over the kid's regular clothes. Each team should also select two or three balloon stuffers.

When the kids are ready, throw out an equal number of balloons to the two teams. The team members must blow them up (all the way), tie them, and pass them to the stuffers who try to stuff all of them into the long johns. The object is to see which team can stuff the most balloons into their person's long johns within the given time limit. Usually about two minutes is long enough. After both contestants have been sufficiently stuffed, stop the two teams and have the two people in the long johns stand still. (Now would be a good time for some pictures.)

To count the balloons and determine the winning team, begin with the one who appears to have the fewest balloons and pop them with a pin (through the long johns), while the team counts. (Be careful you don't stick the contestant with the pin.)

Mad Ads

For this game you need to buy four copies of the same magazine. It should be a magazine with a lot of advertisements in it. Magazines like *Good Housekeeping* are usually loaded with ads. After you buy the magazines, go through one of them and make a list of around 50 advertisements. Include a combination of large (full page) ads and real small ads (which you will usually find in the back).

To play the game, divide your junior highers into four groups and have them get in the four corners of the room. Give each team a magazine and let them rip it apart so that each person has a few pages. Each team should select a leader who sits in a chair. Then, when everyone is ready to play, you yell out the name of one of the ads. "Hershey Bars!" The kids frantically search through all their pages and whoever finds the Hershey Bar ad hands it to their team leader, who then runs it up to you. The first team to get the ad in your hand wins the points for that round. As you go along, you can keep increasing the number of points you give away, making each ad a little more valuable than the one before. Kids love this game.

The Moral of the Story

Get a copy of *Hot Illustrations for Youth Groups* or *More Hot Illustrations for Youth Groups* by Wayne Rice (Youth Specialties/Zondervan) and read one of the stories to the group, leaving out the "moral of the story" (the application) at the end. Challenge each person to write what he thinks the moral of the story would be. They can then share them and discuss. It's amazing how many different things you can learn from one simple story.

Musical Hats

Pick six or more junior highers to stand in a circle, each facing the back of another person. In other words, they would all be looking clockwise, or all counterclockwise. Five of the kids put on hats (or you can use paper paint buckets) and when the music starts (or at a signal), each kid grabs the hat on the person's head in front of her and puts it on her own head. In this way, the hats move around the circle from head to head until the music stops (or until the next signal is given). Whoever is left without a hat is out of the game. Remove one hat and continue until there are only two kids left. Have the last two kids stand back-to-back, grabbing the hat off each other's head, and when the music stops, the one wearing the hat is the winner.

The Narrow Road

Here's a fun game that will help your kids understand the meaning of commitment. Make a long trail around and through the church with duct tape. The longer the better. Tell the kids that they are to follow the duct tape trail for the entire distance—by keeping at least one foot on the tape at all times. That's the only rule. If they will press on and finish the course, they will receive a prize at the end (Philippians 3:14).

Send the kids out one by one, so that they aren't following each other too closely. What the kids don't know is that along the trail, there are candy bars and other temptations just out of reach. There are also several obstacles that they have to climb over or under, while keeping one foot on the trail. There are monsters that attempt to scare them off the trail by jumping out at them unexpectedly, and finally there is a leader who informs them that the game has been called off—they don't have to finish the course after all. Of course, this is a false prophet.

After the kids have returned, you can discuss their experience along the trail. What happened? Were they able to resist temptation? How did they deal with the obstacles and dangers along the way? How can this experience be compared with living the Christian life?

Personalized Letterhead

When you send out letters to members of your junior high group, make up some official youth group letterhead with the names of all the kids in the group on it. With computers and desktop publishing programs, this is easy to do and easy to update periodically. Your kids will be impressed and it will make them feel more like they are a special part of the group.

Pew Races

Ask permission before you do this one. This game is played in the sanctuary. Divide the group into teams and have them line up behind the back row of pews. Each team has a leader who stands in front of the first row. On a signal, the leader rolls a die and calls out the number that is rolled. If it's three, then the team crawls under three pews toward the front and stands up. Once the whole team is standing, he rolls the die again, and calls out a new number and the teams crawls under the appropriate number of pews again. This continues until one team reaches the front.

Phoney Phone Calls

For your next junior high youth group meeting, make a few phoney phone calls to kids in your group, disguising your voice as a rude telemarketer wanting to sell them a membership to a health club, or a radio DJ telling them they have won a trip to Hawaii, or a member of a cult trying to convert them, etc. Use your imagination and have fun. Record the phone calls when you make them and then play them back during your youth group meeting for some great laughs.

Photo I.D. Required

For your next camp or retreat, tell the kids that they have to turn in a photo with their registration form. This will allow you to make copies and give photos to all your adult volunteers, camp counselors, and staff, so that they can learn the names of the kids. This makes a huge impression on the kids. Another way to do this is to conduct short video interviews with each member of your junior high group and make copies of the video for all your adult leaders.

Prayer Candles

This idea will help your junior highers to pray together (and for each other) more effectively. Have the entire group sit in a circle (in a darkened room or outdoors at night) with everyone holding a candle. One candle is lit, then the person holding that candle silently or aloud prays for one other member of the group in the circle (preferably someone across the circle). After completing the prayer, that person goes over to the person she just prayed for and lights that person's candle, then returns to her seat with the lighted candle. The one whose candle was just lit then prays for another in the circle and does the same thing. This continues until all the candles are lit and the leader closes in prayer. All the candles can be blown out simultaneously. The symbolism involved can be very meaningful.

Progressive Worship Service

Here's a creative way to involve junior highers in worship. It can be done in a church, in homes, or on a weekend retreat. There really is no limit to its possibilities. It works just like a progressive dinner.

A worship service has a variety of elements, just like a dinner does. By taking each element of worship separately and in a different location, you can teach kids the significance of each one:

Fellowship. Begin with some kind of group interaction or sharing that provides a chance for the kids to get to know one another better. Something that would put the kids in a celebrative rather than rowdy mood would be appropriate.

Spiritual Songs. At the next location, have someone lead the group in a variety of well-known hymns or favorite songs of worship.

Prayer. Move to another location that provides a good atmosphere for prayer. If outside, a garden would be nice, as Jesus often chose a garden for prayer. Have the kids offer prayer requests and thanksgivings, and have several kids lead in prayer.

Scripture Reading. At the next location have several kids read a lesson from the Old Testament, the New Testament, and perhaps the Psalms. Use a modern English translation, like Eugene Peterson's *The Message.*

Teaching. The next stop can be where the Word of God is proclaimed (the sermon). If you prefer not to be preachy, substitute a dialogue sermon, a film, or something of that nature.

The Breaking of Bread (Communion). The last stop can be around the Lord's Table—a communion service. Conduct this however you choose, but it should be a time of celebration.

There are other ingredients that go into worship (like the offering) that you can incorporate into the others or take separately. Design your own progressive worship service, and you can be sure that your junior highers will never forget it.

Pull Yourself Together

This is a learning game that makes a great discussion starter on how we are all members of the body of Christ. When your junior highers arrive, give everyone a slip of paper with a part of the body written on it, such as ear, nose, foot, kneecap, hand, or eye. You should try to distribute these so there will be enough parts to make up two or more complete bodies. In other words, if you have 30 kids, you might want to have three bodies, each with 10 parts.

When you say "go," have the kids try to form complete bodies as quickly as possible by getting into groups. The body that gets together first is the winner. A complete body has, of course, only one head, two arms, two legs, and so on. If a body has three legs, then obviously something is wrong.

Once the bodies have formed, you can proceed with some small group discussion or other activities that require those bodies to work together as a team to simulate how the body of Christ works. An experience like this can help kids understand passages like 1 Corinthians 12 much better.

The Put-Down Potty

Get a child's potty chair and decorate it as your Put-Down Potty. Keep it in a prominent place in your junior high meeting room and get the kids to agree to this rule: Anyone who puts down another person with an unkind or vulgar remark will be fined 25 cents (or whatever amount you think is appropriate). The money will go in the Put-Down Potty and be used to support a mission trip or some other worthy cause. This can be a light-hearted way to help kids remember that your junior high group is a Put-Down-Free Zone.

Rake and Run

Here's a great way to involve junior highers in a ministry to the community if you live in a neighborhood with a lot of deciduous trees. Load up all the kids in a bus and "arm" each with a lawn rake. Go along streets and whenever you see a lawn that needs raking, everyone jumps out and rakes all the leaves up. No pay is accepted for any of the work. It is all done in the name of Christ. You could also find out the names and addresses of shut-ins who cannot rake their own lawns. It can be fun and rewarding for the kids. During the winter kids can shovel snow in the same way. You can call it "Snow and Blow."

Rumor Game

Here's a good way to open up a discussion on gossiping. Choose three kids to leave the room and wait until they are called back in. Another junior higher in the room is shown a simple drawing of a face and is asked to copy it (as well as he can) on a piece of poster board.

When he is finished, one of the three junior highers outside comes in and is also asked to draw the same drawing, only using the first person's drawing as a guide rather than the original.

The next person comes in and draws her drawing from the second person's. When finished, the last person draws one final drawing, using the third one as a guide.

Now compare the last person's drawing with the original. Of course, there will hardly be any resemblance. The game is fun, but it is also a great way to show kids that when we spread rumors, we usually end up distorting the truth very badly.

Sardines

This old favorite is basically Hide-and-Seek in reverse. The group chooses one person to be "it." This person hides while the rest of the group counts to 100 (or a signal is given). Now the group sets out to find the hidden person. Each person should look individually, but small groups (two or three) may look together. When a person finds "it," he hides with "it" instead of telling the rest of the group. The hiding place may be changed an unlimited number of times during any game. The last person to find the hidden group, which has now come to resemble a group of sardines, is the loser (or becomes "it" for the next game).

Scavenger Food Hunt

This game is fun, and it can also make a significant contribution to a poor family (or families) in your local area, especially around Thanksgiving. The group is divided into teams and is given a list of canned goods or other food items to collect from homes within a specified area. Whichever group collects the most items on the list is the winner, but the real winners are the people who receive the donated food. Each home that contributes should receive a thank-you note, which can also serve as a receipt. It is best to work through a local welfare agency or other organization that can help with the distribution of the food.

Scripture Scavenger Hunt

Here's one that combines a lot of fun with some solid Bible learning. Teams try to bring back items that can be found in the Bible. For example, they might bring back a stick (Moses' rod), or a rock (the stoning of Stephen), or a loaf of bread (the Last Supper). Every item must be accompanied by a Bible verse to prove that it can be found somewhere in the Bible. The team that returns with the most items is the winner.

Secret Sound Videos

Before your next youth meeting use a video camera to film some short segments (five seconds) of things that make sounds, like a staple gun, a lawn sprinkler, a computer game, an elevator door opening, etc. At the meeting give all the kids a pencil and paper and play the video with the screen covered so they can't see it. Have them listen to the sounds and guess what they think they are. Then play it again, this time letting them see what made the sounds. Whoever guessed the most correctly is the winner.

Sense Scriptures

Here's a good way to add a new dimension to your next Bible study or lesson that involves a Bible passage. To begin, read the passage to the group and then explain that you are going to read it again while they close their eyes and tell you what they sense from the story or situation. In other words, you want them to put themselves into the actual scene of the incident being described as you read. Then they are to tell you what they see, hear, smell, taste, and feel. With the active imaginations that most kids have, the results are usually pretty interesting.

For example, when Jesus calmed the storm in Matthew 8, responses might sound like this: "I *see* dark clouds, lightning, big waves, sea gulls. . . I *hear* thunder, splashing, men shouting, a boat creaking . . . I *taste* water, salt, cottonmouth (fear), lunch coming up. . . I *feel* seasick, afraid, very cold. . . I *smell* the rain, the salt water, the wet people, body odor, the fish." This approach can really help young people relate to the Bible in a fresh and intimate way.

Servin' Safari

Divide your junior highers into teams (each team gets a car and an adult driver) and let them go out for an hour or two to places around town where they can serve others. They need to be creative and think of ways they can help someone—and then go do it. They can go clean somebody's house, wash a car, carry groceries, clean windshields at a gas station, or whatever they want. They need to stay busy for the entire time, and then report back to the church or meeting place. You can then let the groups share their experiences and talk about what they learned about servanthood.

Shuffle Your Buns

Here's a wild game your junior highers will enjoy playing over and over again. Arrange chairs in a circle so that everyone has a chair. Each person sits in a chair, except for two people that stand in the middle, leaving their two chairs vacant. The two in the middle attempt to sit in the two vacant chairs while the seated players keep "shuffling" from chair to chair (taking the vacant chairs). If one or both of the two in the middle manage to sit in a chair, the person on their right replaces them in the middle of the circle.

Supermarket Blitz

Here's another way to collect food for needy families. Station a small group of kids outside the entrances to supermarkets in the area. Be sure to get permission first. The kids should have large containers in which canned goods or other food items can be deposited. They ask people going into the store if they would purchase one extra item of their choice to be donated to a needy family in the area. Make sure the people know that a legitimate church or other agency is involved in the food distribution program, and give receipts to those who desire them. It's a pretty effective way to collect food and to help others in Christ's name.

Technicolor Stomp

Here's a wild indoor game. You will need lots of colored balloons. Divide into teams and assign each team a color (red, blue, orange, yellow), then give each team an equal number of balloons of its color. It would be best to give each team about three times more balloons than players. For example, if a team has 10 players, they should get about 30 balloons of their color. The red team gets red balloons, the yellow team gets yellow, and so on. They first blow up all their balloons and tie them. Then, when the game starts, the balloons from all the teams are released onto the floor. The object of the game is to stomp and pop all the balloons of the other teams while attempting to protect your own team's balloons. After the time is up (probably two or three minutes), the popping of balloons stops, and each team gathers up its unpopped balloons. The team with the most balloons left is the winner.

Tour of Your Life

This day-long field trip is great with junior highers and gives them an opportunity to view life somewhat more completely and realistically. Begin by visiting the maternity ward of a local hospital (prearranged, of course) where the kids can see newborns and new moms. Perhaps a doctor can tell about the birth process. Next, take the kids to a local elementary school, then to a college or university campus and show them around. The next stop should be a factory, an office, or any place where people are working. At this point, you can discuss careers and the meaning of work.

Then visit with older folks in a convalescent home or some other place where senior citizens live. Allow the kids to share with them in some way and allow the seniors to share with the kids. The last stop on the tour should be a mortuary or funeral home. The funeral director may show the kids around, explain what happens to the corpse when it is brought in, the types of caskets available, and so on. Close the experience with a meeting or discussion in the funeral chapel (if there is one) or elsewhere if you wish. Other places can be added to this tour depending on how much time you have or the types of places available to you. Allow kids to think about the kind of life they want and how they are going to achieve their goals.

True-False Scramble

Here's a great game that can also be educational. You will first need a list of true-false questions. Divide your players into two teams seated across from each other in two rows. Have them number off, so that players on each team have corresponding numbers. There will be two one's, two two's, two three's, and so on. Between the two teams, place two empty chairs. One is labeled TRUE and the other is labeled FALSE.

To play the game, you simply read a question and then yell out a number. The two players with that number (one from each team) jump up and run to the chair that represents the correct answer to the question (true or false). The first to sit in the correct chair wins a point for his team. It's a wild game, especially if you throw in a few hard questions.

TV Ratings

Print up a simple form that can be used by your junior highers to evaluate the TV shows they watch. The form can ask kids to rate programs on everything from the quality of the acting to how many times bad language was used. The form could also include a list of biblical principles (commands, promises, models, etc.), as well as instructions to check off any of the biblical principles that were broken and kept during the course of the TV show. Let the kids report back to the group on what they found. This can teach kids to watch TV with discernment.

Wake-Up Call

Get up real early on Saturday morning and visit a few members of your junior high group while they are still asleep. If you dress up in a scary costume, you'll get some great reactions when you wake kids up. Of course, you'll also have a youth group "film crew" with you, taking videos to be shown at the next youth group meeting. Be sure to get the parents' permission.

World's Largest Bucket of Popcorn

The next time you plan to have a movie night for your junior highers or if you want to create a refreshment for your next special event, try this. Announce ahead of time that you will have the World's Largest Bucket of Popcorn. The kids will come just to see if you can deliver. You'll need to get lots of popcorn popped, of course. For the bucket, use a molded plastic, child-sized swimming pool. Fill it with popcorn and your kids will be duly impressed.

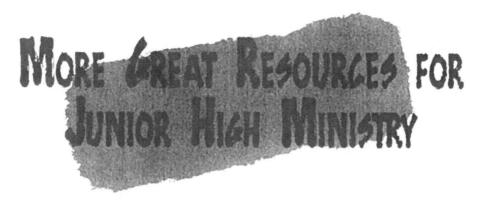

MORE GREAT RESOURCES FOR JUNIOR HIGH MINISTRY

- *Boxed In and Bored: How Middle Schools Continue to Fail Adolescents—And What Good Middle Schools Do Right,* Peter Scales (Search Institute, 1996). This booklet presents a brief overview of early adolescent development and assesses how middle schools are responding to their needs.

- *Creative Programming Ideas for Junior High Ministry,* Steve Dickie and Darrell Pearson (Youth Specialties/Zondervan, 1992). Steve and Darrell offer some excellent advice on how to put together a developmentally appropriate junior high program in the church.

- *Developing Spiritual Growth in Junior High Students,* Ray Johnston (Youth Specialties, 1994). Ray suggests a variety of ways in this book to help junior highers grow in their relationships with God. Very practical with lots of ideas.

- *Early Adolescence: Understanding the 10-15-Year-Old,* Gail Caissy (Insight Books, 1994). Written primarily for parents, this book presents an excellent overview of early adolescent development with parenting tips.

- *Early Adolescence: Perspectives on Research, Policy and Intervention,* Richard M. Lerner (ed.) (Lawrence Erlbaum Associates, 1993). If you are interested in academic research on this age group, you'll find plenty of it in this book.

- *Early Adolescent Ministry,* John Roberto (ed.) (Don Bosco Multimedia, 1991). This book provides practical ideas on junior high ministry for youth workers in the Catholic church.

- *Enjoy Your Middle Schooler,* Wayne Rice (Zondervan, 1994). I wrote this book for parents of young adolescents. Much of the material in *Junior High Ministry* is also in this book.

- *Family-Based Youth Ministry,* Mark DeVries (InterVarsity Press, 1994). Perhaps the best youth ministry book written in the last 10 years. Get it.

- *Help! I'm a Junior High Youth Worker!* Mark Oestreicher (Youth Specialties/Zondervan,1996). This little book contains 50 tips on working with junior highers, written by a youth pastor who knows what he's talking about.

- *Junior High Game Nights* and *More Junior High Game Nights,* Dan McCollam and Keith Betts, (Youth Specialties/Zondervan, 1991, 1992). These books contain some of the wildest, zaniest junior high games and special events you'll find anywhere. A companion video teaches you how to play the games.

- *Junior High Talksheets* and *More Junior High Talksheets,* David Lynn (Youth Specialties/Zondervan, 1988, 1992). Talksheets are one-page reproducible handouts you can use with junior highers to stimulate discussion and learning. These books contain dozens of them on every conceivable topic.

- *Junior High Ministry* (Group Publishing). A subscription to this magazine delivers a steady stream of articles, ideas, and teaching strategies for junior high workers in the church.

- *Learning How to Kiss a Frog: Advice for Those Who Work with Pre- and Early-Adolescents,* James Garvin (New England League of Middle Schools, 1988). This hard-to-find little book contains some wonderful wisdom from a middle school principal.

- *The Middle School Maze,* Cliff Schimmels (Chariot/Victor Books, 1996). Written for parents, this book offers wise solutions to dozens of common problems concerning early adolescent behavior.

- *One Kid at a Time,* Miles McPherson and Wayne Rice (Cook Communications, 1995). This kit provides everything you need to get a mentoring program up and running at your church. Includes mentor handbooks and a training video.

- *The Quicksilver Years,* Peter Benson, Dorothy Williams, and Arthur Johnson (Harper & Row, 1987). This book contains an analysis of the findings of Search Institute's research on early adolescents from the 1980s.

- *Quicksilvers: Ministering with Junior High Youth,* Carole Goodwin (Twenty-Third Publications, 1992). This is a helpful book on junior high ministry written primarily for youth workers in the Catholic church.

- *Raising Self-Reliant Children in a Self-Indulgent World,* H. Stephen Glenn and Jane Nelson (Prima Publishing, 1988). This is the best resource on how to help children and young adolescents develop what Glenn calls "the significant seven"—three perceptions and four life skills that every person needs to become a capable and self-reliant adult.

- *Reaching Kids before High School,* Dave Veerman (Victor Books, 1990). An excellent book on how youth workers in the church can effectively reach and teach junior highers.

- *Reviving Ophelia,* Mary Pipher (Ballantine Books, 1994). Written by a clinical psychologist, this book deals with the unique problems of growing up as a teenage girl in today's world.

- *The Scapegoat Generation,* Mike Males (Common Courage Press, 1996). This enlightening and thought-provoking book offers a positive, balanced look at the research often used to condemn today's kids.

- *Toward Adolescence: The Middle School Years,* Mauritz Johnson (ed.) (University of Chicago Press, 1980). A gold mine of research and articles on early adolescence by such luminaries as David Elkind and Joan Lipsitz.

- *Understanding Your Teenager,* Wayne Rice and Ken Davis (Youth Specialties/Zondervan, 1993). This video curriculum can be used to help parents understand and respond appropriately to their early adolescent children.

- *Up Close and Personal,* Wayne Rice (Youth Specialties/Zondervan, 1989). I wrote this book to help youth workers build community in their youth groups. Lots of ideas and a curriculum on community are included.

Resources from Youth Specialties

Professional Resources

Administration, Publicity, & Fundraising (Ideas Library)
Developing Student Leaders
Equipped to Serve: Volunteer Youth Worker Training Course
Help! I'm a Junior High Youth Worker!
Help! I'm a Small-Group Leader!
Help! I'm a Sunday School Teacher!
Help! I'm a Volunteer Youth Worker!
How to Expand Your Youth Ministry
How to Speak to Youth...and Keep Them Awake at the Same Time
Junior High Ministry (Updated & Expanded)
The Ministry of Nurture: A Youth Worker's Guide to Discipling Teenagers
One Kid at a Time: Reaching Youth through Mentoring
Purpose-Driven Youth Ministry
So *That's* Why I Keep Doing This! 52 Devotional Stories for Youth Workers
A Youth Ministry Crash Course
The Youth Worker's Handbook to Family Ministry

Youth Ministry Programming

Camps, Retreats, Missions, & Service Ideas (Ideas Library)
Compassionate Kids: Practical Ways to Involve Your Students in Mission and Service
Creative Bible Lessons from the Old Testament
Creative Bible Lessons in 1 & 2 Corinthians
Creative Bible Lessons in John: Encounters with Jesus
Creative Bible Lessons in Romans: Faith on Fire!
Creative Bible Lessons on the Life of Christ
Creative Junior High Programs from A to Z, Vol. 1 (A-M)
Creative Junior High Programs from A to Z, Vol. 2 (N-Z)

Creative Meetings, Bible Lessons, & Worship Ideas (Ideas Library)
Crowd Breakers & Mixers (Ideas Library)
Drama, Skits, & Sketches (Ideas Library)
Drama, Skits, & Sketches 2 (Ideas Library)
Dramatic Pauses
Everyday Object Lessons
Games (Ideas Library)
Games 2 (Ideas Library)
Great Fundraising Ideas for Youth Groups
More Great Fundraising Ideas for Youth Groups
Great Retreats for Youth Groups
Greatest Skits on Earth
Greatest Skits on Earth, Vol. 2
Holiday Ideas (Ideas Library)
Hot Illustrations for Youth Talks
More Hot Illustrations for Youth Talks
Still More Hot Illustrations for Youth Talks
Incredible Questionnaires for Youth Ministry
Junior High Game Nights
More Junior High Game Nights
Kickstarters: 101 Ingenious Intros to Just about Any Bible Lesson
Live the Life! Student Evangelism Training Kit
Memory Makers
Play It! Great Games for Groups
Play It Again! More Great Games for Groups
Special Events (Ideas Library)
Spontaneous Melodramas
Super Sketches for Youth Ministry
Teaching the Bible Creatively
Videos That Teach
What Would Jesus Do? Youth Leader's Kit
The Next Level
Wild Truth Bible Lessons
Wild Truth Bible Lessons 2
Wild Truth Bible Lessons—Pictures of God
Worship Services for Youth Groups

Discussion Starters

Discussion & Lesson Starters (Ideas Library)
Discussion & Lesson Starters 2 (Ideas Library)
Get 'Em Talking
Keep 'Em Talking!
High School TalkSheets
More High School TalkSheets
High School TalkSheets: Psalms and Proverbs
Junior High TalkSheets
More Junior High TalkSheets
Junior High TalkSheets: Psalms and Proverbs
What If...? 450 Thought Provoking Questions to Get Teenagers Talking, Laughing, and Thinking
Would You Rather...? 465 Provocative Questions to Get Teenagers Talking
Have You Ever...? 450 Intriguing Questions Guaranteed to Get Teenagers Talking

Clip Art

ArtSource: Stark Raving Clip Art (print)
ArtSource: Youth Group Activities (print)
ArtSource CD-ROM: Clip Art Library Version 2.0

Videos

EdgeTV
The Heart of Youth Ministry: A Morning with Mike Yaconelli
Next Time I Fall in Love Video Curriculum
Purpose Driven Youth Ministry Video Curriculum
Understanding Your Teenager Video Curriculum

Student Books

Grow For It Journal
Grow For It Journal through the Scriptures
Teen Devotional Bible
What Would Jesus Do? Spiritual Challenge Journal
Spiritual Challenge Journal: The Next Level
Wild Truth Journal for Junior Highers
Wild Truth Journal—Pictures of God